Food Cultures of Israel

Recent Title in
The Global Kitchen

Food Cultures of the United States: Recipes, Customs, and Issues
Bruce Kraig

FOOD CULTURES OF ISRAEL

Recipes, Customs, and Issues

Michael Ashkenazi

The Global Kitchen

BLOOMSBURY ACADEMIC
NEW YORK · LONDON · OXFORD · NEW DELHI · SYDNEY

BLOOMSBURY ACADEMIC
Bloomsbury Publishing Inc
1359 Broadway, New York, NY 10018, USA
50 Bedford Square, London, WC1B 3DP, UK
29 Earlsfort Terrace, Dublin 2, Ireland

BLOOMSBURY, BLOOMSBURY ACADEMIC and the Diana logo
are trademarks of Bloomsbury Publishing Plc

First published in the United States of America by ABC-CLIO 2021
Paperback edition published by Bloomsbury Academic 2025

Copyright © Bloomsbury Publishing Inc, 2025

For legal purposes the Acknowledgments on p. xiii constitute
an extension of this copyright page.

COVER PHOTOS: Mahane Yehuda market, Jerusalem, Israel.
(Yadid Levy/Alamy Stock Photo); World flags vectors. (pop_jop/iStockphoto)

All rights reserved. No part of this publication may be reproduced or
transmitted in any form or by any means, electronic or mechanical,
including photocopying, recording, or any information storage or retrieval
system, without prior permission in writing from the publishers.

Bloomsbury Publishing Inc does not have any control over, or responsibility for,
any third-party websites referred to or in this book. All internet addresses given
in this book were correct at the time of going to press. The author and publisher
regret any inconvenience caused if addresses have changed or sites have
ceased to exist, but can accept no responsibility for any such changes.

Library of Congress Cataloging-in-Publication Data
Names: Ashkenazi, Michael, author.
Title: Food cultures of Israel : recipes,
customs, and issues / Michael Ashkenazi.
Description: First Edition. | Santa Barbara : Greenwood, 2021. | Series: The Global Kitchen |
Includes bibliographical references and index.
Identifiers: LCCN 2020007976 (print) | LCCN 2020007977 (ebook) |
ISBN 9781440866852 (Hardback) | ISBN 9781440866869 (eBook)
Subjects: LCSH: Cooking, Israeli. | Israel—Social
life and customs.
Classification: LCC TX724 .A835 2021 (print) | LCC TX724 (ebook) |
DDC 641.595694—dc23
LC record available at https://lccn.loc.gov/2020007976
LC ebook record available at https://lccn.loc.gov/2020007977

ISBN: HB: 978-1-4408-6685-2
PB: 979-8-2163-8622-3
ePDF: 978-1-4408-6686-9
eBook: 979-8-2160-8575-1

Series: The Global Kitchen

To find out more about our authors and books visit www.bloomsbury.com
and sign up for our newsletters.

Contents

Series Foreword		vii
Preface		ix
Acknowledgments		xiii
Introduction		xv
Chronology		xli
Chapter One	Food History	1
Chapter Two	Influential Ingredients	27
Chapter Three	Appetizers and Side Dishes	71
Chapter Four	Main Dishes	85
Chapter Five	Desserts	103
Chapter Six	Beverages	113
Chapter Seven	Holidays and Special Occasions	125
Chapter Eight	Street Food and Snacks	157
Chapter Nine	Dining Out	171
Chapter Ten	Food Issues and Dietary Concerns	187
Glossary		203
Selected Bibliography		207
Index		211

Series Foreword

Imagine a typical American breakfast: bacon, eggs, toast, and home fries from the local diner. Or maybe a protein-packed smoothie, sipped on the go to class or work. In some countries in Europe, breakfast might just be a small cookie and a strong coffee, if anything at all. A South African breakfast might consist of a bowl of corn porridge with milk. In Japan, breakfast might look more like dinner, complete with rice, vegetables, and fish. What we eat varies from country to country, and even region to region. The Global Kitchen series explores the cuisines of different cultures around the world, from the history of food and food staples to main dishes and contemporary issues. Teeming with recipes to try at home, these volumes will delight readers by discovering other cultures through the lens of a treasured topic: food.

Each volume focuses on the culinary heritage of one country or one small group of countries, covering history and contemporary culture. Volumes begin with a chronology of major food-related milestones and events in the area, from prehistory to present. Chapters explore the key foods and meals in the country, covering the following topics:

- Food History;
- Influential Ingredients;
- Appetizers and Side Dishes;
- Main Dishes;
- Desserts;
- Beverages;
- Holidays and Special Occasions;
- Street Food and Snacks;
- Dining Out; and
- Food Issues and Dietary Concerns.

Chapters are textual, and each chapter is accompanied by numerous recipes, adding a hands-on component to the series. Sidebars, a glossary of important terms, and a selected bibliography round out each volume, providing readers with additional information and resources for their personal and scholarly research needs.

Whether readers are looking for recipes to use for classes or at home, or to explore the histories and traditions of world cuisines, the Global Kitchen series will allow readers to fully immerse themselves in other cultures, giving a taste of typical daily life and tradition.

Preface

"I would like to use the term 'Israeli diet' to describe the foods that Israelis eat, while reserving the term 'Israeli food' or 'Israeli cuisine' to describe foods that relate to an image of the nation and national culinary landscape."
—Bernard-Herman, 2014

This book is about both of Bernard-Herman's terms, something I shall call throughout "Israeli food culture." About three-quarters of the text of this book is devoted to describing what Israelis eat, whether in the form of a pictured description, or of recipes that the reader can follow at their leisure. The remaining quarter, interwoven within the descriptive element, is an attempt to answer the question of *how* Israelis eat. I am less concerned here with the issue of meaning, although that emerges from the analytical part as well.

I think it is useful also to note what this book is *not*. This is not a cookbook (there are plenty of excellent Israeli cookbooks, many referenced in the Bibliography). This is also not an academic treatment of Israeli food culture. Rather, this book intertwines some analytical comments with a great deal of observational data about Israeli food, how to make it, and how to consume it as Israelis do.

Pronunciation Guide

Hebrew and Arabic are both difficult to pronounce for nonspeakers. Since the two languages are similar, most remarks here are true for both, except that the pronunciation of Arabic is more guttural. Most of the comments here refer to Hebrew, but unless noted, can be taken for Arabic as well. The orthography of Hebrew and Jewish words is contentious and confusing. I have tried to be consistent, but often a common word goes against this practice, whereupon I have followed the more widespread convention. Thus, "Hanukkah" rather than the more proper "Khanukkah."

- There are two glottal stops: a soft alef/alif, similar to the starting vowels a, i, u, e, o in English; and a throaty stop 'ayin/'ayin pronounced somewhat like a choke in the back of one's throat, 'a, 'i, 'u, 'e, 'o. The 'ayin is represented here by ', for example, '*amba*.
- "r" is rolled and throaty, rolled from the back of the palate.
- A "kh" sound—a hard "h"—(written here kh or ch, since the common orthography is inconsistent. The English "ch" as in "cheek" does not exist) is a throaty scraping like the "ch" in German.
- The accent is almost invariably on the ultimate or penultimate syllable.
- In Hebrew, plurals are generally formed by the suffix ". . . im" for male nouns and ". . . ot" for female. Thus, *kibbutz* (singular, male) and *kibbutzim* (plural, male), but *moshava* (singular, female) and *moshavot* (plural, female).

Israeli and Palestinian

Just to preempt argument. The term "Palestinian" for Arab residents of the West Bank, Gaza, and refugees who left the area of Israel emerged only in the 1960s. Previous to the establishment of the State of Israel, Israeli Jews called themselves "Palestinians." For sake of clarity, in this book, "Israelis" refers to all Israelis: Jewish and Arab citizens of Israel. "Israeli Jews" is obvious. "Israeli Arabs" and "Arab Israelis" refers to those Arabs who are Israeli citizens, most being descendants of those who did *not* flee (or were ejected, depending on version of story) during the War of Independence (1948–1949). "Palestinians" refers to Arab residents of the West Bank and the Gaza Strip who do not have Israeli citizenship and aspire to their own state. This book is about Israeli food culture, which includes many foods and practices common to Israelis and to Palestinians. Palestinians and Arab Israelis have similar, but different, food cultures for sociological and historical reasons. One hopes that a similar book on Palestinian food culture will be published in the future.

A Note on Recipes

Most of the recipes are commonly known recipes that I have cooked for family and friends since my late teens. Although not a professional cook, cooking and studying food culture are something that have engaged me for decades. Very few of the recipes here are "authentic" in the sense that they are the one-and-only way to cook the dish: experimentation and variations are what make a great cuisine. All the recipes here are based on four

Preface

diners. All can be changed to suit larger or smaller numbers. Some varieties of vegetables differ from American ones. For example, the large American cucumbers are almost unavailable in Israel, where smaller, crisp varieties are common.

For all recipes, fresher spices are better than those that have been hanging around for a time. Unless stated otherwise, herbs should be fresh. As a matter of course, Israeli foods based on Middle Eastern or Mediterranean dishes tend to be spicier, whereas those originating in Eastern Europe tend to be sweeter. Adjust according to preference. Israelis argue incessantly about the "best" food or drink. They rarely argue about authenticity, and there is an, at least subliminal, acknowledgment that there are as many ways to make any particular prized dish as there are Israelis willing to try it.

So, if you want to attempt a recipe, don't hesitate to change items, within a fairly broad set of boundaries. Israelis will happily tell you the best of the dish you have made is to be found in a tiny shack, down a lane, in a marginal neighborhood of some city. But they will almost never tell you it is "not authentic." The answer to the authenticity issue, which takes up so much time and so-called scholars' ink, is, to cite a friend of mine: "This is the way I like it. . . ."

Beteavon/Enjoy.

Notation

The abbreviation "q.v." is used in the text to indicate terms/recipes that are discussed in more detail elsewhere in the book. The index will assist the reader in locating these discussions.

Further Reading

Bernard-Herman, Benjamin. 2014. "'It's Not Israeli but You Eat It in Israel': Power and Difference in the Production of Israeli National Cuisine." Undergraduate thesis, Swarthmore College.

Acknowledgments

While I take all responsibility for errors and omissions, this book would not have been possible without the contributions, suggestions, and comments by many people. Zafrira Ashkenazi contributed insights on Israeli cooking, and several recipes, anecdotes, and comments. Tamar Backner did sterling service as local representative, gave access to her library, and contributed from her wide knowledge of Israeli customs and culture, and of the herbal and vegetable resources available to Israeli cooks. My other sisters—Orna, Yael, and Miri—contributed from their experience, and helped by asking their friends for suggestions.

Thanks are due to Fida Nijim-Ektelat for suggestions about Ramadan customs. Gali and Shahar Yehoshua were kind enough to spend several long hours discussing and explaining Samaritan customs and food ways, for which I am very grateful. David Shawgen at Kfar Kama, guided us through the intricacy of Adyghe/Cherkess life, knowledgeably discussed food customs, and suggested some potential recipes. For this, many thanks. Particular thanks are owed Nihaya Halabi for her recipe for Druze *majadarah*, which reached me through her student, my daughter Maayan.

Mikan-no-hime, Sachi-no-hime, Buff, Mandarin, Calico, and Jinjit helped in writing this book by dancing up and down the keyboard at critical moments or demanding to sit in my lap purring while I was writing. Hunter and Binibini were there to distract me with demands for a scratching, and cold noses shoved into my armpit. Thank you all.

Most importantly, I am incredibly grateful to my partner in many culinary and travel adventures, occasional coauthor, and spouse, Jeanne, who contributed to and critiqued my writing while working on her own writing project.

Introduction

Israel, founded in 1948, is like many other countries, relatively new as a nation. Like other new nations, its food history is complex and wound together from many strands. Like the United States, the Israeli population combines immigrant groups that arrived at many different times, blended with locals, left, came back again, and created a vibrant, modern amalgam. The food that the people consume is affected by two main factors: the local topography and climate, and the various cultural preferences practiced by the population, many of which originated elsewhere.

Two things must be kept in mind trying to understand Israeli food practices. First, there are many strands of Israeli food, as people eat both commonly desired foods and foodstuffs and the foods that they learned to accept and like under social settings such as the family. Second, the hot and relatively arid climate means that certain types of agricultural products have been prioritized over others. This latter point must be modified because in the past thirty years at least, Israeli agricultural science has made Israeli agriculture a byword for innovation, both in the technologies of food production and in horticultural development.

All over the Middle East, locals have accepted and modified common foods. Thus, there are Syrian, Lebanese, Egyptian, and other variants of the famous falafel (bean fritters), as well as Israeli variants. Politics notwithstanding, the claimed origin of these foods is a moot point; but the specific local nuances create Lebanese falafel, Egyptian falafel, and Israeli falafel as legitimate variations. In Israel in particular, given the vast heterogeneity of the population as well as population blending, nuances can create great variety in specific "national" dishes, and one cannot claim that this or that recipe is the only "real" dish. So what *is* Israeli food? Israeli food is that branch of Middle Eastern food eaten in Israel, heavily influenced by and blended with non–Middle Eastern, largely European food practices, as well as by religious influences.

Climate and Topography

Climate and topography determine, over a lengthy period of time, what foods are possible and which become incorporated into the daily diet. The climate and topography of Israel are very varied for such a small area (8,000 square miles), which means that even though over half the country's territory is desert (roughly from the town of Kiryat Gat southward), given sufficient water and attention, many subtropical, tropical, and even northern crops are possible somewhere in the country. In addition, there are a great variety of wild plants that have been, and still are, exploited for food.

Temperatures all over the country are warm Mediterranean (about equal to southern California), with warm winters everywhere but in the high hills, and hot, dry summers, except in the Sharon plain and the Jordan valley, which tend to be very humid. Rains fall (if they do—drought is common) between October and April, with occasional showers in May. Snow falls in the higher hills in the Galilee and in Jerusalem. The Arava valley—the strip running from the southern shore of the Dead Sea to the Gulf of Eilat—is hot or warm all year round.

Well-Watered Galilee

The Galilee is heavily cultivated, providing a variety of fruit, ranging from lychees and avocados on the coastal plain to excellent dates (for which the Beit Shean valley along the Jordan is famous) and vegetables of all sorts. The Jezreel valley, which connects the Mediterranean Sea to the Jordan River, is cultivated in grains, fruit, and vegetables produced by a mix of kibbutzim, moshavim, and Arab villages. The hilly areas produce milk products from sheep and goats (and several well-known artisanal cheesemakers), fruit such as apples, and grapes for the table and for wine. Olive groves have been cultivated in the Galilee for millennia, and ancient olive presses have now been replaced by modern, automated machinery. Farmers still bring their harvests individually to be pressed at any one of the many presses.

The climate is warm in the summer and cool in the winter, with occasional snowfall in some years. Although the hills are rocky and difficult to cultivate, the valley areas have rich black soil and produce everything from subtropical to desert fruits and vegetables. There are a few relatively small cities, including Nazareth, and the population and settlement patterns are highly heterogenous. Arab (Muslim and Christian), Druze, and Circassian villages rub shoulders with kibbutzim and moshavim and with cities, some (such as Akko and Nazareth) of great antiquity.

The Coastal Plain

The coastal plain from Rosh Hanikra, where chalk cliffs reach the sea north of Nahariya, to the border of Gaza, and its cities, such as the Tel Aviv conurbation, are hot and humid. Winters, except in the northern part which is cold, tend to be cool and comfortable, summers humid and hot. The soil is a fertile, red, sandy clay called *hamra* ("red" in Arabic), which can produce almost any crop that will tolerate the heat and humidity. Most of the plain is flat, with low hills rising to the east. The plain is heavily populated and contains the Tel Aviv conurbation in the center, with a population exceeding two million.

The coastal plain is the agricultural powerhouse in many ways. Citrus groves used to be the main crop, but the growth of cities has made large-scale silviculture prohibitive. Crops range from strawberries, tomatoes, peppers, cucumbers, and herbs, through citrus, lychees, avocados, sweet persimmons (a locally developed sweet seedless variety is called *Sharon Fruit*, after the central portion of the coastal plain), pecans, olives, almonds, pomegranates, and so on.

Northern Negev

Roughly the area between the cities of Kiryat Gat to the north and Beersheva to the south is a rolling low plain cut by occasional dry riverbeds—*wadis*—which flood in rainy winters. The temperatures are high in the summer, and winter is brief and only slightly cool. Rainfall is uncommon. The northern Negev is bordered on the east by the Judaean hills, and on the west by the coastal plain. Agriculture is possible with irrigation. The population includes largely Jewish cities, kibbutzim and moshavim, and Bedouin tribal settlements. The major city (and road junction) is Beersheva, which has been populated since Chalcolithic (New Stone Age) times.

Most of the agricultural area is dedicated to wheat and other grains, fruit trees, flowers, and melons. With irrigation, the area produces many kinds of fruit, salad vegetables, melons, and other field crops. Red peppers, most of which are exported to Hungary for the production of paprika, are raised as well. Sheep, goats, and camels are raised, and there is some small artisanal cheese production. Many farms specialize in raising chickens, for meat and eggs; and turkeys, which have become a cheap substitute for beef and mutton.

Southern Negev

The southern Negev lies between Beersheva to the north and the port city of Eilat to the south. The western side is mountainous, rocky, and cut by deep gullies and three enormous craters. It is bounded on the west by the Sinai desert and the Egyptian border. The east is composed of the arid Arava valley and the Dead Sea. A unique agricultural product of this area are *kmehin,* otherwise known as *desert truffles.* These fungi, which grow in desert areas of North Africa and the Arabian Peninsula can only be found by the trained eye, and though expensive, they are snapped up by buyers at the market in Beersheva.

The Arava valley is hot and sometimes muggy, with the shores of the Dead Sea being salty as well. Temperatures hover over 100°F in summer and rarely drop below the mid-60s (°F) in winter, allowing a perfect environment for raising export and tropical crops for winter markets, notably in Europe. Along the Arava, a number of kibbutzim and moshavim have made a virtue of necessity. Using modern technology and an intensive breeding program, they have developed table vegetables ranging from cherry tomatoes through circular cucumbers, melons, and other heat-intensive produce that ripen in the winter. Mostly for export, this production ensures a plentiful supply of fresh vegetables in Israeli markets during the winter as well.

The Mountains

The Mountain area consists of ranges of chalk hills that rise east of the Coastal Plain. The hills, which had been largely bare for centuries, have been reforested in the past fifty years. The area is perfect for almonds, which are planted in terraces throughout. The city of Jerusalem is the center of this area, as well as the seat of government. Temperatures are hot in summer and cold in winter, with occasional snow. Jerusalem's population is highly heterogenous, with Jews, Muslims, Christians, and others rubbing shoulders and enjoying one another's food. Smaller settlements include kibbutzim, Arab villages (the most famous of which is Abu Ghosh, on the main road from Jerusalem to Tel Aviv, which is also a Mecca for foodies for its excellent restaurants) and moshavim, most of which raise fruit, poultry, and notably almonds.

Population

As of 2019, the Israeli population stood at about 9 million people. About 75 percent are registered with the Ministry of the Interior as Jews, 18 percent are Muslims (mainly Sunni, a few Shi'a), and 2 percent are Christians, mostly Melkite Greek Catholic and Eastern Orthodox rites, with a scattering of other denominations. About 1.6 percent of the population are Druze, an endogamic sect with roots in twelfth-century Shi'ism. There are scatterings of other ethnic groups, the most prominent are about 5,000 Cherkess (Adighye), who emigrated in the nineteenth century from the Caucasus Mountains, and a few hundred Shomronim (Samaritans), whose religion is similar to Judaism. Around 14,000 Baha'i, people of many nationalities that follow a non-Islamic offshoot of Islam, whose holiest places are located in Israel (Haifa, and between Akko and Nahariya). Baha'i either live in these areas or visit Israel on a regular basis. And, of course, like most modern countries, there are large numbers of expatriates—people whose occupations have brought them to Israel—ranging from American and European company representatives to Jain gem traders.

Jews

Judaism consists of a canon of agreed-upon ritual precepts based on the written Torah, a set of prescriptions and proscriptions codified in the books of Genesis and Deuteronomy in the Bible. A set of interpretations and interpolations—the Mishnah—was formulated by religious experts (rabbis) in the second century CE and added to the canon. This in turn was added to in the Gemara, a component of the Talmud created in the fourth century, and it too became part of the canon. These three bodies of literature are immutable and unchangeable, and they form the basis for later rabbinical legal decisions. Over the subsequent two millennia, rabbis made legal and ritual decisions to fit the canon to daily life, but they observed two principles. First, nothing could be accepted that denied or contravened the Torah or the Talmud (i.e., Mishnah + Gemara + some later interpretations). Second, changes and decisions had to be accepted by consensus, as there was and is no central Judaic authority.

Following what was laid down in the Torah, a great deal of space is allocated to the issue of food: what is allowed, what is not, when, and under what circumstances. Decisions were made by individual rabbis or by colleges of rabbis. As time passed, Jewish communities across the world accepted, rejected, or were completely ignorant of some of these decisions, giving rise to specific communities of ritual practice involving food.

The two largest communities of ritual practice are the Sephardim, which encompasses North African, Portuguese, Turkish, and Balkan Jewish communities, as well as their offshoots in the New World (the original Jewish community of Spain was wiped out after 1495 by the Spanish crown), and Ashkenazim (sons of Ashkenaz, the grandson of Noah), which encompasses most Jewish communities in Western and Eastern Europe and their offshoots in the New World. In addition, there were many other communities of ritual practice: Tsarfati (Provençal), Italki (Italian), Catalan (related liturgically to the Tsarfati), Teimani (Yemeni), Bene Israel (Indian), Beta Israel (Ethiopian), Bukharim (Bokharan) and many others. All of these adhere to the basic principles defined in the Torah and Talmud, but interpretations and food permissions and restrictions may differ. Jewish ritual law is therefore complex, multilayered, and, in some cases inconclusive and contradictory.

Many centers of greater and lesser religious authority emerged, rose, and fell over the twenty-odd centuries since the process started. Traditions were established that are held by the residents of certain geographical areas. There are differences in style and ritual niceties, rather than in beliefs. Overall, individuals usually follow the tradition of their families, although with some quibbles, the essential practices of all styles are considered acceptable to all, and each individual practicing them is as Jewish as the next. Because the preparation and consumption of food are dealt with in Jewish ritual in great detail, and decisions regarding foods affected a wide spectrum of permissible and impermissible foods in defined occasions, these different ritual styles affect their food choices to this day.

In Israel, Jews identify themselves by the degree to which they adhere to the ritual prescriptions and proscriptions, with three practices being symptomatic: keeping the Shabbat, eating kosher, and keeping the fast of Yom Kippur (the Day of Atonement), the most solemn day on the Jewish calendar. Individuals and families may keep all the ritual rules in these three domains, and are thus orthodox, or none at all (secular). Israeli Jews *also* identify themselves (though to a lesser degree than in the past) by *eda*—essentially, the community of ritual practice they or their family identifies with.

The problem is either complicated or simplified (depending on one's point of view) by the growing frequency of marriages between Israelis of different communities of ritual practice. Which tradition the descendants adhere to (if any) depends more on intrafamily dynamics than on rabbinical fiat, and very often also on the fact that many people are not highly orthodox and will eat what they like and can afford, without much regard for tradition. However, stringently ultra-orthodox individuals and families still follow the "our tradition only and always" philosophy.

Orthodox

Orthodox Jews are those who adhere to the 913 requirements of being Jewish. The orthodox amount to about 25 percent of the Jewish population in Israel. Crucially, orthodox Jews in Israel and elsewhere ensure that their food is *glatt* (absolutely) kosher, and no compromises are permitted. Many orthodox are members of a particular rabbinical court and may follow additional commands that come down from the current rabbi or from his predecessors (usually male antecedents) in the court. Some courts came into being in the seventeenth century and carry the weight of making legal and ritual decisions to this day. Others are relatively new, with slightly different forms of courts existing among Ashkenazi and Sephardi orthodox, and so minute differences, in addition to the basic ones, may separate the practices of a particular family from those of other families.

Shomrei Mitzvot/Masortiyim (Observant/Traditional)

This term encompasses a wide range of Jewish religious practices, also called *Shomrei Masoret* (keepers of tradition) and *Masortiyim* (traditional). They constitute about 30 percent of all Jews in Israel. The less observant will fast only on Yom Kippur, while the more observant will attend strictly to the three significant ritual practices (sabbath, *kashrut*, and Yom Kippur). In the middle are people who perform certain ritual behaviors as a matter of course but generally ignore others. Because the degree of observance varies both between individuals and over an individual's lifetime, this category is relatively loose, with boundaries that are not clearly defined. For example, an individual might not wear a *kippa* (skullcap) but still fast during Yom Kippur. Even among those who keep *kashrut*, there are fine gradations in terms of food, between those who adhere to all the food requirements (which are complex and lengthy) and those who choose to eschew certain foods (pork and seafood in particular) from their diet but do not otherwise adhere to all the dietary rules.

Secular

Secular Jews do not adhere on a regular basis to the major dietary or other requirements of Judaism (though some will fast on Yom Kippur or eschew pork or shellfish, claiming to do so for health reasons or by simple preference). They thus interpenetrate the observant group. Between 50 and 65 percent of Israeli Jews define themselves as nonreligious or secular.

In terms of food, this group includes both those who are culinarily adventurous and large numbers of food conservatives, who, though they do not adhere to *kashrut*, nevertheless will rarely eat strange or unfamiliar foods.

In twenty-first-century Israel, religious decisions in the food realm have become less important. The 25 percent of the Jewish population who are deeply orthodox, are loath to adopt so-called strange food habits that could potentially contravene rabbinical injunctions. Moreover, marriages between members of different liturgical communities are now so common as to be the norm, and these new families largely ignore the inconvenient demands of their liturgical community.

The ritual differences between liturgical communities in Judaism include differences in ritual food practices. Thus, Sephardim, who lived in countries where rice was an important grain and where beans were a crucially important mainstay, will eat these foods during Passover, whereas Ashkenazi rabbis, for whom rice and beans were not economically important, forbade them during Passover for fear of fermentation.

Arab Muslim

The largest minority in Israel is composed of Arab Israelis, most of whom are Muslim. The total Arab population of Israel is about two million (amounting to 21 percent of the population). Muslims constitute 90 percent of this population, and they are mainly Sunni, with the rest being Christians. The majority of Arab Israelis live in villages (many of which have become towns due to their population growth). There are two clusters of such villages: one in what is called "the Triangle" in central Israel, northeast of Tel Aviv, and the other in the Galilee in northern Israel. In the past, most of the population in villages were farmers and artisans. Today, they have a range of occupations, both white- and blue-collar. There are also many city dwellers in this demographic, whose way of life has been urbanized for centuries. Jaffa (now a part of Tel Aviv), Akko, and neighborhoods of Haifa have large Arab populations, as do smaller towns in the Galilee. The third large category of Israeli Arabs are the Bedouin nomads. The Bedouin of the Galilee are largely urbanized and have been so for many decades. The Bedouin of the Negev have only recently given up their transhumant way of life, and many of the older people still live in goat hair tents whenever possible, though this custom is dying out.

The Muslim part of the Arab population tends to adhere to Muslim food strictures (no pork, for example). Christian Arabs often raise pork for home consumption and to sell at market. Villagers and former villagers and Bedouin tend to make much use of gathered herbs, which can still be

Introduction

found on the verges of cultivated lands, and there is a large market for nostalgia foods: the wild greens and bulbs that were a mainstay of the poor village and nomadic populations in past decades.

Christian Arabs (around 2 percent of the population) differ from their neighbors from our perspective, largely because they do not celebrate Muslim holidays (and the foods that go with them), and, more important, they raise pigs and eat and sell pork.

Druze

The Druze, whose communities can be found throughout the Levant (in Syria, Lebanon, and Jordan), originated in an offshoot of the Shi'a branch of Islam in the thirteenth century. Centuries of oppression by Sunnis and others combined with religious secrecy and fierce endogamy has meant that though they speak Arabic, they are a distinct ethnic group. About 100,000 Druze live in eighteen Druze villages (some ethnically mixed, some homogenous) in Israel. However, because the community is well integrated into Israeli political and economic life, while they maintain a religious separation, they tend to follow Israeli trends more than do the Arab population. While they maintain Muslim food strictures, due to their self-imposed isolation, they have also evolved specific Druze takes on food, which have interpenetrated Israeli society as a whole.

Cherkess

Originally from the Northern Caucasus Mountains, the Adyghe people, whom the Russians (and the rest of the world) call "Cherkess," were massacred and hounded out of the Russian empire in the mid-nineteenth century. Many settled in the Ottoman Empire in Syria and Turkey itself. A small number established three villages in the Galilee, two of which still exist: Rehaniya and Kfar Kama. Most are Adyghe (the language) and Hebrew bilinguals. The total population consists of about 5,000 people, and though they are Muslims, they are not Arabs. They are endogamous to a great degree, and with the support of the Ministry of Education and Culture, maintain schools that teach their traditional language, culture, and practices. The schools are also centers for teaching Adyghe culture, including food practices, to both Israelis and non-Israeli Adyghe visitors from around the world. For obvious reasons, food practices are an adaptation of their historical homelands' customs to Levantine ones. The food reflects a mixture of these two influences.

Traditionally, the Adyghe placed great emphasis on martial prowess, reticence, and bravery. Their cuisine reflected this as well, including quick, high-energy meals of milk products (e.g., cheeses and yogurts of up to

> ### Khaluzh (Cherkess Cheese Turnovers)
>
> *Yield:* Serves 4
>
> 2 cups flour
> 1½ cups water
> 1 tsp salt
> 1 Tbsp olive oil or other vegetable oil
> 1 cup firm white cheese (the higher the fat content, the better) or use feta
>   or mozzarella in a pinch, crumbled
> Oil for deep frying
>
> 1. Mix flour, water, salt, and oil, and knead to form a smooth, elastic dough.
> 2. Divide dough into a dozen sections and roll them into round balls.
> 3. Flatten each ball on a floured board to about 1/8". thickness.
> 4. Place a teaspoon of cheese just off the center of each dough disk.
> 5. Fold one-half of the disk over the cheese, making sure that the edges of the disk meet in a half-moon shape. Pinch the edges together to seal well.
> 6. Heat the oil to about 200°C (400°F).
> 7. Fry the *khaluzh* a few at a time, ensuring that they do not touch until they achieve a golden color.
>
> *Serve hot on their own, with sweet tea flavored with cinnamon, with honey, or with homemade fruit jam.*

80 percent fat) which made up 60 percent of intake, vegetables, pulses, and grains (making up 30 percent of intake) and some meat (less than 10 percent intake, mainly in feasts). Being thin meant being fighting fit, and traditional clothes emphasized narrow (50-cm) waists for men. Restraint at the table and small portions are cultural imperatives. Many dishes are unique to the Caucasus Mountains, and the Adyghe in particular. Others have been adopted from Turkish and Levantine cuisines. The Cherkess Cultural Center in Kfar Kama promotes Cherkess food through the internet and local tours and hospitality.

Shomronim/Samaritans

Samaritans (*Shomronim* in Hebrew) are a small sect derived from or perhaps emulating Judaism, which is believed to have originated in the surviving population of Samaria after the destruction of the Kingdom of Israel by the Assyrians (approximately 740 BCE). While many of their practices are similar to Judaism, Samaritans maintain a completely separate religious identity. The community numbers about 800 people, divided more or less equally among those living in Holon, Israel, and those living near Nablus in Palestine, on the slopes of their holy mountain, Mt. Grizim. Due to their small numbers, endogamy is not possible, and most Samaritan adults today marry non-Samaritans, although their children are raised as members of the group and faith. The Samaritans have absorbed the food customs of their neighbors—Israelis and Palestinians, respectively—as well as adding new foods introduced by their in-laws. Pesach, Shavuot, and Succoth are the main festivals, as they are the three traditional pilgrimage festivals.

The Sabbath (Shabbat) is maintained as a day of rest and prayer, when no fires or productive work can be done (although domestic tasks are permitted). For the Sabbath, Samaritans retain a set of strict rules that forbid the use of fire, and thus the consumption of hot food. Devices such as timers, commonly found in Jewish orthodox homes, are not used. Instead, Samaritans eat a great many salads, which may be prepared during the Sabbath. Fruit and nibbles are available during the day, although no work is carried out.

Today, the older generations prefer the food that has been passed down from their parents and grandparents—often foods normally consumed by Palestinians and Israelis—but the younger generation prefers more fashionable trends. The Samaritans living around Nablus, among the Arabs, use traditional Arabic names for foods: *molokhiya*, *siniya*, and *makluba* are popular traditional foods, and in Israel, Russian, Georgian, or other foods are mainstays, depending on one's affines.

Kashrut, Halal, and Penguins

Two of the major religions practiced by the Israeli population have strict requirements for the kind of food that may be eaten. In Judaism, these foods are called *kasher*, and the general set of regulations *kashrut* (from which the English word *kosher* is derived). For Muslims (including Druze), permitted meats must fit the rules of *halal*. While the population adheres to these rules to lesser or greater degrees, the religious establishments constantly attempts to extend and strengthen their control over food choices. Some 40 percent of the population who are secular tend to ignore these rules as much as possible.

Kashrut

In Jewish religion, strict regulations indicate permissible and forbidden foods and include a set of rules about time and usage. These derive from restrictions first indicated in the Bible (Leviticus and Deuteronomy, specifically) and elaborated upon by the rabbis (ritual-religious experts) in the Talmud and later exegesis over more than two thousand years. The general principles for food are as follows:

- The meat of all four-footed animals with a cloven hoof who chew cud is permissible. All others are forbidden, with special mention of camels, pigs, and rabbits as strictly forbidden.
- Blood and suet are completely forbidden. The first is removed by orthodox Jews by draining and salting, and the latter is cut out. The flesh of mangled carcasses, or those not properly slaughtered, is likewise forbidden.
- The flesh and eggs of all fowl who have a crop may be eaten. All others (the ostrich and vulture are named prominently) are forbidden.
- Fish that have both fins and scales are permitted. All others (which includes eel, shark, catfish, and, controversially, tuna) are forbidden.
- All other animals are forbidden to eat, except for locusts, which, since they constitute a pest that, when swarming, can destroy an entire crop and bring about famine, are permitted.
- The slaughter of all animals for food must be done quickly and cleanly, cutting the jugular with a very sharp knife (there are regulations dictating precise dimensions and measures of the instrument) while reciting a prayer. The animal is then inspected internally to ensure that it is not diseased or otherwise imperfect, and all blood is drained from the body and discarded. Slaughtering is usually done by professional slaughterers (*shochet*), but it can be done by anyone who adheres to the rules.
- There must be no mixing of milk (or its products) with meat (or meat products) in the same storage place, or eaten in the same meal or with the same utensils. There must be a pause (lasting six hours) between consuming meat and consuming milk or vice versa.
- All agricultural produce is permitted, though once every seven years, the land must rest and may not be cultivated. Once every fifty years (a Jubilee), the land must not be cultivated at all, and no crops brought in.
- From sunset on Friday to sunset on Saturday, lighting fires (and thus cooking) is forbidden, following the Tenth Commandment, which forbids work on the Sabbath. As a consequence, all Jewish communities have evolved either long-cooking stews (fires can be left lit, so long as they are not tended) or cold collations for the Sabbath.
- During Passover, when Jews are required to eschew leavened grain, no bread, beer, or other fermented grain products may be consumed, or even owned; nationally, all *hametz* (bread and other fermented and leavened products) are sold notionally to a non-Jew.

In practice, not everyone adheres to these rules with great vigor. On the other hand, many ultra-orthodox communities and individuals practice even stricter observances. For example, in some ultra-orthodox communities, *matza* (the unleavened flat bread required for Passover) must be prepared within 18 seconds to avoid the slightest hint of leavening.

Kashrut requirements have major positive and negative effects on Israeli food culture. Due to the Israeli election system, small parties, which can join a government coalition, can have a disproportionate effect on government survival and legislation. While the orthodox Jewish community is a minority in terms of numbers, it has always been able to muster enough Knesset (parliament) representatives to play a kingmaker role in elections. The trade-off has always been that these parties have demanded control over all issues related to *kashrut* (as well as other religiously charged issues, such as marriage). As a consequence, the official government rabbinate has a monopoly on deciding whether a product or service is kasher. Restaurants, food vendors such as supermarkets, the military, and most public food services may acquire a *kashrut* certificate (which must be displayed prominently and renewed annually). Because most of the population, while not zealous about *kashrut*, do feel it necessary to adhere to some parts of it (e.g., not consuming pork), most establishments go with the flow. Until the start of the twenty-first century, for instance, few restaurants would not have a *kashrut* certificate unless they were non-Jewish owned (e.g., Arab restaurants) or set out from the start to serve nonkasher foods: even Chinese, Japanese, Thai, and other restaurants had to decide whether to market for the general public (and acquire a certificate) or eschew the certificate and serve dishes that include pork, shrimp, and other nonkasher foods.

Kashrut certificates are not expensive, and most businesses can easily afford them. But there is a catch. For a business to *retain* the certificate, its premises must be inspected by an inspector licensed by the local municipal or rural government rabbinate. These inspections, done daily (or at least weekly), cost a great deal of money, adding a hefty percentage to the price of foods in Israel. Moreover, because the appointment of a *kashrut* inspector is a perk of the local rabbinate, these positions are often awarded on the basis of nepotism, political support, or outright bribery. While many inspectors undoubtedly carry out their well-paid jobs conscientiously and honestly, there are also many cases of inspectors demanding that the proprietor purchase raw materials from certain suppliers or make life difficult for competitors of their protegés. As a consequence, Israelis who feel hampered by *kashrut* requirements flock to non-kosher establishments, notably during Passover, when nonorthodox Jewish Israelis buy fresh pitot at Arab

> ### The Kibbutz and the Penguins
>
> The grilled meat boom in the early 1960s included not only religiously permitted meats, but also a demand for pork. The religious parties in the Knesset strongly opposed the raising of pigs. Kibbutzim, responding to the government's urging to diversify agriculture, soon hit on the idea of eating pork. To avoid the religious establishment's inspections, kibbutz members found two workarounds. In most cases, agriculture licenses (required in order to receive water and land quotas, both controlled in resource-limited Israel) were sought for "pig skin for skin-burn and skin-replacement therapies." Very few could quibble with that. The leftover side product, such as meat, was sold in the market.
>
> An unverified urban legend says that one kibbutz in the early 1950s went even further. Reasoning that few Jewish religious people had ever seen a pig, they requested a license to import a breeding stock of . . . penguins. The penguins were round, pink, and made an "oink" sound. Because Israel has a warm climate, no one had seen a genuine penguin either. Thus, in popular parlance, pork is sometimes known as "white meat," "penguin," or "Norwegian sheep" (which happen to be hairless and rather pink . . .).

communities, or they eat there in preference to *kashrut*-maintaining establishments, or they eat at non-kosher restaurants that serve pork

In summary, *kashrut* has had many ramifications for Israeli food culture. First, certain foods and practices are habitually maintained throughout the country, in large part by *kashrut* demands. Second, the formalization of the *kashrut* system raises food prices and affects food choices made by Israelis—not just those who are religious, but those who are not but do not have a choice of what food to eat. Third, the *kashrut* system is a major source of corruption, both financial and political. Finally, *kashrut* has driven many Israelis to search for nontraditional food alternatives as a simple act of rebellion against orthodox dominance in the private and public spheres of life.

Halal

In Islam, strict but simple regulations determine what is edible and how animals must be slaughtered:

- The meat of all animals, except those prohibited, are acceptable as food. Some animals—sheep, goats, and camel calves—are particularly valued.

Introduction

- The pig and dog are specifically prohibited for consumption, and their flesh is considered polluting.
- The slaughter of all animals for food must be done with a sharp knife passed across the throat, with the animal facing Mecca, and the slaughterer must recite the *shahada* (the profession of faith).
- Blood must not be eaten.
- Live slaughter is enjoined on Muslims for festivals and special events, though not all can afford, or are otherwise unable, to follow this requirement fully, and so they must rely on charity or community support.

In rural areas, notwithstanding the weak protestations by health authorities, ritual slaughter is carried out in Israel, when ritually required and possible, by both Muslims and Jews. In urban areas, slaughter is much more problematic, and many traditions that require slaughter—Muslim, Jewish, or Samaritan—do so only in special enclosures during mass holiday events.

One issue with slaughter is the often-harsh treatment of animals, cared for, if at all, by indifferent keepers. This has raised problems in Israel, with accusations and counteraccusations flying back and forth essentially between modernists, who want to see animals treated more humanely, and traditionalists, who insist on their right to act according to religious strictures at a reasonable cost.

Meals and Performance

Mary Douglas, a British anthropologist, was one of the pioneers in food studies; she worked during the twentieth century and showed that food events—meals, snacks, and feasts—were also forms of cultural performance. Food, she argued, has significance beyond the mere fact of the human body absorbing fuel. Following up on this idea, she suggested that meals have structures that are repeated in any given culture for any particular meal and meal type. The following discussion gives a brief introduction to this idea, developed from Khare (1980). The analysis focuses on six domains of activity, which can be formalized into a number of brief questions: What is eaten? How is food consumed? When is it consumed? Who prepares the food? With whom is the food consumed? Why have this combination of food, personnel, time, and presentation?

What Is Consumed?

A question this book addresses in some detail is, "What foods are eaten in Israeli food culture?" That is, what are the basic materials, and where do they come from? The choice of foods in any given culture depends on three limiters: the ecology, trade, and choice of cultural limiters.

The ecology of Israel—Mediterranean dry and large desert areas—has dictated a selection of plant and animal foods that have been exploited since the Chalcolithic, perhaps even before. This includes tree crops such as olives and dates, grasses such as wheat and barley, and herbs for flavoring and sustenance ranging from wild oregano to artichokes.

Trade, both throughout history and in the modern era, has introduced the area to new crops and foods, some of which arrived in antiquity and have prospered, such as citrus, eggplant, potatoes, and peppers. In the late twentieth and early twenty-first centuries, commercial interests have brought Israeli farmers and agroscientists to consider and adopt many crops that had not been known before (hence the introduction of new fruits and vegetables and new breeds of food animals such as the turkey and carp). Trade limitations have also had an effect: the nation was generally relatively poor in the first decades of its existence, so virtue was made of necessity. As a result, fresh vegetables form a large part of the Israeli diet. Short-term milk and milk products—milk, yogurt, soft cheeses, and others—became a source of energy and even protein for much of the population.

Finally, cultural choice also selects which foods are eaten. Many Jews and Muslims—the majority of the population—eschew pork and pork products for religious reasons, so pork is not an item on menus in most cases. Meat selected and prepared to be absolutely kosher (i.e., edible by Jewish religious standards) is expensive, so turkey and chicken became more common than beef and mutton.

A significant marker of food culture is the question of elaboration. All food cultures elaborate their food with special rules, food sources, preparation rules, and serving roles on special occasions. However, how elaborate is food, both on a daily basis and in general?

Israeli food preparation is often simple, with few dishes relying on more than one cooking method sequentially. Aside from fresh vegetables or fruit, often in a salad, food is usually simmered, grilled, or baked. A cook may add decorative elements—minced parsley, *za'atar*, *tsnobar* (pine seeds), sugar, pomegranate seeds, sumac, paprika, or cinnamon, depending on the dish—but most food is served without much fuss or elaboration. Food is often heavily spiced and may contain hot peppers, as Israeli men in particular pride themselves on their ability to eat hot foods. Foods with multiple ingredients cooked separately and then mixed are also uncommon outside luxury restaurants.

Introduction

Even baked goods—cakes of European or Middle Eastern origin—tend to be less elaborate than their originals overseas. This may be partly because of the history of the *tsena* (rationing) period, when both fuel and expensive foods such as cream were in short supply. And perhaps it is because this is an element of the desirable Israeli cultural quality of being straightforward and unfussy, called *dugri* ("straight/forthright," from the Arabic).

How Is Food Eaten?

Certain foods, under certain circumstances, may be controlled by more or less rigid rules about how to present and to consume them. For example, consider inviting your family to a meal and insisting that everyone sit on the floor, facing away from one another. The choice of eating utensils ranges from using one's hands, to specific utensils made of specific materials in a specified way. The order of food in a meal is significant as well, and woe betide the individual or guest who violates these rules egregiously.

By and large, Israelis eat using what is called "Russian settings" in the same way as most of Europe and the United States: one or more plates/bowls for each diner, a knife, fork, and spoon, and possibly a dessert spoon and/or fork. There is also a drinking container. There are specific rules governing which utensil/container is to be used for what, how, and in what order—try raising your soup bowl to your lips and drinking directly from it during a formal, European-style meal, if you wish to test this last proposition. Similarly, the meal proceeds in some regularized form ("from soup to nuts" is the English expression): the pre-main dish is generally savory, including starters and soups; and then there is a main dish of cooked vegetables and carbohydrates, with meat if allowed, affordable, and available; and the meal ends with a sweet and then perhaps a savory item.

Israelis of non-European or North African backgrounds do not always adhere to European settings, utensils, or order of dishes, though they are usually aware of them. Israeli Arabs and *Mizrahim* (which means anyone with roots in Middle Eastern or Asian cultures) may eat on a floor covering, sharing food from common dishes placed before them. Some, such as Bedouins, eat with their right hands only, and men and women eat separately. In such settings, there are often no separate courses or removes, but all food, except perhaps the final coffee and sweet, is placed on the floor cloth together, and diners help themselves as they will.

Note that an order exists in the daily service of food, as well as weekly, monthly, and annually. Daily meals tend to be simpler than special-event meals such as the Sabbath, and annually, there are special meals in which greater elaboration and ceremony are expected.

Table Settings

In Western-oriented meals, foods are ladled/transferred from a central bowl or serving dish to a diner's individual plate, and then consumed with the aid of a knife, fork, and spoon. More often than not in Israel, meals are served at a table in the European manner (picnics, informal snacks, and eating in front of the TV are exceptions). In Middle East–oriented meals, plates, basins, and bowls of various foods are presented together, sometimes on a table, often on a special floormat or carpet, and diners help themselves from common dishes using their hands, or spoons for items such as soups.

Most Jewish households in Israel will maintain, if possible, at least two sets of dishes: daily dishes and special dishes. Daily dishes may be mismatched pieces, made of different materials (glass china, ceramic, plastic, or metal) and may be used for all meals where only family are present. Special dishes may be used for ritual events, ranging from social entertaining through the Friday-night Sabbath meal, culminating in the Passover Seder. In religious Jewish households, the Passover set of dishes and utensils, which must be free of any taint of leavened foods, may be used only for Passover, for fear of leavened contamination. And even so, they are usually boiled before use. Some orthodox Jewish religious movements, in an attempt to ritualize supposedly better (according to them) Jewish behavior, offer free boiling services in many secular neighborhoods.

Arab Israelis may maintain European-style utensils and dishes for occasions with Westernized peers, but because standard dining practices are based on shared dishes, they always have sets of small dishes for serving common foods, from which diners help themselves with pita or other flatbreads. Large basins made of metal or ceramic hold central dishes such as meat, rice, and other principal foods. Instead of metal utensils, traditional diners eat with their hands.

Water or other drinks are served in whatever the household has handy for daily meals, and in drinking vessels that are as elaborate as they can afford—glass, china, metal—during special events.

Timing: What Rules Determine When Foods Are Consumed?

In the United States, dinner is served at around 7 p.m., give or take. This is unreasonably early for Spaniards, who don't really consider having dinner before 9 p.m. Timing is also calendrical: to test this point, try serving roast turkey, sweet potatoes, pumpkin pie, and all the trimmings in April, or serving hot dogs and relish for Christmas dinner.

For Jewish Israelis, there may be rigid timing rules on a weekly and annual basis, which are defined by the ritual demands of the Sabbath and of the annual religious cycle, which makes both obligatory and customary requirements of the individual and family with regard to food. Significantly, for religious Jews, ranging from the less strict *masortiyim* to the ultra-orthodox, who strictly maintain all religious prescriptions and proscriptions, the daily, weekly, and annual meals are maintained with specific foods enjoined or forbidden at specific times and days. To make things even more complicated, various liturgical communities, ranging from the broadly defined Mizrahi (Easterners), Sephardi (Spanish), and Ashkenazi (Western and Eastern European) to different religious schools and movements, have their own preferences about how to carry out specified prescriptions and how these are expressed in food preparation and service.

Broadly speaking, Israelis eat three full meals and two snacks a day. Breakfast is had early, before work or school, a midday meal at around 1 p.m. to 2 p.m., and an evening meal whose time varies from 7 p.m. to quite late, notably when entertaining or eating out. In addition, when possible, Israelis eat a snack and coffee around 10 a.m., appropriately called *aruchat eser* (ten [o'clock] meal) and another at around four in the afternoon, *aruchat arba*. Other occasional snacks are also possible, such as an ice cream bar or a bag of sunflower seeds; these impromptu snacks are also known as *nishnushim*, a Hebraicization of the Yiddish *nosh*. While some 40 percent of Israelis do not adhere to religious proscriptions on mixing meat and milk at a meal, light meals tend to be based on milk products, whereas heavier meals include meat (assuming the family can afford it, is not ideologically opposed to meat, etc.). This may well be a product of the *tsena* period, when meat was scarce and milk products and vegetables were eaten instead.

The weekly rhythm is defined for Jewish Israelis, religious or otherwise, by the Sabbath. Most services and merchants are closed, so purchases must be accomplished before sundown on Friday. For most Jewish families, Friday night is a family meal. This is usually more formal than the daily evening meal (even in nonreligious households), often with wine and greater elaboration of both the settings and the number and quality of the foods offered: more often than not a meat dish, possibly a fish dish, some form of starter, and dessert. Saturday lunch, which for observant Jews takes place after Saturday prayers at the synagogue, is also a special meal. In observant households, where lighting fires and working are prohibited from Friday evening on, the meal usually consists of one of the many ethnic variants of *hamin*: a stew that has been on a low fire since Friday before sundown; because lighting or extinguishing a fire is ritually defined as work, it is forbidden on Saturdays.

The annual round provides more specific food requirements. There is one major fast in Judaism—Yom Kippur—when the observant fast from sundown to sundown, and several lesser ones. Special foods are served before and after, but not during the fasts, and the foods are generally meant to enhance the fasting occasion. Other holidays (e.g., Passover) have either prescribed foods, in which the foods and their order are defined specifically, or foods that are traditionally consumed, even if not prescribed, such as cheese and milk-based foods during Shavuot, the spring harvest holiday. Even Israel's one secular holiday, Yom Ha'atzmaut (Independence Day), now has its own foods—specifically *mangal* (grilled meat over charcoal), to which many families adhere.

While the Jewish holidays are not followed by the Muslim and Christian population, they are bound to some degree to the Jewish calendar in two ways. First, outside large Christian/Muslim population centers such as Akko and Nazareth, businesses, including supermarkets, are closed. Second, and perhaps no less important, nonobservant Jews turn to their non-Jewish neighbors as a source of eating out. Arab restaurants do heavy business during Jewish holidays, notably Passover and even Yom Kippur, when food restrictions on publicly available food are at their strongest. On the days before Passover, when Jewish-owned supermarkets and shops stop selling *hametz* (everything leavened, ranging from beer to bread to baked snacks), Arab-owned pita bakeries sell masses of pita and other breads wrapped in plastic for convenient freezing, enough to last the Passover holiday.

Depending on the sect involved, food prescriptions may be far less onerous for Christian Israelis. Coptic followers have many fast and meatless days, which are relatively easily catered to. Easter is commonly celebrated with traditional dishes by the various branches of orthodox Christianity. Christmas and Easter are celebrated with specific foods, those required by the faith or simply habitual for a particular ethnic group.

For Muslims, 'Id al 'Adha and 'Id al Fitr, which bracket the holy fasting month of Ramadan, and Ramadan itself enjoin special foods to start and break the fast and to celebrate with the sacrifice of a slaughtered sheep. Friday, which is the day of common prayer, also requires a celebratory family meal after the prayer.

Finally, for all communities, special events require special foods, some prescribed by religious practice and others customary for a given ethnic or origin group. Events ranging from birth through circumcision (practiced by both Jews and Muslims), coming of age, marriage, and death demand specific foods that are adhered to, to a greater or lesser degree, depending on family practice and community expectations.

Who Prepares?

Daily meals are normally prepared, all over the world, by housewives: "the woman of the house." It is not only considered by many to be part of her duties, but also an expression of family values, love, and domesticity. Serving food in the domestic sphere is mainly a female occupation as well. Exceptions are in collective forms of dining, kibbutzim, the army, and in restaurants where male waiters commonly serve food.

In most households in Israel, women do most of the cooking and much of the shopping. In younger households, men participate more in the cooking. Similarly, those with a European background are more likely to share domestic work, including cooking and grocery shopping. In religious households, shopping, cooking, and presenting food are a woman's domain: the housewife and her daughters. The same is true when considering religiosity: religious men rarely, if ever, do domestic chores, including culinary ones.

Who Dines?

The rules of commensality—who eats with whom, and under what circumstances—vary from one culture to another. For example, with whom does one buy and share ice cream cones? Certainly not with a guest who is one's boss. Whereas a five-course dinner, from soup to nuts, is usually not served to underage children, it may include one's social or business superiors. Rules that determine commensality are complex and varied in every society. The variables include the social status of the potential diners, their relationship, the event, and the ongoing social situation. In Israel, where roles and positions are often fluid and multiplex, this complexity is even greater because there are few hard-and-fast rules to go by.

Most Israeli families make efforts to have at least one meal (and if possible more than one) together. This may include only a nuclear family (parents and minor children) or, notably with special events such as Friday night or Saturday midday dinner, it may involve the extended family, including married children and their families, possibly in-laws, and other close relatives. Celebratory meals, including both calendrical events and life-passage events such as weddings, involve much of the extended family, friends, and often work colleagues and other significant others.

Friday night dinner is one meal in which the entire Jewish family is expected to participate (whether the household is religious or not), and even in secular households, it is often a festive meal, with special place settings, wine and wineglasses, and good cutlery and plates. Often the table is decorated with flowers and Jewish symbology: *challah* bread, candles, and spices. Special foods, such as extra meat, more elaborate dishes, and a greater selection of dishes than is usually consumed, also mark the Friday night meal. There is also often an attempt to include relatives—notably the older generation, who may live apart from the household in question.

At the individual level, where food events are usually (but not always) snacks, different rules apply. Because displays of generosity are important in Israeli culture, the idea of sharing food, albeit by strict rules, is commonplace. Children often have unwritten rules regarding sharing treats. Thus, for instance, a child with a treat may declare, "Bli kibudim!" ("No sharing!"), which exempts her or him from sharing the treat, unless a peer has declared, "Im kibudim!" ("With sharing!") previously, in which case the treat must be shared with those who were present at the call (anyone who arrives later is left out if the owner once again declares, "Bli kibudim!").

At a later age—and certainly among young men—one is expected to share as a matter of course. Here, the Israeli preference for common dishes that can be distributed easily helps when creating shared food. Hummus, that quintessential Israeli food, allows a number of people to share, each one mopping up some hummus with a piece of pita. The same is true for other snacks such as *pitzuchim* (nuts and seeds), though not for such items as falafel, which is difficult to share. It is common to see a group of friends sitting at a café or restaurant and sharing some *mezzes*, all of which can be eaten with the hands, with a fork, or soaked up with a pita. The table will likely include at least hummus, a small salad, and mixed pickles, and the food is viewed as a common snack.

In some environments, shared meals include many potential strangers. Army messes (to which most Israelis are exposed at some point), kibbutz meals, and the tables (*tisch*) of famous rabbis are examples in which individuals of defined status share a common meal, sometimes with formal acknowledgment and great ceremony (a rabbi's *tisch*) or as a matter of course (a kibbutz meal). All in all, Israelis move easily among different forms of communal meals and have no problem sharing food with others. Given that meals are considered a social event in which conversation and

Degrees of Variance

The rigidity of food practices is a useful indicator of aspects of a food culture. In some food cultures, rules are absolutely inflexible: in many East Asian societies, for instance, a food event in which rice is served is a meal, while every other food event is a snack. This has social and cultural implications that go beyond the meal itself (Ashkenazi and Jacob, 1999).

The ways in which food is presented, the order it is consumed, and other rules tend to be relaxed in Israeli food events. This, however, excludes holiday meals, which are often prescribed in minute detail by religious practice. Not everyone adheres to these minutiae (in fact, many Israelis schedule holidays abroad during Pesach precisely to avoid these iron-clad requirements). On the whole, people expect a meal to end with some kind of sweet—whether fruit, a cooked dessert, or some pastry, with coffee—and to have foods designated as *pitzuchim* to be excluded from a meal, but included in a snack. The former is more formal, and the latter less and may be impromptu.

Different sets of rules are in force during religiously mandated food events. The degree to which these are observed depends on two factors: the religiosity or traditionality of those concerned (to what degree do they adhere to the religious strictures?) and the particular event. For Jews, Rosh Hashana, Yom Kippur, and Pesach are the three most prominent holidays, and thus the most rigid in their food rules. Highly religious people will adhere to all of them, and the nonreligious will not (they may, for instance, eat *hametz* during Passover, or refrain from fasting during Yom Kippur). Muslims and Christians have far fewer religiously determined food choices, though for Muslims, foods preferred by the Prophet Muhammad have greater status and demand.

Where People Eat

By and large, the more formal a food event is, the more public it is as well. While formal food events do take place within the household, they often become semipublic by virtue of a preference for participation in such events of friends and family. One such formal food event most often celebrated within the household—the Passover Seder—is officially a public event, as the ritual meals starts with opening the door to the outside and inviting "every poor [person] is invited to eat, anyone in need, invited to share the Pesach." I have never known this broad invitation to be accepted by a stranger, but still. . . . Informal food events tend to be private but may be consumed in public. As a rule, meals are more formal, snacks less so.

Informal, Nonpublic Food Events

For most people, most of the time, food is eaten at home. Daily family meals are most often eaten in the kitchen around a table or, in more affluent/larger homes, in a dining alcove or dining room next to the kitchen. However, even in the household, there are alternative locations. Guests may be fed informally in the living room around a low table that characterizes most Israeli living rooms, or formally around a dining table. Many Israelis live in apartments in multistory, multifamily buildings, all of which are equipped with an outside balcony by law. The balcony, if large enough, is the site of snack consumption (with or without guests), and even the occasional barbecue. Those living in a house with a garden will also barbecue outside, of course.

Snacks, including light meals, may be consumed within the framework of some food producer, such as a café or a bakery. It is just as common to eat some foods—hand meals such as falafel or a handful of *pitzuchim*—while walking on the street, sitting on a curb or in a bus station, or on a park bench or at the beach. Such meals, including drinks, may be indulged in at any time and in almost any location.

Barbecues and picnics may take place anywhere (and often do, to the surprise of outsiders). They may be consumed at any time, but at a higher frequency during holidays and on Saturdays. They tend to peak during nonreligious holidays, when even orthodox Jews will engage in a picnic (as the rules against labor, which include cooking, lighting fires, and driving are not in force during secular holidays).

Formal Public Food Events

Formal food events, usually tied to special functions ranging from official receptions to weddings to business meetings, take place in a dedicated area, which may be permanent or may be erected for an occasion (see Succoth and Mimouna q.v.) such as a national holiday. The courts of orthodox and ultra-orthodox rabbis hold *tisch,* which the followers of the particular rabbi or court will attend if they can, and at which specific blessings, a sermon, or other ritual activity might take place. The rabbi's food choices are paramount, as is his sharing of items of food with particularly favored disciples.

Informal Public Settings

The most common informal public setting is the myriad of restaurants, cafés, and bars found throughout the country. They cater to all levels of society. A large niche is reserved for so-called Mis'adot Mizrahiyot (Eastern restaurants), a codeword for restaurants that serve Levantine foods—*mezze*, grilled meats, and others—many run by Israeli Arabs and serving a modified Israeli-Arab menu. Other restaurants run the gamut from French haute cuisine to nouvelle cuisine to "exotic" foreign cuisines, Argentinian grilled meats, seafood specialists, Japanese and Thai restaurants, Persian and Indian foods (at varying economic levels), pizzerias, and a wide net of American and American-like food chains. Few people eat at restaurants all the time, but virtually everyone (perhaps excluding the ultra-orthodox) has eaten at one once (depending, of course, on the individual budget).

Life-cycle events ranging from births through weddings and deaths are signified by all Israelis by some commitment to joint food production and consumption. Weddings, in particular are celebrated in a wedding hall or some other public venue, with many people trying to "keep up with the Joneses" in terms of the fashionable food available, and the cost and formality of the proceedings. Considering that many people may be invited (in Arab villages, kibbutzim, and the entire village may participate in some moshavim), absolutely formal proceedings are unlikely.

Further Reading

Ashkenazi, Michael, and Jeanne Jacob. 1999. *The Essence of Japanese Cuisine: An Essay on Food and Culture*. London: Curzon Press.

Khare, R. S. 1980. "Food as Nutrition and Culture: Notes Towards an Anthropological Methodology." *Social Science Information* 19(3): 519–42.

Chronology

c.300 BCE
Laws of *kashrut* codified.

123 CE
Most Jews exiled from Land of Israel after the Bar Kochva revolt.

200 CE
Reestablishment of Jewish religious communities in Galilee and Mesopotamia. Mishnah is codified.

200 CE
Seder codified.

400 CE
Gemara is codified.

684 CE
Conquest of Jerusalem and its Byzantine province by the Muslim Arabs. Subsequent decay of the Jewish community.

1880–1903
First Aliya. Yemenite and Eastern European Jews immigrate and settle, founding moshavot and semi-urban communities.

1904–1914
Second Aliya. Eastern European (mainly Russian) members of socialist movements settle in then-Palestine. First kibbutzim emerge along with less-collectivized moshavim agricultural communities.

1936–1939
Third Aliya: German Jews fleeing the Nazis. Mainly settle and develop new urban areas.

1945–1950
Post-WWII European Aliya.

1949–1957
Mizrachi aliya. Mass settlement of Jews expelled from or voluntarily leaving Arab countries settle in Israel.

1947–1960
Rationing of imported foods as well as meat, coffee, and other foodstuffs.

1970–
Israeli agricultural technology takes off.

1980–
After decades of modest circumstances, Israeli economy and consumption patterns start to emulate developed countries.

2000–
Israeli food becomes known worldwide thanks to the establishment of gourmet Israeli restaurants abroad (United States, London, Amsterdam).

CHAPTER ONE

Food History

Israeli food culture is largely shaped by three historical factors.

First, it is useful to start with a book compiled some 2,500 years ago: the Bible. A great deal of the Bible is devoted to food and agricultural production. A number of early descriptions of dishes can, in principle, be followed today. Thus, in Genesis 18:3–8, Abraham slaughters and prepares a calf for honored guests and serves it with cheese and curds and freshly baked bread. To this day, nomadic Bedouin will prepare sheep this way for the feeding of important guests (with some differences, such as the inclusion of rice). More significantly, perhaps, is that the Bible describes commonly used crops that are still highly valued. "The Seven Species" of harvest—wheat, barley, grapes, figs, pomegranates, olives, and dates—are all highly desirable today, and to which a number of Jewish rituals are connected. They are also important elements in modern Israeli food consumption.

Second, Israeli culinary history is also characterized, and largely formed, by waves of immigrants who have entered the country since the nineteenth century. Each of these waves of immigrants (as well as smaller groups and families who immigrated to Israel before and throughout all this time) brought with them culinary ideas and practices. And while the acceptance of these innovations by the general population took time, by the first decade of the twenty-first century, new foods had begun to flood the market, so that even *sabras* (native born Israelis, traditionally rough, not known for refinement or fine taste) were accepting new foods ranging from Yemenite fried-dough *malawach*, through Ethiopian *wot* stew and Druze *labaneh* cheese, to American cupcakes.

A third major culinary influence is Middle Eastern food. Jews immigrating from Middle Eastern countries—principally Lebanon, Egypt, Syria, and Iraq—and local Arabs contributed their culinary preferences, which have become an integral part of Israeli food culture, for both Jews and Arabs of all categories. Some Middle Eastern foods such as hummus and falafel have become identified, within the country as well as internationally, as quintessentially Israeli, although they are eaten all across the Middle East.

The violent relations between Arab Middle Eastern countries have not affected the picture much. Israeli food tends to be more varied than Palestinian for the reasons cited previously. The effect of Arab foods on Israeli cuisine is much greater than the reverse. On the whole, Israelis have learned more from their neighbors' culinary habits than have the citizens of the Arab states learned from Israeli cuisine. Israeli-Arab food has always been popular, and a mainstay of the restaurant business. Most Israelis who enjoy their food expect to find the best Middle Eastern food in Arab restaurants (Israeli-Arab or Palestinian) and this recognition is not much affected by the political or security situations. Many Arab dishes—Syrian, Lebanese, Iraqi, Palestinian, Egyptian—have become staples of Israeli food, adopted from locals or brought by Jewish former residents of those countries. In the past two or three decades, there has been a greater appreciation for traditional foods—Arab and Jewish—and the traditional foods of places such as the Druze villages, Galilee Arab villages, and Old Jerusalem now have devoted followers.

Prehistory: Rhinoceros, Ostrich Eggs, and the Bread You Eat

Israel is located at the intersection of several major topographical features. It serves as the single land bridge between Asia/Europe and Africa, which means that various species—humans, animals, and plants—have left traces and descendants as they migrated between the two continents. It is also part of the Eastern littoral of the Mediterranean Sea and the final western reach of the great Arabian Desert. Finally, it sits on the shores of two seas: the Mediterranean to the west and the Gulf of Aqaba/Eilat, a branch of the Red Sea, to the south.

Traces of early hominins, including Neanderthals and prehumans, have been excavated in numerous sites in Israel. And their remains include foods and food sources. Remains of kitchens and middens found include many animal sources that are not found today, such as rhinoceros and ostriches, as well as crocodiles (the last Nile crocodile in Israel was shot by an overeager Briton in the nineteenth century). A variety of seeds—many that later became domesticated in the form of wheats and barley—were eaten. Honey was a food source, along with greens that are eaten today.

About ten thousand years ago, a revolution occurred in human living conditions, as people began systematizing the protection and development of food sources. This, the development of agriculture—known as

Food History

the "Neolithic Revolution"—allowed for the rise of large populations, differentiated economies, innovations such as writing, and cities: by the third millennium BCE, the first cities that produced city records such as Ur had been established in Mesopotamia and others in Egypt. This happened several times in different places: China, Vietnam, India, the Caucases, and the Fertile Crescent lands of the Middle East: an arc stretching from Egypt to Mesopotamia. A number of food plants still immensely important for the food culture of the area, which includes modern Israel, became major, regular, sources of food. This includes what the Bible later calls "The Seven Species."

Cities emerged in Canaan and the rest of the Levantine coast as well, and although under the shadow (and sometimes actual rule) of the greater empires, they flourished and their population practiced both irrigated and dry agriculture. Small and larger industries—winemaking, olive oil presses, and fruit drying—were present and functioning during all times of peace.

Biblical and Archaeological Sources

What we know about the early history of the area that is now Israel comes from two sources: modern archaeological research and the Bible. While in many instances these two sources are in agreement, both the interpretation of the data, and the data themselves, are contentious. The food described in the chapters of the Pentateuch may well reflect foods eaten at the time the Bible was written and compiled, during the later years of the Judaean Kingdom (eighth[?]–sixth centuries BCE). Nevertheless, since change was much more gradual at the time, the Bible does represent a valuable resource when it discusses food sources, presentation, and specific dishes. For example, early menus are described in Genesis, when Abraham prepares a feast for visitors, offering them cooked calf, bread, cheese, and what is probably yogurt, and when Abraham's grandson Jacob cooks a lentil stew.

Food, or rather, food sources, feature prominently in the Bible and in archaeological remains, so a great deal is known about culinary practices from that period. Grain and other foodstuff were harvested using simple tools, often of flint. Products were stored in large pots. Cooking took place in clay pots resting on stones in a hearth, which tended to be the center of the home. Simple dome ovens were developed later, which made baking bread economical. Stone-ground bread was the staple of life. Herbs and edible greens were collected and commonly eaten with olive oil and bread. Meat was a luxury, roasted, grilled or boiled, and normally served only during festivals or to honor a guest. Fish were available, both freshwater from the Sea of Galilee (St. Peter's fish is still caught there) and marine fish. These were eaten fresh and probably dried as well. Spices—initially only local herbs and spices such as nigella and cumin—came later, as trade developed, and spices from other places such as Egypt and even the East were commonly used. Salt, a very important condiment, was mined at the Dead Sea (a practice some people still resort to today) and transported throughout the Levant.

Eating utensils consisted of shallow and deep bowls and cups (or goblets among the wealthy). Although the fork was known, it was used as a ritual implement: people ate with their fingers. If possible, people ate three meals a day, but given the vagaries of the weather, famines were fairly common.

Greeks and Romans

The Jewish polity that emerged around the eleventh century BCE continued on-and-off until the Roman era as a political entity, although a Jewish community in Roman Palaestina (the name chosen by the Romans for political reasons: to destroy the vestiges of Judaean autonomy) endured for several centuries later, until the Arab era. The conquests of Alexander the Great and the subsequent rise of the Hellenistic kingdoms of Seleucid Syria and Ptolemaic Egypt meant that the Jewish population of the Holy Land was exposed to Hellenistic culture. Even the rise of the independent Hasmonean kingdom did not stop the exchange between Jewish and foreign cultural systems. One piece of evidence can be found in a major Jewish ritual, the feast of Passover eve, called the Seder. The Seder is a ritualized feast combining storytelling, actions, prayers, songs, and specified foods. The script for the feast—called the *Haggadah*—is a Jewish reflection of a Greek symposium. So much so that parts of the Haggadah have Greek words, and possibly some of the foods traditionally presented and consumed have Greek origins (e.g., the consumption at specific points in the ritual of required glasses of wine, *haroset*, a mixture of fruit ground to a paste, and consumption of the *afikoman,* or last course).

The Roman Empire, which succeeded the Greek kingdoms throughout the Mediterranean Sea basin, brought with it a variety of imported goods, many of which remain available today. Fruit and vegetables, including carrots, citrus, and apples, were introduced into local agriculture. Other new fruit and vegetables were also introduced during the Byzantine (Eastern Roman) Empire.

The Arab Conquest

The population of Israel was in decline during the constant turmoil from the third to the seventh centuries CE as the Byzantine and Persian Empires fought for supremacy. In the seventh century, Muslim Arab armies erupted from Arabia and defeated both exhausted rivals. The Arab Muslim conquest around 692–694 CE stamped the character of the Middle East and of the Holy Land to this day. Christians and Jews were converted to Islam, fled, were tolerated but oppressed, or were killed. Social structures were overturned, and the character of the Middle East as it is today began to jell. While the original Arab conquerors presumably ate relatively simple foods, by the tenth century, cuisine—a development related to aristocratic societies—was developing in centers such as Cairo and Damascus, and spread throughout the Levantine coast among the wealthy and powerful. Thus, simple foods were elaborated upon with expensive, preferably imported ingredients and elaborate cooking processes and presentation. The Arabs and their successor conqueror cultures served as channels for the introduction of new forms of food to Europe from as far away as China, and some of these new products also took root in the Land of Israel. Notwithstanding the eruption of the Crusades (1096–1272) and a relatively brief Crusader "Kingdom of Jerusalem," the Land of Israel remained a cultural and economic backwater throughout this period and throughout the rise of the Ottoman empire (1299–1920).

The Ottoman Empire

There were a number of waves of Turkic conquerors throughout the Middle East. The last and most powerful wave was that of the descendants of Othman, known in history as the Ottomans. With the conquest of Byzantium in 1453, they established an empire ruled from Istanbul (the former Constantinople), which lasted until after its defeat in World War I (1920). The Turks absorbed many of the foods of their conquered peoples, and also contributed their own culinary dishes to the mix: a mix that is still evident today throughout the Middle East. In addition to many different Christian and Muslim groups, the Ottoman Empire also included Jewish communities in many places. Turkish, Syrian, Iraqi, Egyptian, Libyan, Tunisian, Greek, Rumanian, Bulgarian, and other Jewish communities developed their cuisines under Turkish influence, creating a variety of dishes whose common denominator was adherence to Jewish dietary laws and the festive calendar. Many such Jewish communities originated from the Iberian Peninsula, from whence they were ejected by edicts of Ferdinand and Isabella (1494), but welcomed by the Turkish sultans. This brought Spanish influences into Ottoman Empire cuisine.

During the late Ottoman period, the Jewish community in Israel was increased by Jews from Europe in scant numbers, and by Jews from Asia in larger numbers. By 1860, there was a sizable community of Bokharan Jews settled in Jerusalem. In 1880, Yemenite Jews immigrated, settling largely in Jerusalem but also in Jaffa. Strongly orthodox Jews from other countries had been immigrating in a steady trickle, settling largely in the holy cities of Jerusalem, Tsfat, and Tiberias. These communities generally kept themselves apart, even from their co-religionists. Although they shared the same religion, they spoke different languages at home, and their rituals, while similar overall, were from different ritual communities. There was a major chasm between two groups of immigrants. On the one hand were the Bokharan, Yemenites, and European religious Jews whose motivation for living where they settled was based on messianic motives: the hope of resurrection in a holy city, and the desire for the arrival of the Messiah. On the other hand, starting in the late nineteenth century, Eastern European settlers arrived with Zionist, nonreligious motives: a desire to be free of anti-Jewish oppression in Eastern Europe and elsewhere, and, with the Second Aliya, a desire to revive the Jewish commonwealth, initially only socially and economically, later politically as well, and a desire to return to working the land.

The urbanization of the Ottoman "Jerusalem Sanjak" (Jerusalem province) and the subsequent British Mandate of Palestine also added to the Arab population as job opportunities increased with development: Bedouin tribes from as far away as Libya, and landless farm workers from the Khauran (southwestern Syria east of the Golan Heights) migrated and swelled the population. Poverty was, however, the rule rather than the exception, and dishes evolved to provide food under harsh circumstances.

The British Mandate

In 1919, under the League of Nations, Britain was assigned a governing mandate over the area that was to become Israel, Palestine, and Jordan as a single geographical entity (Syria and Lebanon were assigned to the French). Very quickly, the British government tore off the Trans-Jordan areas to become the Hashemite Kingdom of Jordan, as reward for the participation of its ruler in WWI on the British side. The Mandatory area, for which the British officially revived the Roman/Crusader name "Palestine," contained both Arab and Jewish populations.

By the first quarter of the twentieth century, the Jewish population of what had become the League of Nations' Mandate of Palestine (a name chosen partly because it would not be inflammatory for any of the communities involved) was growing. Landless Arab peasants also were attracted by the work opportunities brought about by the new settlers, as well as non-Jewish Europeans with a religious interest in settling in Bible lands. The small towns and villages that had characterized the landscape soon became larger and more prosperous, and the prosperity in turn brought about more immigrants, Jewish and Arab. In 1909, a new suburb of the ancient city of Jaffa was founded in the dunes to the north, and eventually matured into the city of Tel Aviv. Other new, modern cities soon followed. The growth of the Jewish population was accelerated by the Nazi rise to power in German in 1933, with further *aliyot* after WWII, and after Israel's independence. The Jewish population also developed new forms of communal agricultural settlements: kibbutzim (the first, Degania, was founded in 1909) and moshavim (Nahalal was founded in 1921).

The Mandate (1919–1948) coincided with nationalist ferment across former colonial empires. It also coincided with the rise of Nazism, which brought about two waves of Jewish immigrants: German Jews who fled Germany between 1936 and 1939, known as the Third Aliya, and the period following the war (1945–1948) when Jewish remnants who had survived the Nazi regime in concentration camps, tried, against British and Arab opposition, to immigrate to Israel (the only community that welcomed them en masse).

The British renounced the Mandate and withdrew their forces from Palestine during 1947–1948, after a United Nations (UN) declaration of the division of the Mandate into Jewish and Arab zones. This was followed by the establishment of the State of Israel, which name change also meant that Palestinian Jews (and many Arabs, resident in the area that had become Israel) became Israelis.

The State of Israel

The State of Israel was declared in 1948 following the UN partition declaration and a subsequent war against a military coalition composed of irregular fighters and armies from Lebanon, Syria, Iraq, Jordan, Egypt, and local Arabs (Arabs who had lived under the Palestine Mandate did not generally name themselves Palestinians, and in fact many rejected the term until two decades later). Israel was faced with the need to provide food and basic services for refugees of the Holocaust, which doubled the population of the country in a year. Soon after the War of Independence

(1948–1949), Arab countries, including Morocco, Algeria, Libya, Egypt, Syria, Lebanon, and Iraq, confiscated Jewish properties and expelled all, or most, Jews. Many of these settled in Israel, swelling the population by another half, mostly destitute.

The population of Israel—of which 20 percent were Arabs, and the rest a mixed bag of refugees, many of whom had arrived in dire poverty, and long-time "Palestinians" now "Israelis"—had a wide range of food preferences, but fairly limited choices. The modern population of Israel is thus largely a nation of incomers, which has had a major influence on the food culture of the country. It was only after several decades of hardship and hard work that the Israeli population could start to afford the development of a true cuisine, characterized by plentiful foodstuffs, imported scarce spices, flavorings, and a well-differentiated food and entertainment sector.

All food cultures are subject to social forces that permeate the society. The more unsettled the history, the more varied these influences tend to be. The social history of the State of Israel is complex and can only be touched upon here, with emphasis on those aspects that have shaped the food culture.

Post WWII: Refugees (European, North African, Iraqi, Yemenite)

Following WWII, more than 700,000 displaced people were encouraged to immigrate from Europe to the country. During the period of the British Mandate of Palestine, this was opposed by the British government, and refugees from the horrors of the Nazis were forcibly repatriated to Europe, some to Germany itself. With the end of the Mandate and the independence of the State of Israel, encouragement of immigrants became official policy. Refugees from the Nazis from all over Europe and North Africa, many of whom had been saved from extermination camps, were brought into the country.

Slightly later, in the early 1950s, the Israeli government undertook several clandestine rescue missions to bring Jewish populations from hostile states to Israel, who were the victims of local persecution, legal and otherwise, and actual pogroms. Operations "Magic Carpet" (Iraq), "On Eagle's Wings" (Yemen), and others in Egypt, Syria, and Morocco brought most of the despoiled Jewish populations of those countries to Israel. The process—of immigration and of absorption—was not smooth, and problems percolated down the decades. Nevertheless, in culinary terms, the immigrations from East and West enriched Israeli food culture, even though some of the best results are only being seen today. Another issue that emerged from the mass immigration in the late 1940s and early 1950s was a lengthy period of national rationing—called *tsena*—which affected everyone in the country for a decade and more.

Tsena (Rationing) 1948–1970

The foundation of the State of Israel was followed by a period of war, as Israel's neighbors attacked the new state militarily. The new state was barely able to feed its population, and the treasury unable to import anything but basic foodstuffs. Thus, a decade of rationing emerged. Meat, fats, sugar, and a variety of other consumption items were rationed heavily. One result of this process was the development and publication of new recipes and menus as the government attempted to make Israelis—of varied origins and food cultures—adapt to the necessities of their new existence. Women's organizations (most cooking was expected to be done by housewives) and government agencies published and distributed menus and recipes that used poorly regarded foodstuffs, such as eggplants, which few of the European immigrants had had any experience of. This also continued the incorporation and absorption of local Arab food customs, as they were heavily vegetable based, and the foods used were commonly grown locally, albeit unfamiliar to many new Israelis. Meagre foods were the order of the day. As one elderly Israeli put it ". . . at every house that had visitors there was always cheese mix that could be spread on matziyot (crackers) . . . Add to that a small glass of wine and a raucous political argument, and a good time was had by all" (Zafrira Ashkenazi, personal communication).

Tsena ended officially in the late 1970s, although it had been moribund for years before that, as Israeli agribusiness and technology took off, and as the country's economic position improved. By the middle of the 1960s, rationing started dying down. Rye bread, rice, and a few other products were under price control for a time, but these were also reduced and eliminated altogether when the Israeli populace became more affluent.

The State of Israel, as a national policy and ideology, continues to encourage the immigration of Jews from around the world to Israel today. Great efforts were made to rescue those communities who were at risk of dissolution, whether cultural or physical. Georgian and other Jewish communities from the Caucasus mountains (then a part of the USSR), Moroccan and Libyan communities, Indian Jewish communities, and later Ethiopian and Burmese Jewish communities were assisted in immigrating to Israel. The largest group of post-*tsena* immigrants—several hundred thousand of them—were from the former USSR during the 1970s.

Eggplant Chopped Liver Spread

Yield: Serves 4

1 medium eggplant
1 sweet white onion, finely minced
Oil for frying
1 hard-boiled egg, mashed
Salt and pepper to taste

1. Roast pierced eggplant on a metal plate until soft. In Israel, one can buy pierced metal plates for the purpose. Otherwise, grill under medium heat, turning eggplant as a side burns.
2. Cut eggplant lengthwise, open, and scrape pulp to a wire sieve to drain.
3. Mash and drain again.
4. Fry finely minced white onion in oil until pale gold and soft.
5. Add the eggplant and fry on gentle heat until all the oil is absorbed.
6. Add salt and pepper to taste and the mashed hard-boiled egg.

Serve cold or warm with bread or crackers.

Tsena Cheese Spread

Yield: Serves 4

1. Mix 1 tub 5 percent fat cream cheese with 1–2 cloves garlic squeezed through a garlic press, a little salt, and a tablespoon of tomato ketchup.

Spread on any type of simple nonsweet cracker, or on pieces of matza for authenticity.

Four cultural communities of this later emigration wave have had the most influence on Israeli food culture. Immigrants from the USSR, collectively known as "Russians" although many were from other parts of the USSR, were largely secular. They brought with them demand for their familiar foods and foodstuffs, ranging from salt smoked fish for *zakushki* (drinking snacks), through high alcohol usage, to a demand for pork and its products. Pork products and pork product shops became mainstream, rather than being semi-clandestine under the heavy influence of religious political parties. And although, like most European immigrants, they soon shed the preference for heavy noonday meals, they retained the demand for familiar foodstuffs such as *kasha* (buckwheat) and smoked salmon.

Georgian immigrants, like all Georgians (Georgia in the Caucasus, not USA) brought a lengthy culture of feasting and wine-making with them. Georgian restaurants and foods percolated throughout the cities in which they resided, and have become familiar to many Israelis. Ethiopian immigrants, whose story and practices aroused much emotion in Israel when they started immigrating en masse in the 1980s (Ashkenazi and Weingrod 1984) brought completely different traditions. In Israel, they ate Ethiopian food, modified by Jewish culinary rules (*kashrut*). Shops catering to their specific needs—*tef* grain, hot chilies, and some specialized spices—sprang up in cities in which they settled. The arrival of Jews from India brought about a rise in the availability of specialty Indian spices and foods, notably in the cities of Dimona and Ramle where many settled. American immigrants, a steady trickle since the birth of the state, introduced and encouraged the development of familiar American foods ranging from hamburgers through pizza (which many Israelis consider an American, not Italian, food) to cupcakes, and the introduction of American-style franchise chains.

The Grill Craze

The first signs of Israel's growing prosperity occurred in the early 1960s, but accelerated by the end of the decade. This was evidenced in the street food scene, as commercial meat grills became popular, then ubiquitous. In the early 1960s, cooks equipped with little more than a small charcoal grill, a cooler of meat and bottled drinks, a stack of pita pocket bread, and a mixed-spice shaker, set up shop in the evenings along some of the major roads. They would sell small steaks grilled on the spot over charcoal, and slipped into the pita. As time went by, some of these "establishments" became kiosks, then full-fledged grill houses. Many of the grills were non-kosher, selling "white meat" (pork) steaks. Others claimed to be kosher. Given the high price of meat at the time, this was a luxury item, yet one available to most of the population. Certain parameters determined the form of the product. The steaks were thin, rarely as thick as ⅓" so that they grilled fast, were small so they could be slipped into a pita, and they were almost always spiced with a mixed spice composed usually of ground coriander, cumin, pepper, and salt, dispensed liberally from a large shaker in the interest of speed, and of flavoring meat that was cut from frozen. These practices did, however, shape Israeli taste, and although there has been much variation and change since then, as well as routinization of the producers (not the least because they became fully regulated by the public health and municipal authorities), the flavor principles used, as well as the form of the meat, became basic to Israeli meat grilling.

Additional recipes were added with time to the original forms of grilled meat. *Shawarma*, a vertical spit with layers of mutton and mutton fat, which was turned in front of a charcoal (now electric or gas) broiler, was imported as an idea from Turkey, and, served like steaks in a pita, became a national favorite, although turkey meat was substituted for much more expensive mutton. Affluence brought with it even greater refinements. Some restaurants specialized in goose and turkey hearts grilled on spits and served in wraps, although with the traditional Israeli *salatim* (salads) and pickles, as falafel had innovated decades before. Argentinean immigrants brought with them the idea of broils of mixed meats. Crucially, grilling meat became a household festive dish, with Israeli men taking responsibility for the cooking (although not preparation) of family picnics in nature, indicating the social importance of consuming grilled meat.

Collective Foods

Unlike the United States, collective life is viewed as natural, and in some ways superior or at least evaluated as equal to individual life. Israel was the first nation to actually make collective living work effectively and efficiently, and three major types of collective farming communities exist to this day: kibbutzim, which are complete collectives with all means of production held in common; moshavim, in which each family works their own plot, but major means of production—from tractors through silos to marketing—are held in common; and moshavot and villages, where family plots are completely autonomous, but water is controlled collectively as a unit. While the population of all these forms has never been more than 5 percent of the population, they have had an inordinate effect on cultural life, including food culture.

Another collective institution is far more extensive and pervasive. About 70 percent of males, and 50 percent of females do compulsory military service when they reach the age of eighteen. This means that for about two years for women and about three years for men (length of service has been tinkered with over the years), they all eat the same foods on the same schedule. This develops a certain amount of unanimity in the Israeli population's food habits, whether from the mess, choices in the Shekem (army stores that sell snacks and small necessities to soldiers on bases), or what is offered by outside traders.

Collective Living: Kibbutz Innovation

A *kibbutz* (plural *kibbutzim*) is a collective settlement in which all (or most) property is held collectively, from housing and businesses (originally only farming, today a mix of farming and advanced industry) to food. While the specifics of the 200-odd kibbutzim in Israel has changed over the years, most kibbutzim in the past, and many today, adhered rigidly to the collective ideal, which meant, among other things, that food provision was a common affair, with a single central kitchen and dining hall. Breakfasts at kibbutzim had to be unfussy, filling, and varied to ensure food for people who might work at odd hours, often starting before dawn doing hard manual labor. Thus, the kibbutz breakfast.

Early in the morning, the kitchen staff (a job taken on by rotation) will prepare huge bins and dishes of what the kibbutz could afford or would offer. Fresh vegetables, each type in its own bin, cheeses in many varieties, eggs, and several types of bread and drinks such as coffee and tea are the staples. Other foods were added with the times. As in any cafeteria, take a tray, plate, and silverware, and fill the plate with whatever you wanted, as often as you wish. In the Israel of rationing, and even afterward, this was a cynosure. And the "Israeli breakfast" was born.

Today, while many kibbutzim have moderated the collective lifestyle, a buffet breakfast is still a must for people working in the fields during harvest or other rush times. Guests who are non-kibbutz members would also normally eat at the dining room, so the knowledge of a kibbutz breakfast (now often labeled "Israeli breakfast" for the tourists) has been widespread. Changes include wider choices, the inclusion of non-European type dishes such as hummus and eggplant dips, and pastries. Most hotels will offer an Israeli breakfast, which has opened the practice to the rest of the world.

The Military Experience

Universal draft is the reality of life in Israel. At the age of eighteen, most young Israelis, women as well as men, must join the army. Rabbinical students, married women, women from religious homes, Muslim Arabs, and Christian Arabs are exempt but may volunteer. Druze, Muslim Cherkess, and all Jewish males are, in principle, conscripted. And, for many decades, the military served as a mixing, if not melting pot, for the culinary culture of the Israeli populace. In the first two decades of the country's existence, the military cookhouse was over-influenced by the tastes of the commanders, almost all of whom came from Eastern Europe. With time, tastes (and personnel) in the army changed, and dishes from all over became commonplace, and introduced the conscripts and regular service personnel to food from different parts of the Israeli community. For many poorer Israelis in the 1950s and 1960s, *loof* (canned meatloaf) in the military was their first introduction to regular consumption of meat, and certainly for many men, notably those in field units who had to make do with field rations, their first introduction to cooking, as they tried (and failed) to force the *loof* into edible form, and by doing so, learned, at least to some degree, to cook for themselves.

Opening to the World

The gradual growing affluence in Israeli society (accompanied by growing wealth disparities) has brought international food to Israel. This does not only mean the introduction of new foodstuff, fruits and vegetables in particular, but a growing familiarity and experience with foreign ways of cooking and presentation.

In the first few decades of the state, foreign foods were almost nonexistent, both domestically and publicly. Jewish cuisines from across the world, many of which could be found domestically, notably after the great immigrations of the 1950s, were rarely available outside homes and neighborhood restaurants in centers of particular populations. "Israeli" food consisted largely of Ashkenazi/Central European cooking and what was called "Oriental" cooking: Arab and Middle Eastern food with an emphasis on vegetable dishes and grilled meat/fish. Only gradually did non-Ashkenazi dishes enter the public realm. Even the army, that center of fusion, served almost exclusively Ashkenazi-style food until the late 1960s. Access to foreign foods, notably American, was available to those few who had relatives overseas and could send Care packages, which acquainted Israelis with some American and European foods.

Change arrived partly as result of ethnic and political pressures, partly as Israelis started traveling the world, and partly through happenstance. Both the early State period and the pre-State period (called *Yishuv* period in Hebrew) were dominated largely by Eastern European Ashkenazim, who, for various historical reasons, were the original drivers of the Zionist and Return movements. However, with the arrival of immigrants from Middle Eastern and North African countries, the country doubled its population in a few years, mostly non-Ashkenazim. A few years down the line, and food preferences of non-Ashkenazim became mainstream. The army introduced hummus and *'arissa* hot sauce to its menu, and ethnic restaurants—Moroccan, Persian, Indian—started to proliferate, a movement that has continued. These, together with a growing political voice (and ability to use that voice) made ethnic foods not only respectable, but even in demand, as can be seen in the annual celebration of the Moroccan Mimouna festival, where the Moroccan community (including its politicians) host and entertain members of other communities, not least the old guard of the Eastern European political aristocracy, who had to celebrate and highlight Moroccan food and ritual culture as something of value in itself. Moreover, returning Israelis, first those who went to Europe, and later, young post-army backpackers who went to India, Nepal, and South America (a major rite of passage for many young Israelis), came home with a growing appreciation of foreign foods. Some established restaurants catering to their personal taste that they had acquired abroad. A nudge in the direction of Chinese restaurants, at least, was the arrival of several hundred Vietnamese boat people who had been rescued by an Israeli freighter in the South China Sea, and provided with visas to settle in Israel. Some of them did so permanently, and some of those opened and ran Chinese restaurants even in the less central urban areas, an enormous innovation in Israel.

And, as Israel became more affluent, it became attractive to international chains who opened branches and franchises in Israel. American cuisine, as exemplified largely by fast-food chains, has made a particular impression on the young. Some younger Israelis, with no experience abroad, firmly believe that pizza, for instance, is an American food: its Italian origins are completely obscured by its arrival in Israel via the United States. Adaptations had to be made for *kashrut*, so that cheese-less pizzas became a norm, and cheeseburgers were nonexistent throughout much of the country. Since in the Tel Aviv conurbation, non-kosher food is hardly startling any more, this too has passed, and pizzas with both meat and cheese are available (at least one Israeli food chain runs both kosher and non-kosher branches, and occasionally waiters need to warn diners "This particular branch is not kosher").

The culinary attraction of the United States is neither new nor surprising. The arrival of Care packages from relatives in the United States, which were replete with luxuries such as chocolate bars, coffee, and snacks, and often shared with the extended family and with neighbors, as well as the vision of America presented in popular Hollywood films, disposed many Israelis to see the United States as a cornucopia of desirable foods. Some food places capitalized on this, and included the "Brooklyn Bar," which sold American-style ice cream sundaes and "New York-style pizza," which hinted at American food.

Pizza, Israeli Style

Yield: Serves 4

4 slices white bread, toasted
1 can tomato paste mixed with salt, black pepper, *za'atar* to taste, or alternatively two very ripe medium tomatoes sliced thin and similarly spiced.
4 large slices meltable cheese, enough to cover the bread slices.

1. Place the tomatoes/tomato paste on the bread.
2. Add the cheese.
3. Grill until cheese has browned slightly.

The attraction and penetration of foreign foods into Israel has become a flood over the past three decades. This is entirely unsurprising. Israeli cuisine is a patchwork, one that holds together well, and which is open to foreign tastes, inasmuch as the "original" Israeli cuisine and taste is itself a patchwork.

Developing Water Sources

Nature has been scant with the provision of water throughout the Middle East. In Israel, there are only a few rivers running from the hills of Judea and Samaria/West Bank westward to the sea. The Yarkon, Alexander, Taninim, and Kishon are the only permanent rivers and these are exploited to the maximum. The Jordan River, running North to South (it ends in a large salt-water lake, the Dead Sea, also the lowest natural point on the surface of Earth) provided the most water from the Lake of Galilee, via an artificial National Water Carrier, as far as the Northern Negev. There are several major aquifers under the middle belt of the country. These too are exploited to a dangerous degree. The major source of agricultural water today are the desalination plants, based on Israeli technology, situated along the coast. Eight water desalination plants provide water for domestic and commercial use, as well as agriculture. Another plant in the southernmost city of Eilat provides almost all water for that part of the country.

A strict water recycling regime provides as much wastewater as possible for agriculture. As much as 80 percent of agricultural water used in Israel is recycled (Israel has one of the highest recycling rates in the world).

Some of the recycled water is fed directly into agricultural watering systems. Another part is pumped into sandy areas along the coast to replenish the badly depleted coastal aquifer under the sands.

Additionally, Israel has spent considerable effort in developing better ways to irrigate crops. Most irrigated crops are served by micro-irrigation systems ("drip irrigation") that deliver measured amounts of water (and nutrient additives) directly to specified plants. Salt-tolerant and drought tolerant varieties of vegetables and trees have also been developed, which allow for better water utilization.

The Human Side of Food Production

Given the small size of the country (approximately 62 miles at its widest point, and approximately 250 miles long), agricultural technology is a must if the country is to supply its food needs. Most agriculture is highly technologized, with automated irrigation systems, milking machines, and temperature control being the norm rather than the exception.

The structure of the agricultural population is one of cooperative small farms (twenty-thousand square meters, or about four acres per productive unit is the average) using intensive agriculture. This allows for a great deal of flexibility, given the population is highly educated and willing to try new crops and techniques. While most Arab farming families were originally peasants (low technology, largely subsistence agriculture) this has changed radically in the decades leading up to the 2010s and Arab farmers generally use the same techniques as their Jewish peers.

Since food supply is a critical national resource, the Israeli government has invested hugely in agricultural services, including research institutes, veterinary services, and outreach. This means that new techniques and technology, as well as potential exploitable new crops, percolate quickly throughout the farming sector.

Social Forms for Food Production

Food is produced by a number of types of farmers and farming communities, some of them unique to Israel. The density of agricultural communities is high, except in the Southern Negev.

Peasant Farmers

Until fairly recently, most Israeli village Arabs were peasant farmers, raising both subsistence and market crops. Smaller numbers engaged in trade, the professions, and security services. With time, the number of peasants decreased, with automatization and centralized marketing changing many households from farmers to the professions. Those who remained farmers now worked within the cash economy, producing food for sale nationwide, rather than through exchange and local markets.

Village farmers produce a range of products including wheat and barley, table vegetables, beans and other pulses, olives, and fruit. A small number of cattle, and a larger number of sheep and goats are raised. Pigs are also raised by Christian Arabs. Much of this produce is used domestically, with the rest shipped to markets or sold from roadside booths. With the development of industry and trade in many Arab communities, and a growing number of youngsters going into the professions, agriculture is becoming a side activity, engaged in more by older people than the young.

Shepherds

In the desert area of the Negev in southern Israel, live Bedouin nomads. Due to the small size of the country, and the sometimes destructive nature of nomadism, the nomadic lifestyle is slowly dying out, being replaced by sedentary villages. Most families nevertheless engage in animal husbandry. Sheep and goats, and sometimes camels, are most commonly herded. The original sheep population are a hardy Awasi breed, and goats are a small black variety ideally suited to desert conditions. Nowadays, all these breeds have been improved by imported foreign stock, which helps to raise productivity without risking local hardiness. Milk and milk products are made, normally by women, and beasts are occasionally slaughtered or sold. Many shepherds still collect and use local herbs and fungi to add to the pot. A small number of Jewish freeholders, specializing in artisanal products ranging from meat through cheeses, can also be found, largely in the Galilee, the Negev, and the Jerusalem hills.

Moshavot

The first Jewish farmers in the late nineteenth century settled in villages of independent smallholders. Cooperation, except in issues of local governance and security, was loose. Many such moshavot expanded into cities and only a very small number such as Yavne'el in the Galilee retain their rural setting. Farmers grow fruit and vegetables for the market, and also raise cattle for milk in small numbers. There is minimal cooperative labor, and farmers own and control their own means of production.

Moshavei Ovdim

The ideal of cooperative labor brought about the establishment of semi-cooperative villages. The first of which, Nahalal in the Jezreel valley, still flourishes. In the moshav, families have an allocation of land, on which they grow a selection of crops, influenced by communal decisions. Water, heavy machinery, storage and silage, marketing, and other agricultural services are provided in common. Moshavim produce a large percentage of Israel's agricultural crops. Farmers may sell their produce centrally, or individually at one of the many open-air markets, which means produce often goes directly from farmer to consumer.

Kibbutzim

A socioeconomic settlement pattern unique to Israel and Japan, a kibbutz is a collective agroindustrial community. Population varies from the hundreds to the thousands. All means of production are held in common, as is most consumption. The social and economic forms of the kibbutz vary considerably from some in which the ideal of communal living extends through common eating in a kibbutz dining room, children living together in separate quarters than their parents, and joint social activities; to those kibbutzim that have effectively voted to de-cooperate and turned into villages of autonomous households. Some kibbutzim are purely agricultural, others balance agriculture and industry, mainly in the high-tech sector and agricultural technology. The 200-odd kibbutzim produce a great deal of Israel's food and industrial crops, since they have the benefit of economies of scale. They have also developed and provide a wide range of agricultural technology, ranging from drip irrigation to computerized farming technology.

Urban Farms (Mishkei Ezer)

In a bid to increase food availability between the 1920s and 1950s, the Zionist governing body and later the Israeli government encouraged the creation of urban farming, with somewhat larger lots and water rations provided to those who wished to raise a portion of their own food. These urban farms were established close to major cities to provide urban proletariat with additions to their income. They were designed following the best scientific advice of their times. Some vestiges of these still exist, with a few households going into hothouse development for exotic crops, or raising flowers for local and export markets.

Biblical Crops

The Bible is a primary source for Jewish tradition, and the list of crops mentioned in the Bible is extensive, although some of the names are obscure. The Bible (and the Talmud) takes the agricultural-ritual year for granted, and it constitutes an important background to the action. In modern Israel, where the Bible is very much alive as a cultural history, and where contemporary events take place against the background of biblical names, most people can quote, or at least cite, biblical referents for some of the foods they eat on a daily or at least seasonal basis.

Shivat Haminim

The Bible names a number of crops and food sources. Seven crops are specially noted, and have collectively been named *shivat haminim* ("The Seven Species"). These have both food and ritual importance for Jews worldwide, and they formed the central basis for food in premodern times, and to a lesser degree today. Other available foods from the time have also been interwoven into Jewish rituals that are also kept now, and which, as will be seen in later chapters, still have a strong effect on Israeli food culture.

The ancient Israelites cultivated wheat as a major crop. Together with barley, it is mentioned first in the book of Genesis. The wheat harvest is celebrated in the festival of Succoth, at the end of summer. Wheat is grown today primarily in the northern Negev, and for family use in some family farms elsewhere in the country. With the exception of *frikkeh* (green wheat, considered a delicacy since biblical times) most wheat is milled into white flour for bread, couscous, noodles, baked goods, and other products. Although some wheat is raised in Israel, the country's wheat demand is high enough that much wheat is imported from abroad: Ukraine, Canada, Argentina, and other countries supply wheat depending on the market.

Wheat is eaten mainly as bread, both leavened and unleavened. The price of standard bread had been controlled by the government for decades after independence, as a way to ensure that people were at least minimally fed. The breads consumed are extremely varied, but roughly fall into two categories, which are both consumed by most households and individuals, but in different proportions: flatbreads and risen breads.

Most people of Middle Eastern descent, including the Arab population, consume a high percentage of flat breads, colloquially known as *pita*, although many forms exist, ranging from large, flat *lafa*, which is used for wrap sandwiches, through pocket bread (pita) to thicker Iraqi breads (known unsurprisingly as *pitot iraqiot*). These are usually made from white wheat flour, although full-meal and other handmade variants are available.

Most people of Euro-American ancestry eat mainly loaf (risen and proofed) bread. Standard bread, which was under price control for many years, is bolstered with cheaper rye and has a grayish color and a hard crust. White breads have long since overtaken "standard bread" in daily use, although those who grew up with standard bread still prefer the slightly sour, earthy flavor. A few people bake bread at home, but most bread consumed is made by large bakeries who ship throughout the country.

Barley, a hardy cereal that has coarse bristles sprouting from the ears, is widely cultivated worldwide, mainly for use in brewing and stock feed. A small portion is reserved for the natural foods market, or as grains for soups and stews. The barley harvest has been celebrated since ancient times in the festival of Shavuot, in late spring. At that season, the barley harvested provided surplus for one of the three mandated pilgrimages to Jerusalem.

Grapes were historically used mainly for the production of wine, although they were also eaten fresh and dried for consumption and export. Wine has been a major produce of the area of Israel since ancient times, and industrial-scale production took place since at least the early Iron Age, as attested by archaeological remains. Grapes can be grown in all areas of the country, and Nabatean remains in the area of the Negev mountains show production of grapes was extensive even in those arid conditions. In modern Israel, most wine grapes are grown in the center of the country and the mountainous north, while table grapes are produced almost everywhere. A number of different varieties of red and white are grown for the table and consumption is large. In addition, a successful wine industry has developed for domestic use and export, which relies heavily on locally produced grapes, mostly in the Coastal Plain and the mountainous areas.

Figs were cultivated throughout the Land of Israel and fresh or dried figs were part of the daily diet. A common way of preparing dried figs was to chop them and press them into a cake. Figs are frequently mentioned in the Bible (for example, 1 Samuel 25:18, 1 Samuel 30:12, and 1 Chronicles 12:41). Feral fig trees (the seeds are small and easily distributed by birds) can be found throughout the Galilee, where most of the production is found. Fig production is, however, found throughout the country except in the Arava and southern Negev. Figs are eaten fresh in season, or taken from garlands of dried fruit, or from compressed cakes. Fresh figs are eaten as-is, or incorporated in more-or-less fancy desserts. Dried figs are used in confections, as well as in desserts.

Pomegranates arrived from Persia or Armenia in historical times. The ripe fruit is topped by a crown-like extrusion (the dried flower calyx) and thus the fruit was associated with royalty, and pomegranate images were used to decorate royal buildings, the temple, and other important objects, including Torah scrolls. Pomegranates were usually eaten fresh, although occasionally they were used to make juice or wine, or sundried for use when the fresh fruit was out of season.

The fruit is a large berry filled with transparent whitish to garnet-red arils (seeds coated with pulp within a membrane). Clusters are separated by an inedible white membrane into six sections within the fruit. The juicy pulp varies from sweet-sour to insipid sweet. The deeply red, strongly sweet-sour varieties such as Akko are favored in Israel. Most pomegranates are eaten raw during the season (September to November) and since this season includes Rosh Hashana and Succoth, pomegranates are often used as decorations in the *succah* (leaf-roofed booth that most Jewish Israelis erect for the festival). Pomegranate juice is a favorite drink and a special metal pomegranate squeezer has been developed for those who want freshly squeezed juice at home. A small number of pomegranates are still used to dry the arils for winter consumption. The dried arils (sometimes ground to powder) serve as a souring and flavoring agent in some Arab, Persian, and Bokharan dishes. The juice is also boiled down into thick, tart, semi-sweet molasses, which may be used mixed with cold water or soda water as a drink (*sharab*) that is popular among Central Asian and Arab Israelis. Pomegranate syrup or molasses are sold in bottles in many grocery stores in Israel, both for cooking and for making *sharab*.

Olive oil has been used for food and cooking, for lighting, and for ritual purposes since prehistory. The fruit must be processed for eating or crushed into olive oil. The crushing residue is used as animal feed, fertilizer, and occasionally fuel for fires. The industrial production of olive oil has been a feature of the economy since the late Iron Age, which was enhanced by the invention of the lever press and crushing millstone, although olive oil had been extracted by Neolithic farmers well before that. Large production facilities existed throughout the Coastal Plain, largely for export. The production of olive oil and olives declined drastically throughout the Arab and Ottoman periods and most olive production by the end of the nineteenth century was for local consumption.

Today, olive trees by the thousands cover the hilly areas of the Galilee and, to a lesser extent, other areas. Olive trees grow to a great age, and some olive trees in the Galilee are hundreds of years old and still fertile. Olive trees are kept low to facilitate the harvest, which takes place in the

> ## Opening a Pomegranate
>
> Here is a simple, almost foolproof, way of opening up a pomegranate.
> Hold the fruit crown upward.
> You will feel six ridges (very faintly) running from crown to stem end.
> About 1" from the crown, make a shallow ⅛" deep cut diagonally (45 degrees more-or-less) upward, from the far side of a ridge to the swelling of the next ridge.
> Make another similar cut downward to the next ridge. Make sure the cuts cross one another.
> Repeat for each of the ridges, making sure each cut is crossed by two others, once at its low end, once at its upper end. The end result should be something like this: VVVVVV.
> Gently loosen and pull off the crown cap to expose the bright red or pink aril bunches.
> Make cuts vertically from the lower points of the six Vs, along the crest of each ridge to the stem end.
> Pull the fruit apart into six natural sections.
> Discard all white membrane.
> Eat the arils.
>
> *Note*: It is *barely* possible to eat a pomegranate without staining one's clothes and surroundings. You have been warned.

fall. About one quarter of the produce is intended for the table, with the rest going to oil production, both for domestic use and for the food industry. Around 74,000 acres are devoted to olives, mostly nonirrigated. Olives are raised by individual farmers, as well as large cooperatives. Olive oil is produced commercially by large industrial firms, who contract for olives from farmers' cooperatives. Over the past few decades, more and more Israelis have begun to appreciate artisanal olive oil. Small olive presses are available for those individuals who have olive trees and want to produce their own oil; some of which is for domestic consumption, some to be given as presents, and some to be sold. Table olives need to be picked by hand to avoid blemishes, whereas olives for oil may be harvested mechanically. There are a large number of farmers who, in addition to producing olive oil for their own use, put smaller or larger quantities of fine virgin olive oil on the market, some of it for export. In Israel as elsewhere, olive oil is undergoing somewhat of a renaissance, with people comparing and contrasting the olive oils they use and their source.

Olives are consumed in great quantities, mostly prepared and canned by one or another of the large food companies. Specialist pickle shops found in all markets may sell twenty or more different varieties, sold by weight. Types range from green to black, salt-cured to vinegar, and different sizes. A plate of olives accompanies almost every *mezze* as a matter of course, as well as many street foods. And most domestic minor (that is, nonmeat) meals have olives as one component. Olives are eaten together with bread for a basic breakfast or snack, or accompany any meal as a pickle. Olives are also offered to accompany beer or alcoholic drinks, and no hummus is complete without a plate of olives. Most Israelis take olives for granted as part of a meal and in many restaurants, they are served as a matter of course.

Olive oil is important both as a food source and a ritual product in Israel, as it was used exclusively in the long-lamented (by religious Jews, at least) temple in Jerusalem. Olive oil cruets are common on tables throughout the country. Olive oil is drizzled on plates of hummus, and is a major component of any good Israeli salad. The greenish oil pressed from unripe olives is preferred, although darker yellow oil from ripe olives is also available.

Some families, Arabs and Jews, will take the time to harvest olives from trees that grow wild, or have been planted along roads or in national parks. These are then processed at home into edible olives.

Dates are mentioned in the Bible, and there was a thriving date industry, for local consumption and export in the Jordan valley, until destroyed by the Romans deliberately after the revolts of 70 and 120 CE. The local cultivar went extinct, until a chance find of a viable date seed in Masada, which is now growing. Date palms were introduced in industrial scale into Israel with date seedlings smuggled from Iraq in 1909 to Kibbutz Degania. Since then, a number of new cultivars have been developed attempting to improve the crop and suit the tree to local conditions, including a giant (four times the volume) of the *medjool* variety. Today, date palms are grown in several locations throughout the Jordan River valley and to a lesser extent elsewhere. Date palms are important not only for the fruit. The unopened, undamaged, perfectly formed young fronds are an important symbol in Judaism, and during the festival of Succoth, date palm fronds are supposed to be carried to the Succoth rituals. The mature fronds are traditionally used as a covering for the booths in which religiously inclined people spend most of their leisure time during the eight days of the holiday. Christian pilgrims to Jerusalem, notably during Easter, carry palm fronds in emulation of the time of Jesus. Kibbutzim in the Beit Shean valley earn considerable sums each fall from the export of perfect palm fronds.

The fruit of the date palm has been a major resource throughout the Middle East, and numerous varieties have been developed. The fruit is

Preparing Olives

After harvest, raw olives must be treated to extract the *oleuropein*, which makes the olive too bitter to eat. The ancient Romans, and possibly Judaeans, soaked olives for a few days in ashes (from which lye is produced) mixed with water. The olives are then washed in fresh water, and soaked again in fresh water changed daily until the bitterness is at an acceptable level. Lye wash is most common for commercial olives today. Olives can be soaked in fresh water changed daily for a period of one to three weeks. To quicken the process, they may be crushed lightly under a stone or board, or cut to the stone individually. Black (ripe) olives can be packed in rough salt for a period of three to six months, rinsed, then soaked in fresh water to remove excess saltiness.

Once most bitterness has been removed (a matter of taste and habit), the olives are pickled in a pickle of salt water or vinegar, spices (chilies, garlic, lemon slices, bay leaf, mustard seeds, or any aromatic of choice) and placed in a sealed jar for at least a few weeks, resulting in edible olives.

---

very high in sugar (40 percent in some varieties) as well as protein, and with water can sustain human life. Fresh (*medjool* type) as well as dried (e.g., *deglet noor* type) dates are available. Some varieties require bletting (allowed to ferment slightly to convert starches to sugar), others can be eaten off the tree, but have short shelf life.

Dates are a popular snack, often eaten with a salty nut to cut the sweetness. In addition to eating them raw or dried, dates are used for two products: *silan* (date honey, called *dibs* in Arabic) and stuffing for savory and sweet foods. *Silan* produced in the area for thousands of years is made by boiling down ripe dates and removing the liquid, which stores well. Some argue that the honey referred to in the biblical characterization of the land as a "... land of milk and honey" (Exodus 3:8) is actually date honey, although there is little early evidence for that. Dates are used to fill a number of confections of Middle Eastern, European, and notably North African origin that are popular both as industrial and domestic baking in Israel.

Other Biblical and Historical Agricultural Products

Carobs (St. John's bread, locust tree) are mentioned several times in Jewish and Christian sources and the pods were a famine and hermit's food in both traditions. The seeds are sometimes surrounded by a drop of intensely sweet syrup, which children enjoy.

Leeks, onions, and garlic have been prominent items of flavoring food and are mentioned in both the Bible and Akkadian culinary texts (Bottéro 1995). Onions and garlic were important in Jewish cooking, both in Europe and throughout the Middle East in Medieval and premodern times, and were cited by the Spanish Inquisition as a cause for suspecting a person of being Jewish. Today, all are consumed in large quantities throughout Israel.

Legumes of various kinds are also mentioned in the Bible and have been the food of the poor throughout history. In modern Israel, large quantities of various legumes are consumed as a matter of course, with pride of place going to the chickpea.

Melons and cucumbers, both members of the Cucurbitae family, are also mentioned in the Bible, and have become important foods in modern Israel, although there is no certainty that the fruit mentioned in Exodus is indeed the same fruit as it is today. One needs to keep in mind, however, that the choice of vegetables available in premodern times, before the start of globalization in the sixteenth century, was rather limited, and the transfer of plants to and from the Levant is an ongoing, and by now, conscious, process. This means that what is available today to the average consumer far exceeds biblically familiar agricultural products.

Further Reading

Ashkenazi, Michael, and Alex Weingrod. 1984. *Ethiopian Immigrants in Beersheva: An Anthropological Study of the Absorption Process*. Highland Park, IL: American Association for Ethiopian Jews.

Bottéro, Jean. 1995. *Textes Culinaires Mésopotamiens*. University Park, PA: Eisenbrauns/Penn State University Press.

CHAPTER TWO

Influential Ingredients

Given the great heterogeneity of the climate and topography, as well as the population, it is not surprising that the Israeli food basket has both familiar and unfamiliar (to Americans) products that are eaten as a matter of course. The biblical products listed in the previous chapter are still important today, but are overshadowed in many cases by new agricultural products and additions to the food basket that most people in Israel take for granted, and which are consumed in as great quantities as the biblical food sources.

Grains, Honey, and Nuts

Several non-biblical grains are used in modern Israel for food. Maize, raised locally (notably in the northern coastal plain) is boiled and eaten as corn on the cob, or as a side dish, with or without other vegetables. Maize is also the basis for several snacks and nibbles. Other grains, either raised locally or imported, may be of particular importance to a particular community or tradition. Nuts are a component of the diet in the form of *pitzuchim* nibbles, which most Israelis indulge in to a greater or lesser degree during social gatherings.

Grains

Tiras (maize) is eaten on the ear, as a side-dish, or, largely by Rumanian Jews, as a main starch dish called *mamaliga* (similar to the Italian polenta). Frozen or canned maize kernels are constituents of soups and stews. In late summer, Galilee farmers sell fresh corn ears from small booths along the highways. Boiled corn-on-the-cob is a common street and beach food throughout the country.

Rice is not indigenous to Israel. Rice may have been brought to the Holy Land during Second Temple times (516 BCE–73 CE) from Persia, and was an important export crop during Talmudic times. In modern Israel, rice is second only to wheat as a staple: Israelis consume about 37 lb per person per year. Small quantities are raised in Israel in the Huleh region in the north of the Jordan valley, where a dried marsh makes for good conditions for the grass, but most is imported. Rice is often made into festive dishes. Jews who hold to the Sephardi ritual in Judaism consider rice to be kosher for Passover, and it is served as a major dish during the festival. The Arab population has considered rice to be a high value foodstuff since the Middle Ages. Bedouin feasts invariably are based on rice, most often in the form of a *mansaf*: a bed of rice topped with mutton served in a communal dish.

Most commonly, rice is flavored and even colored. Yellow rice is dyed with turmeric and flavored with cardamom and is a favorite dish. Red rice is flavored with tomato sauce. Fried onions, meat, stock, and other flavorings are also used often. Rice pudding is a common dessert, notably during Shavuot whose food is dominated by milk and milk products.

Specific grains may be favored by a particular community of origin. Buckwheat, for example, although not a true grass, can be included here. It is eaten in households of Russian origin as *kasha* (groats) cooked as a breakfast porridge. Israelis of Ethiopian origin or background import quantities of *tef*, a millet-like grain now raised in the United States as well, for making fermented pancakes called *injirah*, which are a staple of the Ethiopian diet.

Dvash (Honey)

The Canaan into which the Israelites entered in biblical times (whether the story is true or apocryphal) was a land of "milk and honey." There are arguments, some of them weak, that the honey mentioned was really *silan*, a molasses made from dates. Whatever the case, it is clear that honey from bees was a commonly available sweetener. The tradition continues today, with Israeli beekeepers providing large quantities of honey of moderate quality. Honey is used both in ritual (dipping an apple in honey for Rosh Hashana) and cuisine (*lekach* is a well-known honey cake), to symbolize sweetness.

Egozim (Nuts)

Israelis eat a large variety of nuts, most of which are grown in the country. They may be served as *pitzuchim*, sometimes on their own (e.g., pecans in their shells), sometimes with dried fruit (e.g., almonds and raisins), sometimes salted or sweetened, or may be incorporated in various confections, or made into foods such as almond marzipan, for example. Almonds, pistachios, and walnuts have been grown in the area since antiquity, and have always been popular as the base for foods during Passover, since they cannot become *hametz* (leavened).

Pride of place goes to *shkedim* (almonds), both because they have some ritual significance, and because the almond trees, notably those along the roads to Jerusalem, are an annual sight appreciated by visitors who flock to see the first blooms of spring. In spring, the blossoms look like pale pink clouds as the trees bloom.

The sour green fruits, when the nut has a jelly-like texture, are sometimes eaten by children. Largely however, the fruit is allowed to dry into an elongated, pockmarked nut, which is cracked for the interior sweet kernel. Almonds are sold roasted in the shell and cracked, or completely shelled, both salted and not. Sugared almonds of various sorts are available in most markets by weight, and in premeasured bags at groceries. Almonds are also incorporated into a variety of confections and cakes.

Imported from the United States, pecan trees found an ideal climate in Israel, and are now raised throughout the center and north of the country. Toasted, raw, and sugared pecans are available, as well as unshelled nuts which, since they are easier to shell and sweeter than walnuts, have overcome the popularity of the native fruit.

The pistachio tree is native to the Levant coast, although the best fruit bearers are the Persian variety. Pistachios are expensive, much more so than other nuts, and are valued highly. Pistachios, originating from Iran through Syria, have always had a pride of place on Israeli and Middle Eastern tables. The nuts are mostly roasted, salted, or natural. Due to expense, they are not offered lightly. Pistachios are also incorporated into many Middle Eastern confections such as baklava, which is popular in most Middle Eastern-style restaurants throughout Israel. The best pistachios were imported from Aleppo in Syria, and older Israelis may still refer to them as *fistuk Halabi* or *fistuk Sha'ami*. The Arab word *fistuk* is used in Israel in preference to the original Hebrew word *boten*, which is now used for the peanut.

Egozey melekh (walnuts) have been grown in Israel since ancient times. They are available both shelled and unshelled. Local production is small, and most are imported. They have been overshadowed in modern times by the popularity of pecans. Walnuts are an ingredient in some variations of *haroset*, a dried fruit and wine mixture that is a ritually essential component of the Passover feast (the Seder). Hazelnuts, although raised in Israel, are a minor crop and most hazelnuts are imported. They are mostly incorporated into mixed *pitzuchim* and used for confections.

Although not a proper nut, *botnim* (peanuts) are a popular and cheap ingredient, sometimes used inappropriately for confections such as adulterating and bulking up *tahina*, halva, and other foods. The word *botnim* originally meant pistachio nut, but through a linguistic mix-up, ended up as a term for peanuts, an American vegetable, unknown in the times of the Talmud. Eaten as *pitzuchim* (in the shell or out, salted, sugared, roasted, and so on), peanut butter, and candy bars, peanuts are grown both as green manure and as a crop for animal feed, in addition to culinary uses.

A crucial seed for many Israeli dishes is sesame. These are raised by many farmers, and some take sesame seeds to the next logical step: grinding of *tahina* sauce, which is a staple of many Israeli dishes, and a major player in hummus and falafel, both signature Israeli dishes. White sesame is the most commonly used, although there is a small market for black sesame, which is imported.

Whole toasted sesame seeds are scattered over many kinds of breads, both risen and flat. Notably, sweet *challah* (Sabbath bread) in Israel is scattered with sesame seeds (nonsweet, with poppy seeds). Sesame seeds are also scattered over *ka'ak* rolls that are sold hot from the oven by street vendors.

Legumes

Many legumes—some of them indigenous to the Middle East, some newcomers—are eaten regularly in Israel, and beans are prepared both for daily and for special and holiday meals. Legumes of various sorts were and are extremely important in the Middle Eastern diet, as well as historically throughout the Jewish world (so much so that one variety of beans is called *giudea*—Spanish for "Jewish" in Spain to this day). Different legumes were consumed by the poor as a staple in both Europe, the shores of the Mediterranean, and in Central and South Asia. Eating legumes during Passover—forbidden by Ashkenazi rabbis, permitted by all other ritual communities—is one distinguishing mark of non-Ashkenazi ritual communities.

In Judaism, one is forbidden to light, or douse, a fire during Saturday, the day of rest, that is, from nightfall on Friday to nightfall Saturday. How then was a housewife to provide hot food for her family? The solution was a slow-cooked stew, called *hamin* (from the Hebrew *ham* [hot]) in the Talmud, usually containing beans, which, the more they are cooked, the better they taste.

The Hebrew word for chickpeas, which have been grown in Israel since the first centuries CE, is *khimtza*, a word almost unused today. Instead, the

Arabic cognate word, "hummus," evokes Israel's most popular legume, as well as its two most iconic dishes: falafel and hummus.

Green beans are a popular vegetable served in many ways. The form of cooking often depends on the person's inclinations and preferences as much as on cultural background. They may be served hot with a meat course, or cold as a salad.

Ful (fava beans), both young in the pod and dried mature, are one of the main sources of protein for most Egyptians. *Ful* is considered the mainstay of poor rural and urban families, as well as a homely delight for the wealthier. While some Egyptian Jews were Europeanized middle-class, many others were poor, and like most poor Egyptians, relied heavily on *ful*.

Today, *ful* is consumed by Israelis from various Middle Eastern countries, as well as Israeli Arabs, and to a lesser extent, the non-Mizrahi public mainly in the form of a sandwich. Some restaurants offer only *ful*, in which they specialize, somewhat like a *hummusiyah*, a hummus restaurant. As in a *hummusiyah*, *ful* can be ordered in a pita or on a plate. The *ful* is placed on a plate, garnished with *tahina* and salad if desired, and swiped up with a flatbread and either cream cheese or a salty white cheese. In Israel, it is served as a matter of course with a small plate of olives or pickles.

Lentils (red, green, and yellow) are a popular legume because they are easy and cheap to cook and considered easier to digest than other legumes.

"Some of That Red, Red": Modern Continuities of History

One of the earliest cooked dishes mentioned in the Bible is a lentil stew traded by Jacob, Abraham's grandson, to his brother Esau. We have no recipe in the Bible for the lentil dish Jacob prepared (Genesis 25:34). However, one of the earliest collection of recipes in the world comes from the royal archives of Akkad (Bottéro 1995), which places it at about the putative age of Abraham and his sons and grandsons. We don't know exactly what the recipe was in Canaan, but we do know that Jacob's family had roots in Mesopotamia: his mother and grandfather were from that part of the ancient world. As is often the case with ancient recipes, we have to guess quantities and even some of the ingredients such as the spices ("ground flavorful wood" in the original) used, although all the ingredients in the following recipe would have been available at the time. Lentil soups are common in Israel in the winter, and may be similar to that original "red, red" that Esau craved.

Marak Adom (Red Lentil Soup)

This, or something similar, may be the red lentil soup that Jacob served Esau.

Yield: Serves 4

1 large onion, minced fine
½ cup virgin olive oil
1 medium leek, white part only, cleaned and minced fine
2–3 cloves garlic, peeled and crushed
1 tsp cumin powder
1 tsp fenugreek powder
4 cups water
1 cup red lentils, sorted (lentils often have small stones that should be cleaned out) and rinsed
¼ cup clean barley
Salt to taste

The following would not have been available in Bronze Age Canaan but would be added for more familiar taste in modern Israel.

1 tsp sweet or hot paprika
Ground black pepper to taste
1 bay leaf (fresh preferable)
1 carrot scraped and cut into small cubes
Other vegetables such as parsley, celery, celeriac to taste

1. Fry onion in the olive oil until golden. Lower heat, add 1 tsp water, cover and allow onion to caramelize on low heat, scraping bottom of pan from time to time.
2. Raise the heat. Add garlic and leeks, and stir for 1 minute.
3. Add cumin and fenugreek (pepper and paprika if using), and stir briskly for 30 seconds until fragrant.
4. Add water, lentils, barley, and bay leaf (and other vegetables if using).
5. Cover and simmer gently for 1 ½ hours.

Serve with freshly baked bread.

That a three- or four-thousand-year-old recipe still strikes resonance, and is still cooked, with some modern adjustments today, indicates how deep the historical and biblical connection of Israel's cooking is to its past.

Influential Ingredients

In Europe, lentil soup was a commonplace of the poor. In the Middle East, lentils were used to stretch expensive rice and served as substitute for meat. For the often-impoverished Jewish communities, this was a major foodstuff.

The importance of lentils in the Israeli diet has shrunk relative to other legumes, notably the chickpea (*hummus*). Nevertheless, two lentil dishes are commonly eaten and well-liked, partially because they are vegetarian dishes, partially because many students learn to prepare these dishes as an easy and cheap meal, and partly because they provide a feeling of tradition and nostalgia. *Majadarah* is a Middle Eastern dish that can be made vegetarian, or enriched with mincemeat. Lentil soup, in one of many varieties, is one of the winter mainstays for many people: winters in Israel are generally temperate, but cold days do occur notably in the mountains and the north.

Like rice-and-beans or Central American *gallo pinto, majadarah* has many variations, but at the core, it is a lentil stew served on rice: a way to ensure poor people have both carbohydrates and protein.

Nihaya's Druze Majadarah

Yield: Serves 4

1 cup olive oil + 1 tsp sunflower oil
4 medium onions, chopped roughly
3 cups chicken or vegetable stock
1 ½ cups dry washed and picked lentils: brown, green, or puy
½ tsp bicarbonate of soda (baking soda)
½ tsp ground coriander seed
2 tsp cinnamon powder
Salt and black pepper to taste
2 heaped Tbsp bulgur
1 minced onion, fried crisp for garnish
2 Tbsp well-washed and finely minced parsley for garnish

1. Use a large heavy cookpot with a lid. Heat the oils on a low flame.
2. Add the onions making sure they are stewing, not frying in the oil. The onions should bubble, not sizzle.
3. Cover and allow to cook 20–30 minutes, stirring occasionally and making sure the onions are not frying and pot bottom is well-scraped.

4. Once the onions are caramel brown, add the stock and bring to a light boil.
5. Stir in cinnamon, coriander, salt, and pepper.
6. Add the lentils and bicarbonate of soda (to soften the lentils).
7. Cover and allow to simmer for 25 minutes or until most liquid is absorbed.
8. Add the bulgur, cover, and allow to cook until bulgur is cooked soft and all liquid is absorbed for about 5 minutes.
9. Correct seasoning and spicing if necessary.

Serve the stew on freshly cooked rice, with thick yogurt or cucumber and salt grated into yogurt on the side. Top with crisp-fried onions and fresh parsley.

Garden Crops

The first Jewish settlers of the Second and subsequent *aliyot* were intent on adapting themselves to the land for ideological reasons. In addition, they were generally quite poor. They strove to replicate the lifestyle of local Arabs for dogmatic and economic reasons as much as possible, adopting many of their food customs, which were largely vegetarian.

Fresh vegetables are eaten by most of the population on a daily basis, whether as salads or on their own. Israelis consume more fresh vegetables per head than almost any other country. Some vegetables, such as tomatoes, cucumbers, and peppers, are the basis for many dishes, and are consumed daily. Other vegetables may be consumed less frequently. Given the climate and agricultural technology, many vegetables are available in commercial quantities all year-round.

Kinras (artichoke) has been known in the Middle East since Talmudic times, and in some countries is a dish associated with Jews. In Israel, where the artichoke and its relative, the cardoon, grow well, artichokes are eaten throughout the spring, and have been associated in particular with Passover. The outer leaves are too tough to eat, and only the fleshy base of the leaves, and the heart are eaten. Patient cooks will also prepare stuffed artichokes. Italian Jews will prepare *carcioffia ala giudecca* (fried young artichokes) in which most of the flower is eaten.

A popular vegetable throughout the Middle East and Africa, *bamiah* (okra) is made into stews, with meat or vegetable sauces. Only the smaller green varieties are commonly available in Israel. The interior of the pod is

Influential Ingredients

gelatinous, and the finer the fruit is cut, the more gelatinous the result, which is a plus for some, and a minus for others. *Bamiah* is particularly popular with those of Egyptian heritage, although other Middle Eastern cuisines consume the pods with relish.

Recommended in the Talmud as very healthy, *kruv* (cabbage) has been eaten since antiquity. Stuffed cabbage roll is both a traditional Mizrachi and Ashkenazi dish, although they are prepared differently. The rolls may be cooked in tomato sauce (Mizrachi) or in white sauce (Ashkenazi) and the filling may be meat or rice, burgul, and even potatoes. Cabbages are a common item in the Israeli diet, often eaten raw, sliced thin in salads, or German-style sauerkraut. Cabbage soup, both Russian-inspired borscht, and other forms are popular in the winter.

Like most of the brassica, *kruvit* (cauliflower) grows well in Israel, and is commonly eaten at home for both meatless and meat meals. The vegetable is prepared in different ways by much of the populace, and can also be found in restaurants. A popular way of preparing it is baking it in oil, and then adding a dressing of *tahina* or a white sauce.

Shoresh (celeriac) is the bulbous root of some forms of parsley. Peeled and cut into chunks, it is added to stews and vegetable or meat soups. It is very popular among most Israeli families.

Collard greens have been consumed in the Levant since before the common era. They were eaten by Jews in the countries round the Mediterranean and beyond. They are available in Israeli markets, and are particularly loved by Sephardim, who cook collard greens with a sour and hot sauce. Ethiopian immigrants still consume collard greens in large quantities; they are cooked with beans and hot pepper and served when possible with a *wot* (stew) and, of course, *injirah* pancakes.

Melafefonim (cucumbers), which may have been known since biblical times, have been a mainstay of the Israeli diet since early on. They are easy to grow, and became a quick staple in the form of salads and pickles. Since they were familiar vegetables to both European and Middle Eastern immigrants, cucumbers were quickly incorporated into daily consumption. In the late 1940s, Kibbutz Bet Alpha in the Beit Shean valley pioneered a relatively thin, thin-skinned dark green variety named after the kibbutz, which has become the "standard" Israeli cucumber, and is now exported to Europe and other areas. It is characterized by good flavor, crisp texture, and lack of seeds.

Cucumbers and tomatoes became the foundation of the Israeli salad, which started in the *kibbutzim* and migrated to all areas of Israeli cuisine, so much so that many Israelis do not feel a meal is complete without a salad, usually accompanying the main dish, of which cucumbers are an essential part. Cucumbers are eaten by many as a quick snack, sometimes dipped into salt in a twist of paper, sometimes on their own.

The *hatzil* (eggplant), a relative of the tomato, migrated from its Indian origins in early medieval times, and became a popular vegetable all over the Mediterranean. The most common one today in United States and European markets is the large dark purple variety, although green, pure white, streaked, and many other varieties can be found in Israel. The plant is easy to grow, and the flesh is relatively bland, and it absorbs other flavors with ease. It's commonly a poor person's food, and many families with low incomes ate eggplant instead of meat.

Today, eggplants are served in a multitude of ways. There are so many ways that a Tel Aviv restaurant, Abu Hatzil (Father of Eggplant), served nothing but eggplant dishes. The two most common ways one finds eggplant in Israeli homes is as *Hatzilim betahina*/mayonnaise (grilled hatzilim that have been finely minced, then mixed with garlic, parsley, salt, and either *tahina* or mayonnaise) or so-called *salat yevani* (Greek salad): grilled eggplant finely minced together with some onion and garlic, parsley, tomatoes, and salt and pepper), both of which are popular *salatim* or may be eaten as part of breakfast or a light meal. Hatzilim also feature in ratatouille-like stews such as Rumanian *guvetch*, which is a popular staple. Fake chopped liver is also made by grilling eggplant, then frying with onion until brown. A few housewives still make *hatzil* schnitzel, although the generation that grew up with that as a staple during the 1950s either still loathe the dish, or eat it largely out of nostalgia.

A well-loved vegetable is *shumar* (fennel root, popularly also called *finoccio* from the Italian), eaten by almost everyone during the season. The commander of one military base, who had a taste for the vegetable, almost had a rebellion on his hands when he insisted *shumar* be prepared for every meal during the season. The crisp bulb, leaved somewhat like a fat onion, responds well to baking and roasting, and can also be added to soups and stews.

Shum (garlic) has been associated with Jews since antiquity, and has lost none of its popularity since. Cooking with garlic was, according to the Spanish Inquisition, one of the signs of Jewishness, and the herb also featured heavily in Eastern European Jewish cooking. Few dishes in Israel today are prepared without some reference to garlic.

Pilpel[im] harif[im] (hot peppers, chilies) were introduced into the Middle East through Spain soon after the discovery of the Americas. Together with tomatoes, they caused a culinary revolution (oddly enough, potatoes and sweet potatoes, and maize, made a smaller impression: rice and wheat remained the major carbohydrates). Many dishes that had had softer and blander flavors became hot, even fiery hot.

> ## Eggplant Schnitzel
>
> Select a large eggplant of the deep purple-black variety. In choosing an eggplant, make sure to choose the lightest fruit. The weight is made up of a bitter juice that is unusable and can affect the flavor negatively. Slice it lengthwise into ½" slices or thinner, making one slice per person. Place the slices on an inclined board, sprinkle with salt, and allow to stand for 10–15 minutes. Beads of brown liquid will run off the fruit. Rinse the slices, then dry on both sides with a paper towel.
>
> *Yield:* Serves 4
>
> 1 large or two small eggplants, prepared as described previously
> 1 egg, beaten in a soup plate
> 1 cup flour for dredging, in a separate soup plate
> 1 cup fresh breadcrumbs, for dredging, in a separate soup plate
> Oil for shallow frying (eggplant absorb large quantities of oil, so more may be needed)
>
> 1. Soak slices for a minute or two in the beaten egg.
> 2. Dredge each slice in flour, then in breadcrumbs.
> 3. Lay each slice into the hot oil. Add as many slices as there is room ensuring that each slice has plenty of room and does not touch its neighbor.
> 4. Fry gently for about 3 minutes (length of time depends on thickness of slice), turn over, and repeat.
> 5. When a slice is golden brown, and a fork slides through easily, remove it from the oil and drain on a paper towel.
>
> *Serve immediately with a lemon quarter, a dab of mustard if desired, and mashed potatoes on the side.*

In both Moroccan and Yemenite meals, the presence of a fiery sauce as a relish became obligatory. The Jews from those countries adopted the new flavors offered by chilies wholeheartedly, and, when Jews from these countries immigrated to Israel, they brought their preference for peppery foods with them. Later, immigrants from India and from Ethiopia, who had also adopted hot chilies, brought additional pepper sauces with them. The two most prominent sauces, ones that virtually all Israelis eat to some degree, are green *zchug*, favored by Yemenites, and red *'arissa*, brought by Jews from Morocco.

In addition to pepper sauces, many Israelis, notably men, will eat pickled hot chilies as a relish, or merely as a snack, with or without bread. Olives and other pickles may be flavored with hot chilies and these accompany many dishes. Israeli males, as a sign of manliness, will also compete (verbally, and sometimes in practice) on their ability to consume truly hot sauces and peppers.

Harshaf yerushalmi, or Jerusalem artichoke, is neither an artichoke nor in any way associated with Jerusalem (the name is result of a mispronunciation of the French *girasol* [sunflower] of which this corm is a relative). It is a popular vegetable, sometimes substituting for potatoes, and can be grown easily in backyards. The corm has a reputation as a good food for diabetics, and thus has a popular niche of its own as a health food.

Loof or *krisha* (leeks), a milder version of the onion, originated in the Middle East and have been popular since before biblical times. They are used in Israel in stews and soups, as well as sometimes on their own as a side dish vegetable.

Molokhiya (young leaves and shoots of flax) is a popular vegetable in Egypt and Sudan, and in Syria and Iraq to a lesser extent. The leafy green serves as a thickener for vegetable or meat-based soups. Like *bamiah* (okra), it gives a soup or stew a gelatinous texture that is well-loved in many cultures, ranging from Louisiana to Japan. *Molokhiya* is best in the spring when the greens are tender, and are often added to soups by many Israelis, Arabs, and Jews alike.

Batzal (onion) have been popular throughout Europe and the Middle East since early history. They feature prominently in most Jewish cuisines. The most common onion in Israel is the white cooking variety, although both red and other salad onions are available. Commonly, finely minced onions are added to fresh salad. Field workers would often take a raw onion to add to tomatoes, cucumbers, and hard-boiled eggs as an early breakfast. Onions simmered in oil serve as the base for many dishes. Fried onions are added as a garnish to many Ashkenazi-origin dishes. Shallots, named for the then-Crusader port of Ashkelon, are also popular in the spring.

Tapuach adama (potato), in all their varied forms, are a major staple in Israel. Chips (French fries) are available in most fast-food places. Mashed potatoes are common in the home as well as collective food places such as army messes. In the summer, many people make potato salad: boiled potatoes with finely minced onion, parsley, and sometimes hard-boiled egg mixed with mayonnaise, as a simple filling food during the hot days.

Chips come as a matter of course as a side for any food, typically grilled meat, fowl, or fish. Falafel and other fast-food stands often make their own chips by frying potato slices, allowing them to dry, dredging them in potato flour flavored with turmeric, then frying them again, which causes

Influential Ingredients

the chips to puff up. These are added to the meat and/or vegetables in pita sandwiches, also often as a matter of course.

Making a bonfire is a common way for children to be free of adult supervision on summer nights. In particular, the cooking of potatoes in ashes comes to a climax during the holiday of Lag Ba'omer, which celebrates the rebellion of Bar Kochva against the Romans in 132 CE. Potatoes also feature heavily in another Jewish holiday: Hanukkah, which commemorates the independence of Judea from the Seleucid Syrio-Greeks. Oily foods are in high demand, including *levivot* (which most Americans will know as latkes): potato pancakes, of central European origin. Although originally an Ashkenazi specialty, *levivot* have become an Israeli commonplace treat for all during Hanukkah. Sweet potato (*Ipomea batata*) known in Israel as *batata* are also eaten and fill an important role in Moroccan cuisine, which took to *batata* rather than the potato.

Tsnon/tsnonit (radishes) are eaten fresh, the large ones on their own or lightly vinegared, the smaller ones as part of a salad. Larger radishes are cut up and made into pickles of various sorts.

Dla'at (squash) have been eaten since antiquity, and are still popular as a vegetable accompaniment to meat dishes. Several varieties are grown and consumed locally, although American pumpkins are more rarely eaten.

Several varieties of *pilpel matok* (sweet peppers) are available on the market. Israeli agronomists have developed a number of colors ranging from chocolate brown to bright yellow and purple, although all taste the same. Moroccan and other North African inspired stews and roasts include red peppers. Diced colored peppers are added to fresh salads. Peppers are pickled, on their own or in a mélange. A very common dish is stuffed peppers, which feature in both Eastern European and Middle Eastern styles of cooking.

Agvaniyot (tomatoes) were introduced into the Middle East after the discovery of the Americas by Europeans. The Hebrew name is a somewhat racy translation of the European *pommo d'amore* (love apple). As tomatoes grow well in hot climates, provided they are watered well, they have become an indispensable fruit for all meals, in Israel as elsewhere. Tomatoes are grown throughout the country. In the north, the fruiting season is in summer, whereas in the Arava valley, many farmers specialize in growing tomatoes that ripen in the local winter heat. Israel has also invested heavily in developing varieties of high-salt tolerance and low water demand tomatoes, including the famous Tomaccio cherry tomato.

Tomatoes may appear at almost any meal, either raw in salads, or cooked into a sauce, soup, or other dish. When a tomato shortage hit in the late 1980s, some Israelis swore they could not eat or live without eating

Torshi (Turnip Pickle)

Yield: Serves 4

2 medium white or yellow turnips, peeled and cut into thick French fry-style pieces
1 uncooked red beet, peeled and cut as described previously (cooked red beet can be substituted)
2 cloves garlic, peeled
1 bay leaf
2 chili peppers, whole (variety depending on preference)
½ cup kosher salt
1 cup vinegar diluted to taste with water. You need enough liquid to cover the vegetables.

1. Layer turnip strips, beets, and garlic alternately in a suitable sterilized glass jar.
2. Heat the rest of the ingredients to a bare simmer, taking care to stir the salt until it dissolves.
3. Pour the pickle liquid over the vegetables until completely covered. Tap the jar a few times to allow air pockets to escape. Top up jar. Place a small clean pebble or something else suitable to ensure the vegetables are all under the pickle.
4. Allow to rest for 3 days, unopened, at room temperature.
5. Keep in refrigerator. Will keep for 10 days after opening.

a tomato at least once a day, whatever the cost. Industrial products include canned tomatoes, tomato ketchup, tomato juice, and tomato soups.

Although rarely eaten raw, *lefet* (turnip) are common ingredients in thick stews, and even more widespread, as pickles since Talmudic times. Turnips are common in the Middle East, and until the arrival of the tomato and eggplant, were probably the cheapest and most consumed vegetable in the Middle East. *Torshi* (pickled turnips), which are often colored red with the addition of beets or radishes, are a popular pickle and may be added as a matter of course to pita sandwiches such as *shawarma* or falafel. They are an essential part of most *mezze/salatim*.

Kishuim (zucchini) are members of the squash family. In Israel, the most commonly available variety is pale green, and they are picked well before they reach maximum size, to preserve the delicate flavor. Zucchini are made into soups, savory puddings, and, most importantly, stuffed vegetables.

A common use is to make them into a *pashtida*, a pudding or deep-bowl bake, with or without cheese. This may be served as a side dish with meat, or as the centerpiece for a light meal.

Wild Greens and Vegetables

As a general rule, poor rural societies tend to rely to a great deal on gathering foodstuffs from the wild, which are, after all, free. This was true of populations throughout Europe and the Middle East in historical times. Once there is access to foods that provide higher energetic rates and better flavors, the knowledge of how to exploit these resources tends to die out. This has happened in Israel as well. The generation that relied, at least to some degree, on collecting wild foods is dying off among Mizarahim, Ashkenazim, Arabs, and Sephardim. Here and there, some individuals and even groups strive to maintain or revive the practice, which includes knowledge of the land and the seasons.

Some new restaurateurs, anxious to provide their customers with traditional new tastes (although older customers would find these greens completely unsurprising) have awakened the market, and offer some of these traditional vegetables. Some wild herbs are still remembered today because they are iconic, or because with growing prosperity there is almost always a desire to reexamine one's roots and old ways.

Khubeza/halamit (wild mallow) is a weed that grows in nondesert areas throughout Israel. The fruits—0.2" flat tomato-shaped—are edible and were served as a staple for a kind of bread during the War of Independence (1947–1948) while Jerusalem was under siege. *Khubeza* remains an iconic food, although few people still eat it. Children sometimes chew on *khubeza* fruit (the name derives from the Arabic word for bread, *khubz*).

A desert truffle (unrelated to the European truffles)—*kmehin* in Hebrew—grows in sandy areas in the Negev and elsewhere on the southern shores of the Mediterranean and in Arabia. It is hugely sought-after during Passover as a luxury, particularly by people whose families came from North Africa. The meat is spongy and slightly sandy, with a strong mushroom flavor. Cooked in broth or grilled, it imparts its flavor to meats and vegetable dishes. With a short season and low availability, it is a luxury food that can be found occasionally in the markets in spring.

Fruit

Israelis eat large quantities of fruit, many of which are grown locally. Fruit are eaten fresh in season, dried, and/or cooked in many different ways.

Several varieties of *anonacea* are popular in Israel, all generally known as *anona*. Some varieties are grown noncommercially as garden trees. A large variety of *anona* is common in the markets in winter, and constitutes one of the favorite dessert fruits. The creamy pulp is scooped out and the hard seeds discarded. The fruit is eaten as is, with a spoon, or is made into uncooked desserts and sometimes drinks.

Tapuchim (apples) have been available in the country for two millennia, originating from Central Asia via Persia. Several varieties are grown today. Besides being eaten fresh, apples are used to make apple juice, which is a popular drink. The most extensive cooking use is for the preparation of apple sauce or cooked apples, and for baking. European-type bakeries make strudels, apple cake, and other apple-based confections.

It is customary during Rosh Hashana (the Jewish New Year) to eat apple slices dipped in honey to wish a Happy New Year. Apples are also used to make a variety of *haroset*, a ritual requirement of the Seder, the Passover meal. In European tradition, apples, dried fruit, nuts, and wine are combined to make the dish.

"*Bukra ful mishmish*" is an Arabic epigram marking anything short-lived. The apricot (*mishmish* in both Hebrew and Arabic) season is short, and the fruit are soon gone. Eaten fresh for the most part, dried apricots, largely imported from Turkey, play a role in the making of fruit soup, a common Israeli dessert. Dried apricots, along with other dried fruit, are offered to guests for a quick snack. *Gogoim*—a game named after apricot stones—are used instead of marbles, with each player attempting to knock out their opponent's pile of apricot stones. *Gogoim* is still played occasionally during the short three-week *mishmish* season.

Avocados were introduced to Israel in the 1950s, where they grew largely in people's yards. In the 1960s, Haas avocados, as well as Ettinger, a larger thin-skinned Israeli cultivar, became a commercial product. Avocados grow well in Israel, notably in the Coastal Plain and the North, and avocados notably of some well-traveling varieties have become a commercial and export success.

Avocados are eaten on their own on bread or toast, made into guacamole, or added uncooked to soups or to salads. Since avocados cannot be cooked, they fit neatly into the Israeli preference for raw vegetables.

Bananas, which were a strange and exotic fruit to new immigrants in pre-State Israel and the early 1950s, have become a common fruit. They are grown in the northern Coastal Plain, in the Galilee, and in the hot Jordan valley by many farms, which supply almost all of Israel's demand for the fruit. They tend to be the first solid baby food, as well as a fruit that is eaten for snacks, and sometimes made into frozen yogurts or other confections. As in much of the rest of the world, the cultivar is Cavendish, which, although not the best tasting variety, is robust and has a lengthy shelf life.

Called colloquially *duvdevan* in Israel, the National Language Committee insists the true name of sweet cherries is *gudgedan*, a nicety most Israeli's cheerfully and rightly ignore. Cherries may have arrived during the Middle Ages, but had largely disappeared until reintroduction in the twentieth century. They are raised in mountainous and cooler areas and the supply is limited, making them an expensive spring fruit, sometimes eaten for the Shavuot holiday.

Pri Hadar (citrus) have been a mainstay of Israeli export agriculture for over a century. Starting with fruit that had been raised by Arab farmers in the Sharon plain and exported via Jaffa port (hence the "Jaffa Orange" name), Israeli farmers and scientists improved the fruit varieties, along the way hybridizing and genetically modifying them for better taste, shelf life, color, and properties. Today, Israel produces oranges, mandarins, grapefruit, lemons, kumquats, pomelos, and others in a bewildering variety of shapes, tastes, and colors. Most are available in Israeli markets, and to a lesser extent, overseas.

Tapuzim (oranges) and mandarins are eaten at any time as snacks or dessert. Some people add grapefruit to this, notably the newer sweeter varieties. Grapefruit are also eaten for breakfast in much the same way as in the United States. Lemon juice is used on salads and many other cold dishes, as well as drinks such as cold tea and lemonade. Other citruses are eaten as snacks or dessert. Pomelos, and the new hybrid called Jaffa Sweetie, are exported worldwide, and may be eaten at any time. Other varieties of citrus—kumquats, blood oranges, temples, and so on—can also be found, albeit in small quantities.

The advent of EU trade agreements and the rise of Spanish and Portuguese (members of the EU) exports, forced Israeli farmers to turn to more exotic citrus crops such as sweeties and kumquats. Although they have lost some of their glory, oranges remain a favorite Israeli fruit and are commonly eaten as whole peeled fruit, in fruit salads, and as elements in bakery products. The thick-skinned Shamouti variety preferred in Israel for its sweetness, juiciness, and durability, also has thick skin, which is used for candying at home and commercially.

Due to their size and easy-to-peel qualities, mandarins and clementines are favored fruits for snacks. They are small and handy enough that some people habitually carry a few in their packs or coat pockets for a quick snack. They are also included in winter fruit salads. Seedless, juicy, sweet varieties such as the Michal are exported in large quantities to Europe and East Asia.

A large variety of lemons are raised in Israel, including a small, thin-skinned variety that is often made into pickled lemons. Sweet lemons, which have little commercial value, and occasionally were found in the Sharon plain, were raided by young boys and eaten straight from the tree.

Lemons have multiple uses. Primarily, they are used as a souring agent for various foods ranging from *tahina* to tea. Lemonade, commercial and household, is a common use for lemons, and most households will keep a supply. Sliced lemons are used to sour and flavor pickles, and even on their own. Pickled, or to be more precise, salted lemons have been a feature of Moroccan cooking, as well as elsewhere in the Middle East. Many households will make them to this day, preferring the small, thin-skinned lemons for pickling.

Kumquats, small thumb-sized citrus fruit, are raised for the taste of their peel, which is sweet and eaten off the fruit. During the winter season when they come to market, many families will make kumquat preserves to use during the rest of the year. Both sweet peel and sour flesh are included in the preserve along with sugar.

Grapefruit have been a major export fruit for more than a hundred years. The original varieties were white and extremely sour. With time, newer varieties have come into being and most Israeli grapefruit today are the sweet pink variety. Israelis eat large quantities of grapefruit, sometimes included in fruit salads, eaten with a spoon, or from the open sections. Peel is preserved by some families in sugar to serve as a sweet snack. Grapefruit juice and canned grapefruit sections are available commercially.

The standard pomelo, the largest citrus, is raised and sold in Israel. However, a new variety, in which grapefruit has been recrossed with pomelo, has the juiciness of grapefruit with the sweetness of pomelo. This, labeled "Jaffa Sweetie" for commercial purposes, but "pomelit" domestically, has proven hugely popular in Israel and overseas, and has eclipsed the local sale and availability of pomelos.

Etrog (citron) is one of the three genetic parents of all modern citrus (the other two being pomelo and mandarin). In Jewish tradition, this fruit has assumed, since the fifteenth century or so, preeminence as a ritual fruit representing well-being and the good of the earth during the Succoth festival. Although inedible, the fruit has a wonderful scent. The very scant pulp is discarded if there is any, but the peel is sometimes candied as a special treat. The best quality citrons in Israel are imported from Italy and Sicily, as the citron does not do as well locally.

Israeli Winter Fruit Salad

Yield: Serves 4

1 orange, peeled, or 1 clementine or mandarin, peeled, as much white pith removed as possible
1 sweet persimmon, peeled and chopped
1 Tbsp roughly crushed almonds
1 apple, rinsed, cored, and chopped
1 guava, peeled, roughly chopped (optionally discard central seed ball)
1–2 *feijoa* (pineapple guava in the United States), flesh scooped out of shell and roughly chopped
1 Tbsp sweet dessert wine (optional)

1. About ½ hour before serving, gently blend all ingredients.

Serve with yogurt.

A prolific tropical and subtropical medium tree, guavas were brought to Israel in the first half of the twentieth century. They proliferated rapidly, and were one of the fruits that became extensively available during the late *tsena* period. The fruit—both pink and white varieties—are generally eaten raw. Some people discard the central, very juicy seed ball, others swallow the hard seeds whole. Guavas are also cooked for foods either for preserving in syrup, or as a part of *marak perot* (fruit soup), which is always popular.

A Brazilian relative of the guava, the *feijoa*—called "pineapple guava" in the United States—matures in winter. The bushy tree grows well in the coastal region, and the fruit is raised for domestic consumption and export. The entire egg-shaped, green fruit is edible and the pungent taste and scent are extremely appetizing. Due to the plant's relatively small size, it is raised in small backyard gardens for home consumption in early winter when the fruit is ripe and falls from the tree. It is not often used as hedging due to the habit of neighborhood kids of helping themselves.

A variety of the jujube has grown in large trees in the Middle East since early times. In Israel, it is not cultivated but grows wild, and the tree often serves as a hangout for young boys who alternatively pelt one another with and eat the slightly floury berry-sized fruit. Chinese jujubes were introduced by some farmers in the 1980s and are grown on a small scale, sometimes finding their way in limited quantities to the markets.

The kiwi, a New Zealand-developed variety of a Chinese vine, grows well in Israel and has become a successful acclimated crop. It is added to fruit salads and smoothies, and is found as garnish in *nouvelle cuisine* restaurants.

Lychees/litchis were unknown in Israel until the 1970s, when some kibbutzim in the north of the Coastal Plain began experimenting with the trees. Today, lychee fruit are mostly exported to Europe, but some still enter the local market. The ripe fruit are strawberry-sized, covered by a crisp red or red and green outer shell, which is easily cracked. The flesh is white, and extremely juicy and sweet with a unique flavor. The internal stone is discarded. Lychees are eaten as snacks or for dessert during the brief spring harvest season.

Mango became popular in Israel during the push to diversify the country's agriculture and find new export products. The most common varieties—Tommy Atkins, and Maya (a local cultivar)—yield medium sized fruit, yellow-fleshed, and not too fibrous. Other varieties that will adapt to relatively cooler Mediterranean climate, such as enormous Keitts, are also found, notably in private house gardens. Mango trees grow to a huge size, and giant mango trees can be seen in the Sharon plain where they do exceptionally well.

Israeli Summer Fruit Salad

Yield: Serves 4

2 cups chopped mixed summer fruit, including (depending on season, preference, and taste) mango, melon, kiwi, grapes, peaches, plums, or other seasonal fruit
Optional: chopped dried fruit
2 Tbsp pomegranate arils
Fresh mint leaves for garnish

1. Mix fruit, including dried fruit, and place in bowl.
2. Scatter pomegranate over salad.
3. Garnish with mint leaves.

Serve with ice cream.

Mangos are eaten in desserts and used as topping for pastries. Elaborate mango desserts enjoyed something of a craze, and, of course, mango can feature in Israel's basic fruit salad.

Melons, notably *avatiach* (watermelon), are extremely popular. Due to agrotechnical advances, watermelons, which were once a summer staple only, are now available most of the year. The U.S.-style long pale green striped watermelons are not as common as small round deep green ones. In the summer, entrepreneurs, young and old, provide watermelon stands piled with round green fruit, which is often sold "on the knife": you can try a wedge of the fruit you are buying before purchase.

Most Israeli males pride themselves on their ability to choose watermelons, apparently strictly a male trait (women buying watermelons will often ask a male customer to check a watermelon for them). The melon is thumped, weighed, listened to, and inspected before it is passed. Truth to tell, few customers know precisely what they are listening to when they put the melon to their ear and thump, but it is an essential part of Israeli maleness.

Cantaloupe melons of several varieties are available and in great demand. The most famous are Ogen with bright green flesh, and Galia, which are heavily scented, medium to small. All varieties of melons are eaten as desserts or snacks, rarely with salt. Melons are also used to make fruit salads, and some households will make candied watermelon peel.

Tut etz (mulberries) grow throughout the country, largely black mulberries of the *Mora nigra* family. Some white variants, sweet but less flavorful, are also found. The fruit are available in late spring but because they are highly perishable, are rarely seen in the market. These are largely children's fruit. An adult who wishes to enjoy mulberries needs to find willing youngsters, provide them with a pot to fill, and allow them free run of a tree.

Afarsekim (peaches), a historical import through Iran from China, are grown in the central part of the country, the north and in rare cases, in the Negev Desert. Kibbutz Sde Boker, overlooking the scarp of the Tsin river, was famous in the 1960s for its yellow peaches, which grew to enormous size and sweetness. They were sold to the public at a small farmer's shop on the main road to Mitzpeh Ramon, and woe to the bus driver who did not stop to allow his passengers to purchase some of the fruit.

Peaches are now common throughout the country, in a number of varieties that have been selected for Israeli conditions. Much of the fruit goes to the canning industry, and canned peaches feature in a number of desserts and even savory dishes.

Afarsemonim (persimmons) are a hugely popular winter fruit, so much so that there are occasional cases of people overindulging in the fruit—3 or

4 kilograms is not unusual—and ending up in hospital. First arriving in Israel in the 1950s, the tree was improved by local agricultural scientists resulting in a seedless, non-astringent, sweet, flat variety that was given the marketing name "Sharon fruit." Most Israelis consume the fruit, skin and all, while it is still firm (in many cases carrying a few about their person in case of sudden munchies). Others prefer it once bletted, which produces a soft, juicy, sticky, and very sweet pulp that can be eaten with a spoon. Persimmons are grown extensively in the northern Negev and the southern Coastal Plain, and in winter the orchards are full of the large golden balls.

The *pitanga*, also called *pitango* (Suriname cherry), is often grown as a hedge. The bush produces hundreds of small (up to ¾" diameter) berry-like fruit shaped like a flat tomato with a single hard large seed. When they ripen, the cherries turn almost black, to the lamentation of many mothers, as the fruit, which are rarely harvested commercially or sold, serve as ammunition for children. The sour-sweet and very musky flavor puts some people off.

A variety of plums appear in the Israeli market toward the end of summer. One of the most in demand is *nubiana*, a large, round black plum with yellow flesh and a small stone. Green, yellow, red, and black plums of various types are raised commercially, as well as in private gardens.

Plums are eaten fresh, made into jam called *povidl* (a term once used for jams in general, now applied almost solely to plum jam) and cakes and other baked goods. The dryer varieties such as Victoria are dried into prunes. The fruit, both fresh and dried, are also used in cooking, the two major products are *tkemeli* a sour-sweet plum sauce that is an essential in Georgian-Israeli kitchens and is gaining traction among other Israelis, and North African-inspired dishes in which dried fruit are cooked together with mutton in the oven.

Khavushim (quinces), a hardy relative of the apple and pear, are mentioned in the Talmud, and are one of the few fruits that must be cooked before eating. Quinces grow in many home gardens, and can be found occasionally in the markets and grocers. The fruit is yellow when ripe, highly aromatic, knobby on the outside, covered with brown fuzz that is easily rubbed off. It has a hard flesh that keeps its shape when cooked, and turns pink or deep red when cooked slowly with a tablespoon of lemon juice. It is made into a paste or jelly, or, more frequently in Israel, cooked with braised or roasted meat to add refreshing sourness.

An iconic fruit, originating in Mexico, the *sabra* (prickly pear) was introduced in the nineteenth century and grows all over the country except in the deep desert. The fruit, the skin of which is covered by tiny spines, must be treated with caution. After removing the thick spongy skin, the interior is a bright orange and full of hard seeds. Very popular as a children's fruit before the 1960s, the fruit lost popularity with the introduction of new, more easily consumed fruit. It is gradually regaining market share as new spineless varieties have been developed. It has been raised commercially since the 1990s and is common in the markets. The term *sabra* is also applied to Israel-born Israelis, with the implication that they are tough and prickly on the outside, and sweet on the inside.

Shesek (loquat), a small, elongated fruit with 2–4 smooth large stones enclosed, grows well in Israel and is a favorite tree for home gardens, as it gives a thick shade and edible fruit. Although present in the area for several centuries, it only became a marketable commodity in the 1970s when larger, sweeter varieties were bred locally. Until then, it was a strictly domestic and children's fruit. A common belief among children until prosperity became the norm was that if one held a *shesek* seed in one's mouth for long enough (weeks, in some stubborn cases), it became chewable like chewing gum (perhaps a misidentification with *mastic* gum).

Most of the very sweet, very juicy fruit is eaten fresh, with the stones discarded. A few people stew the fruit in syrup, although given the availability during the spring season, few people really bother, notably as the taste of the fruit does not keep well.

The *shikma* (sycamore or mulberry fig) fruit, related to the common fig, is known since biblical times. The prophet Amos presented himself as a mere "shepherd and sycamore cutter" (Amos 7:14). The sycamore fruit, which resembles a small, bright red fig when ripe, grows on the boles and branches of this large tree. It was important in premodern times as animal feed during the summer, but the top of the fruit needs to be cut to allow the ingress of the wasp that pollinates the fruit, hence Amos's part-time job. Although the tree is commonly planted for shade along urban streets, the fruit are rarely eaten since, with no one to cut them, few ripen.

Tut sadeh (strawberries) were introduced to Israel during the 1970s as a cash crop. Due to climatic conditions, they have become a ubiquitous winter crop and have been now incorporated into local cuisine as desserts, eaten raw or cooked. Strawberries are used to decorate cakes, produce juice drinks and *gazoz*, and cooked into various desserts such as *marak perot* (q.v.). They have now become available almost year-round, and their distinct identification as one of the fresh fruits available in late winter has been lost.

Bread and Other Basics

Bread is a major food element, and many people would not dream of sitting down to a meal without bread on the table, no matter what else is on offer. Israel has basically two different bread traditions. The European tradition includes mainly yeast-risen bread in loaf form. The Middle Eastern tradition is of flat breads, some lightly risen.

Risen Breads

Loaf bread includes a number of types. *Lechem achid* ("standard bread") is made of a mixture of white and rye flours. Standard bread is price controlled to ensure that this important commodity is available to all. There are also variations of the standard loaf such as seed breads (kümmel [caraway], pumpkin seed, sunflower seed, and others). White breads come in many shapes and forms including ciabatta, French baguettes, baton, and so on.

Challah

A special bread—*challah*—is made on Friday for consumption on the Sabbath, which starts with sundown on Friday. A *challah* is a ritual requirement in most ritual versions of Judaism (Yemenite tradition is one exception) although the braided shape is a European convention. All stores that provide bread—bakeries, groceries, supermarkets—will make *challah* available on Friday. Religious housewives will often bake their own *challah* following whatever is the household tradition. Standard *challah* is available in two versions. Sweet *challah* is baked as a braid and has a mounded appearance. It is usually topped with toasted sesame seed. Nonsweet *challah* is braided but baked in a bread pan, is therefore shaped as a lozenge, and conventionally topped by scattered poppy seeds. Artisanal bakeries will prepare other forms. Ashkenazi tradition—where the *challah* is made of braids—is most commonly visible, whether sweet or not, but other traditional forms can be found at artisanal bakeries.

The custom of baking special bread for Saturday arose from two related religious commandments. The first is to provide a morsel of risen dough as a sacrifice to God, as part of the Friday rituals. The second is a general instruction that one must beautify one's performance of religious regulations. Friday *challah* is thus an elaboration on daily bread. It is woven into braids, sweetened, made of pure white flour, decorated: whatever the housewife can think of.

Influential Ingredients

Even nontraditional Jewish families in Israel often try to ensure that a *challah* is available and prominent on the dining table during Friday's family meal. Customarily in traditional households, the head of the household will break off pieces of the bread (the braiding helps), dip them in salt, and offer them to each participant in turn. A special blessing is said, and each participant consumes the morsel of bread, after which dinner can begin.

Flatbreads

Flatbread of some sorts is the Middle Eastern norm, and there are as many variants on the theme in Israel as there are origin and ethnic groups. Most Israelis will eat pita (plural *pitot*): a pocket bread with strong spongy sides that are used to hold a variety of hand meals. Pitot can be bought from automated bakeries as well as hand crafted. Many households make them themselves when possible. The breads are between 15 and 25 centimeters across, and lightly risen.

In addition to the "standard" Israeli pita, there are a number of ethnic variants. Iraq is an ethnically diverse country, and many ethnicities pride themselves with a local variant of flatbread. Jews, who lived among others in the country, not unnaturally adopted many of the food customs, notably the breads. This means that there are a variety of "Iraqi pita" to be found in Israel, although what most people mean by "Iraqi pita" are a thicker variety of flatbread with no internal pocket. Often, the bread is decorated with nigella grains. *Lavash*, a very thin, large rectangular bread is common in Armenia and northern Iraq. Some bakeries do make them as a specialty, although it is considered by most Israelis to be a variant of the *lafa*.

Lafa are double the diameter of a pita, but much thinner. It is less fluffy than pita, and does not absorb liquids as readily: an advantage with sauces. Originally popular among Iraqi Jews in Israel, the flatbread has become a national favorite used often as a wrap for other foods. *Lafa* are made in a tandoori-like *tanur* (clay oven). Food is placed on one end, the bottom is folded over, and the whole is then rolled up. Anything that can be piled onto a *lafa* in Israel will be, but the most popular is *sabich* (eggplant salad). In some fast-food restaurants, one can choose to have a sandwich in a *lafa* or in a pita. Confusingly, *lafa* are also sometimes termed *"pita iraqit."*

Lahouh, a pancake-like bread made by Yemenite Jews, is also popular. Like Ethiopian *injirah*, it is made by allowing a highly liquid sourdough to froth over a day or several, then cooked over a flat metal or ceramic griddle. The result is a fluffy, slightly sour pancake. Many people dislike the slightly sour flavor (and the lengthy preparation time of the dough) and *lahouh* can now be bought, or made, using a yeast batter and cooked in a skillet. *Lahouh* is served with *hilbeh* (fenugreek relish) and *zchug* (hot sauce), honey, or dried fruit as a snack.

Bourekas

Bourekas originated in Turkey, perhaps under the influence of Sephardi Jews fleeing Spain in the fifteenth century. They have become a major snack time food in Israel. *Bourekas* are rolls or layers of phyllo dough that have been well greased and layered with a filling, whether savory or sweet. Because of their popularity, *bourekas* in Israel have become highly industrialized (with a concomitant reduction in quality). Nonetheless, homemade and artisanal *bourekas* are still to be found throughout the country.

The most common fillings are meat and onion (sometimes flavored with pine nuts), cooked potato and onions, and hard white cheese sometimes with spinach. Small *bourekas* are made as individual portions, scattered with sesame seeds, and can be bought frozen for reheating at home. In artisanal bakeries, *bourekas* are usually made as long rolls that are curled onto a baking pan, and are redolent of oil and spices. *Bourekas* are deeply associated with Sephardi culture in Israel, and a genre of Israeli films that feature popular Sephardi cultural memes are called "*bourekas* films."

Typically, *bourekas* are viewed as a snack, which can be eaten with coffee or a soft drink at any time of the day. Small one-bite *bourekas* also feature in events such as weddings and bar-mitzvahs, although the oil in the leaf dough is reduced (with a loss of flavor). *Bourekas* may also be eaten as a dish in a light meal accompanied by a salad or salads.

Noodles

In Eastern Spain, Jews took to noodles early: by the fifteenth century, they had become a major staple, eaten usually in soup. In the Sephardi world, these were known as *fideus*, by which name they are still known in Eastern Spain. The Yiddish term *lokshen* derived ultimately from a Persian word *lakhsha* (slippery) and refers to strips of dough boiled in water, and consumed in a soup or with a sauce or spicing. In Hebrew, they are known as *itriyot* (*itriya* singular), a word that derives from Latin.

Noodles are eaten as savory and as sweet dishes. In the Ashkenazi world, *lokshen* could be found in chicken soup, or could be flavored with sugar and cinnamon, or baked into a *kugel*, which in Poland was generally

Influential Ingredients

sweet, and in other areas, tended to be savory. Persian and Central Asian Jews still eat *lakhshman* soup, of mutton with pulled noodles, which is eaten almost as a staple. Noodles thus arrived in Israeli food culture from numerous directions. The term *lokshen* by which noodles were known in the Ashkenazi world has echoed through Israeli culture. "*Al ta'achil oti lokshim*" ("Don't feed me noodles") presumably refers to the slipperiness of noodles, and means "don't feed me lies." Salary slips are called *lokshim* since before computer printouts, they were thin long strips of paper, torn off a larger sheet.

Noodles were often made at home, usually once a week, by Ashkenazi housewives. As commercially made noodles of various sorts became available in food stores, this practice declined, and few housewives outside the ultra-orthodox community still maintain it.

As across the world, spaghetti, often in tomato sauce or with a Bolognese ragout, is eaten by most people at some stage, as are nonmeat variants of pasta sauce. Macaroni and other pasta of various types are also available. In some households, *lokshen kugel* (q.v.) are still made.

Meat and Fish

Israelis, in common with many other people, love meat. This presents a problem as the country has little open space for pasturage, and animal feed is noneconomical. Meat is thus expensive, which is made up somewhat by a high consumption of farmed fish and poultry, notably chicken and turkey.

Meat

One not so obvious barrier to meat production and consumption in Israel is the control of the religious authorities over the *kashrut* laws and their application, which means that any meat offered to the general public must meet stringent *kashrut* laws, or have serious problems with import, marketing, and even storage.

Most meat is sold through supermarket chains, although independent butchers can still be found, notably in ultra-orthodox and Arab communities. The former because they do not trust the Israel Rabbinate, which is formally responsible for *kashrut* in publicly sold food, the latter because they do not maintain *kashrut*. Most Israelis are thus unsurprisingly, fairly ignorant about cuts of beef, proper butchery, or storing meat. This is changing as there is a growing sophistication in food choice, as more Israelis are exposed to practices and the choices available overseas.

Beef is sourced largely overseas. To ensure *kashrut*, inspectors from the Rabbinate must be dispatched. To add to the cost, hind quarters, which according to *kashrut* rules would require removing *gid hanasheh*, cannot be purchased, and the forequarters are generally more expensive. (*Gid hanasheh* is a sinew that runs from the rump of the animal to the foot, and is forbidden for consumption. As result of the injury Jacob incurred to his hip while wrestling with an angel [Genesis 32:22–32], the rabbis forbade Jews from eating this sciatic sinew.) All this adds to the cost of meat. Due to the combination of import and *kashrut* laws, beef thus tends to be expensive. Until fairly recently, the government maintained a monopoly on beef imports in an effort to ensure price control.

On the whole, beef is sold as steak meat, ground, stew meat, or roasting meat. Innards, notably liver, are prized, and some people enjoy other internal parts such as lungs, spleen, and brain.

Mutton is considered a desirable—for some, the most desirable—meat throughout Israel, but particularly among those with origins in the Middle East and the Maghreb. Moroccan Israelis and Samaritans will buy a sheep that is fattened for slaughter on Passover (although the national and municipal health authorities frown on the practice). Bedouin, who maintain flocks of sheep, will slaughter one for a feast and cook a *mansaf* of *lafa*-lined bowl with rice flavored with turmeric and *samna* (clarified butter) topped with chunks of stewed mutton.

Mutton is very expensive because grazing land and animal fodder are scarce. Iconic Middle Eastern dishes featuring mutton, such as *shawarma*, are made with cheaper and plentiful turkey meat. The vertical skewer is topped by a piece of mutton fat, which melts in the grill and drips down to flavor the meat. In some communities, the sheep's head is considered a delicacy and either served whole, roasted, or with the soft, delicious face muscles separated and served in soup, and the brains cooked separately.

The most common sheep in Israel is the robust Awasi breed, which is well suited for the dry environment, but does not otherwise compare well with other breeds for milk, wool, or meat. Several new and one ancient breed—Jacob's sheep, which has four horns—have been introduced, sometimes crossbred with the Awasi.

While goat is kosher, it rarely reaches the market, although it is sometimes eaten by flock owners and their families. As adult goats have a strong flavor, kid is preferred, but rarely available.

Camel is non-kosher and thus is eschewed by most Jews, but is in high demand by Muslims. Nevertheless, due to shortages of space and pasture, few camels are slaughtered, except in exceptional circumstances.

Influential Ingredients

White Turf and Pink Surf

Most Jews and Muslims eschew pork. A minority of both faiths insist on their freedom to eat what they please, without the interference of the government political machinations. Christian Arabs, mainly residents of the Galilee, raise pork for their own consumption, but often serve non-Christian customers as well.

Even some secular Jews will not eat pork. Others will not eat shrimp or other seafood. Nonetheless, pork products and seafood are available, and sold in some markets and fishmongers. On the whole, consumption of pork is rather low. Some bacon and ham is made, but most of the meat goes to cuts of meat and occasionally sausages, all of which are available in specialist shops. Until the 1970s, pork was available "under the table" from some kibbutzim and from Christian Arab breeders, often going by the name "white meat." With the massive arrival of Russian Jews from the Soviet Union, more pork products became available as pork was commonly eaten by almost all in that part of Europe. The immigrants from the former Soviet Union had powerful electoral strength of their own, and had been used to eating pork, brought sales more into the open, and in cities with plentiful former Soviet immigrants, stores selling pork and pork products, imported and domestic, soon sprung up. Today, pork meat and other products are available in many dedicated butchers and supermarkets, which are also patronized by non-pork eating secular people, since these stores do not pay the fee for kosher certificates from the Rabbinate.

Shrimp and prawns were plentiful in the Mediterranean Sea, and Israeli fishermen exploited this resource largely for export, which the Rabbinate acquiesced to. Inevitably, some of the catch was sold in Israel as well, as fishermen provided some of their catch to favored restaurants, family, and friends.

With the rise of globalization and the turn of Israeli cooking from necessary to artful, many restaurants, notably in traditional port cities such as Tel Aviv-Yaffo and Akko, have opened offering non-kosher dishes of pork and seafood. Fried calamari and cooked prawns are favorites and can be found in most of the upmarket seaside restaurants.

Fowl

Most of the animal protein in Israel comes from fowl, which are easily raised industrially, and to which fewer ritual difficulties adhere. Two fowls are central to cooking in Israel: chicken and turkey, which are prepared in many forms. Moreover, most Jewish communities throughout the world raised and used fowl of various types for daily cooking, since not much space was required, and thus the prominence of fowl was an established fact from most immigrants to Israel.

Chickens were raised for eggs during the Ottoman period and only slaughtered for special occasions. It was the rise of the kibbutzim and other communal farming styles that allowed the industrial growth of chicken farming. *Tnuva*, the marketing arm of the kibbutz movement, was a major purveyor of eggs, and, once refrigeration technology was sufficiently advanced, chicken carcasses as well. Chickens—whole carcasses and parts—are available in supermarkets, markets, and butcher's stores. Most slaughter is supervised by the Rabbinate, as merchants are reluctant to lose customers who want at least some form of *kashrut*. For the ultra-orthodox, official Rabbinate supervision is not always a sufficient guarantee of complete *kashrut*, and the communities have set up their own slaughterhouses to provide *glatt* (absolute) kosher meat. This has led to ongoing struggles as the state attempts to stamp out these slaughterhouses, often unsupervised and unlicensed.

Chickens, including innards such as gizzards, hearts, and liver, are in great demand. As more Israeli kitchens are now equipped with ovens, roast chicken is a common dish at home, as in restaurants, including at roast chicken takeaways. Chickens may be made into soup or stewed, and even stuffed. Chicken allows a great deal of flexibility, with the potential for both simple and elaborate dishes. It may be served simply for daily menus, or as an elaborate preparation restricted for holidays or special events. As the cheapest form of protein, it is commonly seen on Israeli tables on a regular basis, and few households go without if at all possible.

The difficulty of procuring red meat pushed Israeli farming into looking for alternative sources of animal protein. The solution was the turkey (which had been the main source of animal protein in Mexico for centuries. Ostrich, another option, are not kosher). A program of selective breeding soon developed an optimal bird for local conditions, and a great many farms, both kibbutzim and moshavim, went into raising turkeys for meat (eggs are available, but not in much demand). Turkey meat is generally sold as white meat (breast) or red meat (the rest). The availability of turkey meat at reasonable prices increased meat consumption on one hand, and also brought about innovations in the kitchen, as turkey meat substituted for others. As an example, *shawarma* (meat slices grilled on a vertical spit) were and still are made from turkey meat, rather than the more expensive mutton.

Turkey meat is used for making kababs, minced meat for many purposes, and meat stuffing. A major use is the replacement of veal with white turkey breast meat in the production of schnitzel, which is a major form of meat consumption, both in the home and as a public food in cafeterias, for example.

Geese were raised by famers in the southern Coastal Plain, mainly those with a French or Algerian background. Israeli *foie gras* secured a respectable niche in the French market and worldwide. Once force feeding was forbidden by law in 1976, the availability of geese declined. The carcasses were initially sold at knockdown prices at supermarkets, and for a period were popular with the poor. Later, the meat was processed into various products such as smoked goose breast and mock ham. The mock ham was sold under the commercial name "Jambo," which slyly evoked the French term *jambon* without arousing the ire of the religious authorities.

Fish

Fish are a desirable item in the diet. With the decimation of fish stocks in the Mediterranean Sea, wild fish yields have declined significantly. This is partially made up for by farmed fish, both marine and fresh water. The dietary laws of *kashrut* also mean that many types of fish are available only in limited quantities in places that cater to nonobservant Jews. Shrimp, eel, and shellfish of all sorts are not kosher, although they are caught for sale overseas, with a growing amount being retained for home and (non-kosher) restaurant use.

Marine Fish

With a long Mediterranean coast, Israelis have become accustomed to the availability of sea fish. The gradual depletion of these resources has raised their cost to a great degree. Nevertheless, many Israelis enjoy fresh fish meals either at home or in one of the many seafood restaurants throughout the country. A number of types of fish are eaten, some of them related to North American varieties, although the fish choice of Israelis (and the rest of the Levant) differs from the United States, or even other areas in the Mediterranean.

Grey mullet, known locally as *buri*, is a local favorite. The firm white flesh lends itself to grilling, and most *buri* are grilled with salt or tomatoes. Dried compressed *buri* roe is popular as a snack among Tunisian–Israelis.

Cod is imported, and before the collapse of the cod stocks, *bacalau* (fresh codlings) were a common and desired fish. In the late 1960s, grilled young codlings were sold as "bakalah" in roadside grills, and for a time

> ### Buri al Haesh (Grilled Mullet)
>
> As with many foods, the preferred way of cooking *buri* is to grill it over coals.
>
> *Yield:* Serves 4
>
> 4 *buri* (grey mullet) about 40 cm long each, cleaned, scaled, and butterflied
> Rough (kosher) salt
> 3 tsp minced garlic
> 2 Tbsp virgin olive oil
> Juice of 1 lemon
> 1–2 ripe tomatoes, sliced thin
> 1 medium onion, sliced thin
>
> 1. Place fish skin side up, preferably in a wire fish grill basket, and scatter a small amount of salt on the skin.
> 2. Turn fish over so the flesh and spine are up.
> 3. Mix garlic, olive oil, and lemon juice, and rub thoroughly into the exposed flesh of the fish.
> 4. Distribute onion slices, then tomato slices on the fish, then drizzle with a small amount of olive oil, then salt to taste.
> 5. Grill skin side down for about 5–10 minutes, then flip wire basket over and grill the exposed side.
> 6. Run wooden skewer into flesh to ensure doneness.
>
> *Serve with salads and French fries.*

made inroads into the domain of steaks and falafel. This fish is no longer easy to find. Cod are no longer as cheap as they used to be, but are still eaten by many as a matter of preference.

Other sea fish, notably those that can be raised in controlled conditions, are also popular. They include dorade locally called *denis* (gilt-head bream), *farida* (red snapper), sea bass pronounced *sibess* in Israel, and *palamida* (bonito or Spanish mackerel), which is less popular due to its strong fishy flavor. Commonly, *palamida* fillet is also made into a dried, salted, and oil preserved delicacy called *lakerda*, which, together with dried bonito roe, is popular with Israelis with roots in North Africa, notably Tunisia. Tuna, like cod, is an imported fish. It is rare to find fresh tuna available in the market, and most tuna is imported in the form of canned

Influential Ingredients

fish. As such, it is consumed for light lunches, often in the form of a salad with mayonnaise and finely chopped vegetables (peppers, celery).

Freshwater Fish

Most fish consumed in Israel are freshwater fish. These come from two sources: the Sea of Galilee, a lake that has been a fishing venue since prehistoric times, and manmade fish ponds, which are common along the northern seacoast and in the Jordan valley. The demand for fish, notably carp and *amnun* (tilapia), peaks during holidays, notably before Passover, on Friday, and at Rosh Hashana (Jewish New Year).

Fish farms have been a kibbutz specialty for more than half a century. Certain kibbutzim such as Ma'agan Michael on the Mediterranean coast, Dan, at the Dan source of the Jordan River, and Mishmar Hayarden in the Jordan valley have extensive fish ponds. The two most common fish are carp, which is in high demand by those who want to prepare gefilte fish (stuffed fish) for the Sabbath and holidays and tilapia, which competes with gefilte fish as a Friday treat. The Moroccan version of gefilte fish—*khreime*—has become a welcome treat for many families.

Carp are relatively easy to raise, and can be sold live in fresh water. For many ultra-orthodox families, a live carp to be killed and served for the holidays and the Sabbath dinner on Friday evening is an important item of diet. It is often prepared as gefilte fish (stuffed fish), either stuffing a whole fish with minced carp flesh, or balls of the filling cooked in their juice, which can be eaten hot or cold. The Sea of Galilee—Kinneret in Hebrew—is the home to a local St. Peter's fish called *musht* locally, which has been fished in the lake for thousands of years. It is served grilled or fried in specialist restaurants on the shores of the lake—a popular tourist and pilgrimage area—as it has been for at least two millennia, and due to demand is also raised in kibbutz fish ponds. *Nesichat hanilus* is the commercial name for Nile perch, generally sold frozen whole or in fillets. Sturgeon are prized for their flesh, which is smoked, and even more for their roe, called caviar, which is in great demand worldwide. Kibbutz Dan on the banks of the Dan river, which flows from the Hermon range into the Jordan River, has been raising sturgeon for smoking and for caviar for the past decade. With a can (1 oz.) of the local Osetra caviar retailing for over 100 U.S. dollars overseas, it is one of kibbutz Dan's most profitable branches: the fish ponds produce some 4 tons annually.

Processed Fish

Preprocessed fish were the only fish most Israelis ate during the early years of the state. This came as frozen fish fillets, from northern Atlantic waters, or as canned fish: sardines and tuna. The fish fillets (most likely pollock, although any white fleshed fish would have been possible, except shark [at least legally], which is not kosher) were called "fillet" by most, and as they were on the ration cards, fillet was a standard meal item once or twice a week.

Fillet was most often dredged in egg (if available) and breadcrumbs, then fried in scant oil. An entire generation of Israelis grew up loathing fish due to their experience with fillet. Israeli fishing fleets expanded in the late 1950s, and a greater variety of fish came into the market, notably from the Indian and Atlantic oceans where these fleets operated. Fillet is still available at the cheap end of the market, although it now often includes naming the fish variety. Other processed fish products such as fish nuggets as well as ready-made gefilte fish also became available.

Canned fish, notably sardines and tuna, have always been a staple. Canned tuna is a fixture of *sandwich Tunisai* (Tunisian sandwich), a common street food.

Israelis who served in the army during the late 1970s and early 1980s still recoil from canned tuna. The military quartermaster, in a logic all its own, packed some of the field rations with cans of tuna and almost no other protein. Inventive, bored, and hungry soldiers discovered a way of changing the taste by making "tuna candles."

Tuna Candle

Yield: Serves 4

1 can tuna in oil
A square of clean paper towel

1. Open the tuna can, making sure to not detach the lid fully, to serve as a handle.
2. Roll the paper into a hollow cylinder. Dip into can, making sure it is well soaked in oil, then stand upright.
3. Light the paper and allow to burn (if it doesn't, you may have water-packed tuna).
4. When flame goes out, food is ready.

Pick up using lid and a rag for protection, and eat out of can with a fork with bread or crackers.

Milk, Cheeses, and Eggs

Milk and its products, and eggs, were major sources of protein for much of the population during Israel's early years. This was simplified by the Jewish religious requirement to separate meat from milk, and not consume them in the same meal. Even when meat became plentiful, many people still separated meat from milk meals. As a result, Israel has developed an extensive repertoire of milk products and soft cheeses. Hard cheeses, generally modeled on European originals, are also available. Since Israel is a country of immigrants, unsurprisingly, the cheeses available are borrowed from both Mediterranean and European cheese traditions. The same is true of other milk products.

A large variety of milk products were produced and used by Jews from all backgrounds throughout history. For the poor (and most Jews throughout history were poor), some form of milk product—sour cream and sour milk, soft cheeses, and yogurts—were a major source of protein and fat. In Europe and India, the milk was often bovine, whereas in the Middle East, North Africa, and Central Asia, it was sheep or goat's milk. Camel milk, a common product in the drier areas of the Middle East, is not commonly sold in Israel since the camel is a non-kosher animal.

During the 1950s, as part of a two-headed attempt to increase economic demand and to ensure the health of children, the government started a widespread campaign to increase the drinking of (cow) milk. Advertising slogans were devised and spread via radio and billboards (among other things, serving as catchphrases for local comedy acts). While Israeli milk consumption—178 liter/person annually—is not notably high compared to Finland or Sweden, for example, it is very high in comparison to other Middle Eastern countries. In particular, mothers were encouraged to both consume milk themselves (to increase lactation) and to encourage their weaned children to consume bovine milk. Both objectives were largely successful, with nutritive health of Israeli children being assured (for other reasons as well, of course) and a rise in habitual milk consumption. The army too contributed to the demand for milk by providing quantities of both milk and chocolate milk to serving soldiers, whether in camp or in the field whenever possible.

In the 1950s, milk in Israel was sold pasteurized, but not homogenized, in glass bottles, and could be delivered by a milkman. The tops of the bottles were often filled with clotted cream that rose to the surface, the source of innumerable sibling squabbles over who would enjoy the treat. Later, milk was sold in polyethylene bags of one liter, until the development of waxed paper cartons, which are common today. Like virtually all milk products, milk can be bought in fat free, skimmed, or full-fat versions.

In the growing prosperity of the 1970s, the milk industry became more diverse and sophisticated and the demand for various traditional milk products established a vertically segmented market, ranging from standard industrialized products, through artisanal production, to expensive imports. By the early 1970s, Israel was producing analogs of well-known European cheeses from Emmental through Camembert, and a huge variety of Middle Eastern-inspired fermented milks and soft cheeses.

The diversification of the milk industry has meant that the average food shop offers a wide variety of milk and milk products. Hard cheeses are consumed less than soft cheeses and varieties of fermented milks. These products appear on almost every table at nonmeat meals (breakfast and either lunch or supper, depending on choice). In addition, several religious festivals traditionally require milk/cheese dishes, including Shavuot (spring harvest festival) in which cheesecake is traditionally served, the post-fast dinner after Yom Kippur, Succoth (the Feast of Booths), and *Simchat Torah* (The Giving of the Law) in the fall. Many traditional Ashkenazi and Sephardi dishes are made with cheese fillings, sour cream, or fermented milk, sometimes as a principle ingredient, sometimes as a flavor addition or enhancer. Another element of diversification was the increased availability of sheep and goat milk, and, most notably, their products. Goat and sheep cheeses and some fermented milk drinks are sold by artisanal dairies, mostly located in the Jerusalem area, the Galilee, and the northern Negev. Druze villages in particular have become famous for their production and sale of *labaneh*.

In the nineteenth century, an immigrant from Bulgaria established himself in the Galilee hilltop holy city of Tsfat and started manufacturing a version of *brinza*, a common Balkan hard white cheese preserved in brine, now known throughout Israel as *Gvina Tsfatit* (Tsfat cheese). Other varieties of Balkan semi-cured semi-hard cheeses followed and became common throughout the 1950s. As milk production improved, and butterfat percentages in Israeli milk increased, more butterfat content allowed for the production of better cured yellow cheeses and other fat-dependent foods such as ice cream. (Kibbutz Yotveta, just north of Eilat in the Arava, one of the hottest and most arid areas in the country, has a thriving dairy industry and are reputed to make the best ice cream and yogurt in Israel, as their dairy herd has one of the highest production yield and butterfat content in the world.)

Soft white cheeses are consumed in large quantities in Israel, and because of their relatively slow spoilage have also been popular for picnics and field meals. While choice was limited until the 1960s, there are now a variety of cheeses for every taste. Many Israelis eat some soft cheese every day, and they commonly feature in light meals, whether for spreading on bread or as part of some other dish such as *bourekas.*

With the rise of the Nazis in Germany, many German Jews fled to Israel and settled in then-Palestine. They brought with them customs and manners from Germany, as well as their food preferences. One important German food item is, and was, *quark,* a soft, spreadable fresh cheese made largely from skimmed milk. In 1935, a German immigrant set up the first industrial production of *quark* locally. This relatively cheap food had two consequences. First, it helped in developing the dairy sector locally, and second, the product, labeled *gvina levanah* (white cheese) became a quintessential Israeli food. When the production of hard cheeses became commercially viable, due to improvements in the dairy sector, *gvina levanah* held its place because of its price and great plasticity. *Gvina levanah* is slightly smoother than its original as it is often made of full milk. Besides being spread on bread, there are varieties that have been spiced with paprika, flavored with garlic and herbs, and so on.

Many Israeli-Arab villagers with access to their own herds (cattle, sheep, and goats) still make a soft, unripened white cheese called *jibneh beida,* which is common throughout the Middle East. A few artisanal cheesemakers also offer *jibneh* to the public. It can be made from cow or sheep's milk, and is often used for breakfast for dipping a flat bread or spreading on risen bread.

Labaneh (from the Arabic laban "milk/white") is the common Israeli name for a soft, white semisolid dairy product made by draining the whey from goat, sheep, or cow's milk yogurt. Depending on the degree of draining, *labaneh* can have the texture of sour cream or be as thick as cream cheese. *Labaneh* developed as a method of lengthening yogurt's shelf life and utility. In the Levant, for even longer storage over the winter, *labaneh* was made in a mass quantity, rolled into balls, dried, and stored in olive oil.

Labaneh is used as a spread or as a dip, sometimes as part of a *mezze*. It may be blended with vegetables such as chili sauce or cucumbers, but purists prefer to consume it on its own with a dash of olive oil and a sprinkle of *za'atar. Labaneh* as well as balls of *labaneh* preserved in olive oil are sold in groceries, although as an industrial product are considered inferior to the "real" thing. The women of many Druze villages in the Galilee and the Carmel have become adept at marketing their *labaneh*. Druze *labaneh*—soft, fluffy, sour sold by many Druze housewives from home or at markets—is generally acknowledged to be the best available, with customers flocking from around the country to buy their share.

> ## Labaneh
>
> *Yield:* Serves 4
>
> 1 liter (2 quarts) *good* full-fat yogurt. Preferably ewe's milk (the better the origin, the better the final product)
> Salt to taste
> 1 Tbsp virgin olive oil
> 1 tsp *za'atar*
> Pita, *lafa*, or other flatbread
>
> 1. Mix yogurt with about half the salt.
> 2. Place the yogurt in a sieve lined with cheesecloth over a deep bowl and allow to drain overnight.
> 3. Salt lightly to taste.
> 4. Remove from sieve onto a plate and smooth with a spoon to create a broad, flat crater.
> 5. Drizzle the *labaneh* with olive oil, then scatter *za'atar* on top.
>
> *Serve with flat breads and side dishes of olives, vegetable salad,* salata mechoui, hummus, *and so on. The whey makes a pleasant salty summer drink.*

Yogurt arrived in Israel relatively late, since the food niche had been already occupied by *lebeniyah*, and local tastes initially preferred the more sour product. However, with time and persistence, and with the arrival of large numbers of Soviet Jews in the 1970s, yogurt started taking market share away from *leben*. Today, one can find many kinds of yogurts, fruit and other flavored as well as plain, in Israeli food shops.

Leben is a fermented milk product, similar to yogurt, although produced by a different culture, one that predominated in pre-State Israel. It is slightly thicker and with a rougher texture and sourer flavor than yogurt. A glass, later plastic container, of *leben* was the standard for each person for nonmeat meals, and because of its durability even without refrigeration, often was taken by farmers or workers out to work, and eaten for breakfast. *Leben* is thick enough to eat with a spoon, and many would simply cut tomato or cucumber pieces into the jar to add interest, or prepare a quick vegetable salad and put *leben* over it. A more liquid version, *lebeniyah*, was used as a drink, and eventually mutated into fruit drinks similar to fruit yogurt.

Leben has lost much of its popularity today, due partly to changes in taste, and largely to a more varied choice that shoppers are faced with, notably yogurts. Nevertheless, it is available in Israel in some food stores. The ever-hovering language aunties of the National Language Committee tried, only partly successfully, to change the popular Arab-language name of the food from *leben* to *zivda*, a word that many Israelis are cheerfully ignorant of.

As the milk market diversified, demand for particular varieties of fermented milk allowed manufacturers to provide new products in a saturated market. Buttermilk, the side-product of the manufacture of butter, became available as a summer drink. Notably seized upon by Jews with roots in Northern and Eastern Europe, Israel produces and consumes modest amounts of buttermilk.

Shamenet hamutza (sour cream, sometimes marketed by its Slavic name, *smetana*) derived from the traditions of Eastern European Jewry. Today, in addition as being used as garnish for soups and latkes (q.v.), it is eaten like *leben* or yogurt. Generally, like these other sour milk products, it is sold in small 200 ml individual plastic goblets. *Shamenet hamutza* is also used in the making of cheese cakes of various sorts.

Eggs

The most commonly available eggs in Israel are hens' eggs, although turkey eggs can sometimes be found. Ostrich eggs, which taste much like their hen counterparts, can be bought from one of the ostrich farms in the Negev, although since they are non-kosher, their appeal is limited to only part of the population.

Eggs are, of course, almost essential for *parve* dishes as they are considered neither milk nor meat. They thus feature in many guises in baked goods. They are also important during Passover, and several eggs dishes such as *matzabrei*, called *matziyot* (crumbled matza soaked in beaten egg, then fried) in Israel are a staple for light meals.

Herbs and Spices

Herbs and spices are an essential component of most Israeli foods. The use of herbs collected from the wild is particularly prominent among Arab Israelis and those of Middle Eastern background. Most herbs are collected in spring when rainfall turns some of the country green. Herbal uses include consumption raw in salads, in cooked dishes, and as flavorings.

Baharat is a spice mixture originally from Turkey, that is used throughout the Levant. There are *baharat* for particular dishes, such as lamb, beef, fish, and so on. *Baharat* is generally sweet and aromatic rather than sharp. Different communities and households make different *baharat*.

Cinnamon is a popular flavor. The true Sri Lanka cinnamon and the Chinese cassia are used interchangeably, and arguably, most Israelis are ignorant of the existence of two separate unrelated spices with the same name and very similar flavor. Cinnamon is used heavily in confectionary, and features prominently in Moroccan cuisine.

Kusbara (coriander or cilantro) is an annual herb whose leaves and dried seeds are important both on their own and as part of spice mixes such as *baharat* (q.v.). Both the green leaves and the dried grains are used for cooking. Many people dislike the strong flavor of the herb, but will happily consume foods flavored with the ground seeds. It is common throughout the Middle East and follows only cumin in its importance to local cuisines. Coriander has been available as a local spice since prehistoric times.

Coriander features heavily in many Israeli dishes. A mix of coriander powder and other spices flavors almost all charcoal grilled dishes, many soups, and other cooked dishes. The green fresh leaves are one of the bases for hot pepper sauces, notably Yemenite-inspired *zchug* sauce.

Kamun (cumin) powder is probably the most common spice used in Israeli cooking. Many Israeli and Middle Eastern dishes are made with freshly ground cumin, ranging from hummus through sausages and steaks. The greenish gray powder is sold in groceries throughout the country, although many prefer to buy the sickle-shaped tiny seeds in quantity and grind their own at need.

Leaves of the *dafna* (bay laurel) grow wild, as well as being cultivated domestically all over the Levant and southern Mediterranean. The leaves are used as a matter of course by most cooks in stews and soups. The bush can be found in the wild in the Galilee, which is relatively well-watered.

Introduced from India to Yemen where it is widely used, *hilbeh* (fenugreek) was then brought with Yemenite immigrants fleeing oppression in Yemen. The spice has anti-glycemic properties, and many men of Yemenite descent consume a *hilbeh* soup or tea daily believing it protects them against diabetes and increases virility. The spice also features prominently in Indian cooking, and a walk through any of the neighborhoods heavily populated by those of Indian descent—Ramle, Dimona—gives a strong curry scent typical of the spice. The hard seeds are soaked in several changes of cold water to remove some of the bitterness.

The seed of a small annual, *khardal* (mustard) originates in the Middle East where it still grows wild, although it is hardly a major spice. Seeds are used whole, normally for pickling. European-style ground mustard made

> ### Hilbeh Soup/Tea
>
> *Hilbeh* soup is good for what ails you. It also goes some way to lowering blood sugar for some people.
>
> *Yield:* Serves 4
>
> 6 Tbsp fenugreek seeds
> 1 quart water
> 1 ripe tomato
> ½ garlic bulb, cloves peeled and minced roughly
> 1 tsp cumin seeds
> 1 pinch turmeric powder
> Salt to taste
> Juice of ½ large lemon
> *Zchug* to taste
>
> 1. Soak fenugreek seeds in water overnight.
> 2. Drain and discard water.
> 3. Place fenugreek, tomato, garlic, cumin, turmeric, and lemon juice in a blender. Process well until result is as smooth as possible.
> 4. Season to taste with salt and *zchug*.
>
> *Drink for breakfast, adding water if necessary to make drink more liquid.*

into a paste is also available and eaten at home. The leaves are also eaten in the spring.

Kurkum (turmeric) is a signature spice that is used in many dishes. The spice is a bright yellow powder made from the ground rhizomes of the plant. In addition to dishes—both savory and sweet—in the Indian Jews' cuisine, turmeric is also used to flavor a mixed meat spice that is used on grilled meats, as a prominent flavor in *meorav yerushalmi* (chicken sandwich), in rice dishes, and in *'amba* (mango) relish and to color *jalabi* (fritters). The general rule is that one uses one half as much turmeric as any other spice in a dish, since otherwise the slightly musty taste can be overwhelming.

The extraction of the flavor from rose petals was developed by Avicenna (Abu Sina), a Bokhara-born scientist and philosopher in the Middle Ages. His invention, rose water, is still popular all over the Middle East, and it is used to flavor sweets and cookies. Using the same process, the flavor of orange blossoms is also distilled and used similarly. Orange blossom water is used to flavor "Oriental" (that is, Middle Eastern-derived) confections such as *baklava*. It is available in grocery stores in small bottles, and used with discretion. Rose water, like orange water, is a popular and common flavoring agent for special dishes, some savory, most sweet. It is used often for Middle Eastern sweets such as *rahat lokum*, as well as baked goods.

A sour-bitter spice, *mahleb* is made by grinding the kernels of sour cherry pits. It originated in Persia and is made and used throughout the Levant. It is used to flavor baked goods and sometimes meat and stews.

Na'ana (mint or other *Mentha* varieties) has pride of place for a drink that is available throughout Israel: *té im na'ana*, or Moroccan mint tea. *Té im na'ana* may be indulged in at all hours of the day notably by those who abhor coffee. The tea is normally heavily sugared and served in a glass, not a tea cup. Only fresh mint leaves are used.

Kamun shakhor (nigella or black cumin) is a spice grown since antiquity in Israel, it is now entering a revival after many years of being neglected. The seeds are small and black with a distinct crisp and sharp flavor. In Israel today they are used to flavor crackers and bread, sometimes incorporated in the dough, sometimes scattered on top of savory baked goods.

Paprika, a red pepper powder of Hungarian origin, can be either sweet or slightly hot, and was brought to Israel by European Jews. One kibbutz in the Negev exports much of its pepper crop to Hungary for the production of the best paprika. This relatively mild pepper powder was adopted by restaurants and by Oriental Jews, probably as a sop to European-origin sensitivities to "true" hot peppers. Hummus plates, for example, are almost always served with a garnishing of hot paprika: sufficient to assuage the conscience of those who like hot peppers, but not hot enough to put off those for whom hot peppers are anathema. Thus, certainly in the early years of the state, paprika served as a bridge, or a precursor, to the wholesale adoption of hot peppers, pepper sauces, and so on, that so mark Israeli cuisine today.

Pilpel shakhor (peppercorns) are a favorite spice throughout the world. Pepper is used in many Israeli dishes, of all backgrounds. It is often part of spice mixes such as *ras el hanut* and *baharat*.

Petrozilia (parsley) is one of the most common herbs in Israel. The herb originated in the area and has been cultivated and used since antiquity. In most cases, fresh flat-leaved parsley leaves are rinsed thoroughly, then minced fine and added to cooked soups stews and roasts, scattered as a garnish on both Middle Eastern and European dishes, or included in salads. The herb imparts a freshness to dishes and is used liberally for everything except sweet dishes. It is also used commonly as *karpas*, one of the required ritual mouthfuls during the Seder.

Parag (poppy) seeds are used in Israel both as filling for sweet baked goods, and scattered over rolls, buns, and nonsweet *challah* bread. The most commonly found (and eaten) filling is for *oznei haman*, the triangular pastries eaten at the Purim Carnival holiday.

Shamir (dill) has been cultivated in Egypt and Judea for millennia. The herb grows wild in some places such as the Jerusalem hills, and the licorice scent is noticeable in the spring and summer. It never acquired the popularity it has in Northern Europe. It thus occurs more commonly in Ashkenazic than other dishes in Israel. Vinegar-pickled (as opposed to salt) cucumbers in Israel typically include dill. Some specific dishes such as potato salad also commonly use dill. It is also used to flavor *tzatziki* and other dishes with yogurt.

A very old oil seed, perhaps the first cultivated, *sumsum* (sesame) seeds have been used as a flavoring in the Middle East for millennia, and no less importantly as an oil for cooking and light. Foods flavored with sesame seeds are prominent in Israel, ranging from breads through honey and sesame seed candy bars. A major use for sesame seeds is the making of *tahina* (which originates in a word for "grinding" in both Arabic and Hebrew): a paste that is used for many dishes, and garnishes many others.

Looking somewhat like dark purple crystals, sumac is the crushed dried berries of a large bush. In the late summer, when they turn deep red upon ripening, the clusters of sumac berries are harvested and dried in the sun for several days. Before lemons and tamarinds arrived in the Middle East, sumac was the primary souring agent. Sumac may be used instead of lemon juice to sour a dish, although it has a distinct flavor of its own. It is scattered on various dishes such as roast lamb to provide a refreshing sour contrast. Crucially, sumac is a component of *za'atar*, which is used to flavor dishes including hummus, and is often used as a dip for baked goods such as *ka'ak*.

Although more a pickle than an herb, *tzlafim* (*tzalaf* [singular] caperbuds) are a common addition to fish and other foods that need some tang. The caper bush is a perennial found throughout the center of the country down to about Beersheva. The flower buds are picked and pickled. Otherwise, the bush provides beautiful large white flowers that sprout from rock walls and chalky cliffs.

Hyssop are examples of several small plants that grow over much of the Middle East, and often have medicinal properties. Both plants, which are similar botanically, are called *ezov* in Hebrew. *Ezov* is mentioned several times in the Bible used for purgation. All have a strong, pleasantly fresh smell. As a spice, it is used as *za'atar*, a mix of dried hyssop leaves, sesame seeds, ground sumac berries, and salt.

Za'atar is used as a fresh spice, sprinkled over some foods. Notably, a twist of paper with some *za'atar* almost always accompanies a *ka'ak* (bread bun, somewhat like a bagel) for dipping and flavoring the bread. This is a common street snack, notably in Jerusalem.

Further Reading

Bottéro, Jean. 1995. *Textes Culinaires Mésopotamiens*. University Park, PA: Eisenbrauns/Penn State University Press.

CHAPTER THREE

Appetizers and Side Dishes

The neat distinction between "main" and "side" dishes becomes complicated, and almost irrelevant when speaking about Israeli food culture (and that of the rest of the Middle East). Side dishes and main dishes blend into one another and may well be part of the same dish. So-called side dishes may well *be* the meal, with what would be a "main" dish in Europe becoming merely one element among others.

Salatim: The Mezze

A *mezze* is an eastern Mediterranean tradition that goes back centuries. Essentially an appetizer, a *mezze* is a series of small dishes filled mainly, although not exclusively, with cooked and raw vegetables. *Mezze* are traditionally served in multiples of three, although not everyone adheres to this tradition. In Israel, the *mezze* is generally known as *salatim* (salads), which covers the same territory as *mezze*. The hands down favorite is hummus with *tahina* sauce, olive oil, and a scattering of hot paprika, cumin powder, and fresh minced parsley: a meal in itself, a snack, or part of the *salatim* in a meal with a meat or fish entree. A fresh salad, *salat yerakot*, mainly composed of tomatoes, cucumbers, and onions, chopped, and with the addition of any fresh vegetable in season, is probably the second most popular, and may be eaten alongside any dish except soups and dessert. Arguments still erupt over the proper fineness of the chopping, with some preferring (and swearing by) large cuts, and others insisting on pieces small enough to fit all elements of the salad into a teaspoon.

In the past, less so today, breakfast and supper consisted of little more than a salad or salads, a container of *leben* (q.v.), olives, and bread, perhaps with fruit to follow. Several salads are prominent as they appear in many positions in different meals. And while this or another country or place of origin can lay claim to a particular type of salad, they are generally considered an Israeli fixture by Israelis.

Unlike Western diners, who look askance at repetition of ingredients at a cocktail party or buffet, a *mezze* usually features many items of the same class, such as several relishes, hot sauces, and salads. A *mezze/salatim* is always accompanied by bread, normally *pita,* which is used to scoop the food up. The list of popular *salatim/mezze* items is lengthy, and might include any of the following in addition to hummus, salad, and mixed pickles:

Alei gefen memulaim (stuffed grape leaves)
Baba ghanouj/Hatzilim betahina (eggplant salad in *tahina* sauce)
Falafel
Hatzilim bemayonnaise (mayonnaise eggplant: grilled eggplant flesh dressed with mayonnaise, vinegar or lemon juice, finely minced garlic)
Kibbeh mahshi (fried meat-stuffed burgul croquettes)
Kruvit bethina (cauliflower cooked in *tahina*)
Matboucha (cooked tomato and pepper salad)
Mortadel (filled meatballs)
Muhammara (red pepper relish)
Olives
Pilpel kavush (roasted peppers in vinegar)
Salat gezer marokai (Moroccan carrot salad: lightly cooked carrots in a spicy sauce)
Salat kruv (cabbage salad: lightly blanched shredded cabbage flavored with vinegar, salt, and nigella)
Salat selek (beet salad)
Salat tapuchei adama (potato salad: boiled, peeled waxy potatoes and slices of onion dressed in mayonnaise and vinegar)
Salat turki (spicy Turkish-style tomato salad)
Salat yevani (Greek eggplant salad: grilled eggplant flesh, minced together with tomatoes, onion, and parsley and flavored with olive oil, lemon juice, salt and pepper)
Tabbouleh (burgul and mint salad)
Torshi (mixed pickles)
Yerakot memulaim (stuffed vegetables)

At dairy meals, foods like *labaneh* (yogurt cheese) sprinkled with *za'atar* and goat cheeses might also be featured.

Matboucha (Cooked Tomato Salad)

Matboucha, brought by Moroccan immigrants, has become mainstream and a staple of *salatim*. It is available commercially; although the homemade version is so simple and tastes so much better, it's a wonder anyone

Appetizers and Side Dishes

buys the product. Significantly, *matboucha* serves as flagship in presentations of Moroccan pride in Israel. Since it keeps relatively well, and goes with most Israeli dishes, it is commonly found in restaurants (whether they are serving *salatim* or not) as an appetizer dip, as well as in fast-food stores and of course in many homes, even those with no direct connection to its Moroccan ancestry.

The Military as Food Pioneer: Avocados and Exotic Foods

In an effort to diversify and strengthen both the country's economy and its food sources, farmers turned from more traditional crops—oranges, plums, apricots, wheat, tomatoes—to more exotic fare. Avocados were one of the attempts. However, avocados were unknown both to native-born and most foreign-born Israelis. In some despair, avocado growers in the late 1960s hit on a brilliant strategy. They unloaded tons of some of their first crops as a free gift to army messes. Most of the soldiers had no idea what these strange fruits were. But, in many units, given the diverse nature of the army, those with a family background in Latin America, South Africa, or Australia seized on the fresh oily fruit with glee. The others soon learned, and brought their desire for the new food home on leave with them. Avocados are now a major export crop for Israeli farmers, and are a common staple in many households. They are mostly eaten with salt and lemon juice, although new products often emerge such as avocado sushi. Some other new agricultural products were ingrained into popular cuisine (and consumption patterns) in a similar way.

Matboucha

This simple tomato and pepper relish can, of course, be tarted up, but it is best kept simple. Long slow cooking is essential, as is the red oil.

Yield: Serves 4

1 heaped tsp sweet or smoked paprika
½ cup good olive oil
6 very ripe medium tomatoes, cored and chopped roughly
2 sweet red bell peppers
1–3 hot peppers of your choice
4 cloves garlic, peeled and sliced thin
Salt to taste

1. First make the red oil, an essential ingredient. Place paprika and olive oil in a bowl and beat well. Leave to rest for half an hour.
2. Meanwhile, roast the bell peppers under high heat or over a fire until the skin is well charred. Dunk into very cold water immediately. Remove all papery black skin and core, and rinse peppers of all seeds. Chop roughly.
3. Chop tomatoes roughly.
4. Slice hot peppers if you want a hotter product, else leave whole.
5. Place all vegetables and garlic into a suitable pot. Bring to a boil under medium heat, then lower heat to a slow simmer, stirring all the while.
6. Keep stirring occasionally to ensure mixture does not stick to bottom, until most of the liquid has evaporated.
7. Mix red oil into the tomato mix, and adjust seasoning to your preference.
8. Allow to barely simmer for another 20 minutes.
9. Allow to cool, check seasoning once cool, and serve cold with almost any kind of dish or as part of *salatim*.

Hummusim beMitz Limon (Chickpeas in Lemon Juice)

This is often added to the list of *pitzuchim*, or may be served before a meal. It differs from hummus by the term *hummusim*, which indicates individual beans.

Yield: Serves 4

Juice of 1 lemon
¼ cup virgin olive oil
Ground cumin to taste
Salt and pepper to taste
1 cup chickpeas, boiled until completely cooked but not falling apart (you may remove the translucent shell if sensitive, otherwise they usually stay on), drained, kept warm

1. Beat the olive oil, lemon juice, cumin, and salt and pepper thoroughly.
2. Pour over the *hummusim* (chickpeas) and mix thoroughly.
3. Allow to marinade for at least 30 minutes.

Adjust seasoning and serve with beer, 'arak, or brandy.

Salat Russi ("Russian" Cooked Vegetable Salad)

With the arrival of a large population of Russian immigrants from the former Soviet Union, Russian foods entered the mainstream of Israeli food.

Yield: Serves 4

2 cooked beets, peeled and cut into thick slices, then quartered
2 waxy potatoes, boiled until firm but easily penetrated by a skewer
¼ lb lightly boiled or steamed green beans, cut into 1" lengths
2 medium carrots, peeled, lightly boiled or steamed and coined
1 sweet onion, sliced into rings
2 dill pickled cucumbers, coined, then quartered
A handful or less green olives, pitted and cut into slices
2 spring onions, finely minced

Dressing
2 Tbsp wine vinegar
2 Tbsp olive oil
¼ tsp sugar
Salt and freshly ground black pepper to taste
½ tsp dry mustard powder

1. Beat all ingredients of dressing except mustard together.
2. Drop a little of the resulting liquid into the dry mustard powder and mix thoroughly, gradually adding more liquid until a thick liquid is obtained.
3. Blend the mustard mix into the remaining dressing ingredients and whisk thoroughly.
4. Allow the dressing to rest for at least 15 minutes.
5. Place all other ingredients in a bowl.
6. Drizzle on the dressing and toss gently just before serving.

Salat Yerakot

Yield: Serves 4

Vegetables
It is imperative all the vegetables be absolutely fresh, and well rinsed in cool water, then shaken dry.

> 1–2 large or 4 medium tomatoes, or 8 cherry tomatoes
> 2 crisp Israeli cucumbers, or ½ large European cucumber, deseeded if necessary
> 1 small onion, sweet if preferred, minced fine
> 1 sweet bell pepper (yellow, purple, or chocolate to add color), deseeded and deveined
> Any choice of: peeled carrot, peeled kohlrabi, 2–3 leaves lettuce, 2–4 small radishes
>
> *Dressing*
> 1 Tbsp freshly squeezed lemon juice
> 1–2 Tbsp virgin olive oil
> Salt and black pepper to taste
>
> 1. Beat all dressing ingredients together.
> 2. Allow to rest for 5 minutes or more.
> 3. Cut all vegetables into small cubes about ⅛″ to a side (some Israelis argue for a finer cut. A sharp knife and plenty of patience are required).
> 4. Place in large bowl.
> 5. Beat dressing one more time, then pour over salad just before serving and mix in thoroughly.
>
> *Eat together with a main dish, as part of* mezze, *together with a plate of hummus or as one component of a falafel sandwich.*

A salad in Israeli meals, mainly called *salat yerakot* (vegetable salad), is the senior bit player in all Israeli meals and in many dishes. Israeli salad features as a side dish (rarely on its own as in classical European cuisine) for breakfast, lunch, and dinner. It is also a component in a good falafel sandwich, and rare is the Israeli who will "wipe" a plate of hummus without an accompanying small salad.

Pickles

Pickles accompany most meals and they are known by the collective name *hamutzim* (sours). The most commonly available, aside from olives, are pickled cucumbers. These are either vinegar or salt pickled, and each variety has its partisans. In addition, many Israeli families bring with them their own pickling traditions. Iraqi Jews make 'amba, a mango pickle with whole cardamom seeds. Baltic Jews make dill and sweet and sour pickles

Appetizers and Side Dishes

not too different from those found in New York. Virtually all these specialties are also available in commercial form in stores.

In the cold of northern Europe, pickles—cucumbers, cabbages, or turnips—provided the only vegetables available during long snowy winters. The tradition of pickling for home consumption and for commercial sale was brought to Israel by immigrants from northern Europe, keen to taste traditional delights. That there was little snow or real cold in the winter was neither here nor there. Both dill and cucumbers grow well in Israel, and the use of crisp, small Israeli cucumbers meant that the rather soggy European cucumbers virtually disappeared from the menu, both domestic and commercial.

European Jews, notably those from Germany in the 1930s, brought with them a taste for sauerkraut. As cabbage was cheap and easily available, it soon became a regular pickle in many households. Peculiarly enough, sauerkraut also became a fixture in falafel sandwiches. Aside from the cost factor, there may have been two other drivers: sauerkraut mass is relatively amorphous, and so could fit easily into a pita, and German immigrants in the 1930s settled near Yemenite communities, in both urban settings (e.g., the city of Rehovot) and in some moshavim. For whatever reason, intermarriages between the Yemenite and "Yekke" communities

---

Salted Lemon Pickle

Yield: Serves 4

2 lb, preferably thin skinned, small lemons
½ cup kosher salt
1 Tbsp hot chili flakes
1 Tbsp whole coriander seeds

1. Select a clean, sealable, glass jar. Rinse jar, and if you want the pickle to last longer, rinse again in vodka, or sterilize by boiling in a pot with water to cover for 5 minutes, then allow to cool.
2. Place two thick cutting boards, or large knife handles, a lemon's width apart. Place each lemon on its stem base between the boards. With a very sharp, thin knife, make two or three cuts through the lemon's core, without cutting all the way down.
3. Once all lemons have been cut, stuff some of the salt into each cavity, along with some of the chili flakes.

4. Place a layer of lemons in the jar. Scatter some more salt and chili flakes over the layer and add coriander seed. Repeat until jar is full or all lemons have been used.
5. Place jar on a window sill where it will get plenty of sunshine.
6. Leave jar to pickle, shaking the jar lightly from time to time and rotating it so all sides receive sunshine.
7. After 7–10 days according to taste, the lemons are edible.
8. Remove quantity desired from jar, brush excess salt (or rinse lightly), cut, and serve as any pickle.

were relatively high in the early years of immigration. It is a sociological truism that immigrant communities tend to be endogamous (they marry within the community) for the first two generations. And may become exogamous (marrying outside the community) for the third generation and subsequently. Yemenite–German intermarriages were relatively higher than to be expected from the second generation on. This may have aided in the transfer of sauerkraut as a falafel condiment, since Yemenite immigrants quickly took on the falafel-making niche from early on after their arrival in Israel.

Sauces and Relishes

A condiment or sauce, often more than one, are a necessary accompaniment to most meals. Spicy hot sauces, as well as bland, are spooned (sometimes, ladled) on all street foods, and on many dishes for home consumption.

Tahina

The quintessential sauce for most Israelis is *tahina* (or tahini in the United States). It is made by grinding toasted white sesame seeds (though in Nablus, Palestine, a version is also made from nigella seeds). *Tahina* is made both industrially and as an artisanal product, and several mills, notably in Arab villages in the Galilee, proudly market handmade *tahina* from their own fields' product. *Tahina* comes out of the mill as a thick, gluttonous mass. After some time in storage, the heavy solids separate from the lighter oil on top, which must be remixed before use. To use, the mass must be blended with water and lemon juice to the consistency

Appetizers and Side Dishes

Siniya

Israeli Arabs, who are reputed to make the best *tahina* in boutique mills throughout the Galilee and Sharon plain, often prepare this well-loved dish for breaking the fast during the Ramadan fasting month. During Ramadan, food is strongly spiced to encourage drinking and eating. You may want to reduce the quantity of spices somewhat.

Yield: Serves 4

½ lb minced meat per person, preferably lamb or a mix of lamb and beef
2 Tbsp fresh parsley leaf, finely minced
2 tsp cumin powder
1 tsp coriander powder
1 tsp *baharat*
½ tsp sumac powder (available at Middle Eastern stores)
4–8 garlic cloves according to taste, grated or mashed fine
Salt and black pepper to taste
½ cup raw *tahina* paste
2 Tbsp lemon juice
1 cup cold water
½ tsp salt
1 Tbsp olive oil
½ tsp sumac powder and 2 Tbsp roughly minced parsley for garnish

1. Place meat, parsley, cumin, coriander, *baharat*, sumac, and garlic in a deep bowl and mix thoroughly with bare, well-washed hands until spices are well blended with the meat. Add salt and black pepper to taste.
2. Allow meat to rest for half an hour in refrigerator.
3. Meanwhile, prepare *tahina* sauce. Place *tahina* in a bowl. Add all the lemon juice and blend well with a wire whisk. When the emulsion thickens and darkens, add cold water a little at a time until the sauce relaxes and thins out. Add salt (if mixture thickens again, quickly add a tsp of cold water). The end result should be a thin cream that pours easily from a spoon. Reserve the sauce.
4. Heat the oven to 320°F.
5. Form the minced meat into egg-sized balls or into sausage shapes, then flatten slightly.
6. Place meat balls onto a lightly oiled ceramic or glass baking pan. Pour all the *tahina* over the meat, ensuring the meat is well covered.

7. Bake the dish for 20 minutes, then test for doneness. If meat is still raw inside, bake for an additional 10 minutes. The sauce will thicken and may form a crust.
8. Remove from oven when meat is done.

Garnish dish with sumac and parsley. Serve with rice.

desired: thicker if eaten on its own, thinner if to be mixed with hummus, or almost watery to be added as a salad dressing.

Tahina is also used as a cooking sauce. *Siniya* is a Lebanese dish of mincemeat cooked in *tahina* sauce, which is also popular in Israel. A vegetarian version uses baked cauliflower instead.

'Amba

In the early nineteenth century, Jewish merchants started traveling to India, notably the Mumbai area, on business. Other Jewish communities had been there much longer, largely in rural areas of India, and had become more Indianized. Gradually, a community of Iraqi Jews, who engaged in trade and professions such as translation, grew in the subcontinent. On trips home, they brought with them a condiment called *'amba*, which they had adapted from Indian origins, made from green mangoes flavored with coriander seeds and chilies. When Operation Magic Carpet brought the majority of Iraqi Jews out of the country to Israel, they brought this relish with them, and it has become an inescapable part of the Israeli culinary landscape. Sold in many stores in large glass or plastic jars, the slices of salty-sour mango are eaten as a relish and feature in many falafel kiosks to be added to the sandwich.

Horseradish

The horseradish root is a root vegetable commonly found in Eastern and Central Europe, where it is known as *khren*. It is used by many Jews of European decent as a relish with gefilte fish, for example, and is an essential ingredient in their Passover dish where it features as "Bitter Herbs." Grated, the radish produces a strong front-of-the-tongue burn and piquancy. Among Baltic Jews (Poland, Latvia), this is moderated by adding grated beetroot and even sugar, although purists insist on eating it as is. It

Reuven's 'Amba

My father would make this *'amba* sauce from his own mangoes. It can be eaten as a relish with any savory dish, and is particularly appropriate with *sabich* (fried eggplant sandwich), falafel, *meorav yerushalmi,* and any other Israeli pita sandwich.

Yield: Serves 4

About 2 lb mango flesh. 1 large (*keitts*) or two or more smaller mangoes are usually sufficient. Make sure that they are green, hard, and still sour. Cut flesh with peel from the mango cheeks and the seed edges.
1 whole green chili
Salt to taste
½ tsp mustard powder
About ¼ cup water
1 small green chili, shredded
½ tsp fresh grated garlic
½ tsp grated fresh ginger
½ tsp coriander seed, ground roughly in mortar and pestle
½ tsp fenugreek seed, ground roughly in mortar and pestle
½ tsp mustard seed, ground roughly in mortar and pestle
½ tsp cumin seed, ground roughly in mortar and pestle
½ tsp whole mustard grains
½ cup vinegar
½ cup vegetable oil

1. Slice each cheek and edge piece into slices about ½" wide. Peel.
2. Place in a glass or steel bowl. Mix in whole chili and salt to taste.
3. Mix mustard powder with enough water in a small bowl to make a light slurry.
4. Heat 1 Tbsp oil. Fry garlic and ginger over low heat for 30 seconds or so until fragrant. Remove from heat and set side.
5. In same pan, add a bit more oil, then add coriander, fenugreek, ground mustard, cumin, and whole mustard. Fry until mustard seeds start popping and jumping. Remove from heat.
6. Immediately add fried garlic and ginger and mustard slurry. Mix well.
7. Pour immediately over mango slices. Mix. Transfer mango slices and the rest into a sterilized glass jar. Seal well. Leave for at least 24 hours.

Eat as a side with any savory dish, or as one part of a mezze.

is commonly sold in early spring, when prices go up for Passover, but it's available in jars in shops throughout the year.

Zchug

Yemenite Jews started immigrating to Israel in the 1880s, and en masse from 1948. Fewer than one hundred of them, out of a population of several tens of thousands, remain in difficult circumstances in Yemen.

Yemenites have a number of Israeli culinary achievements to their credit. They were the first to popularize falafel (even though it was unknown in Yemen) and many early falafel kiosks proudly declared their Yemenite origin, true or false. They started a number of culinary fashions including *malawach* (fried bread) and *hilbeh* (fenugreek relish) soup, and they popularized Israel's second iconic hot sauce: *zchug*.

Zchug

Zchug must be made fresh every day for the best result. Some people prefer more, some less, coriander leaf. Adjust to your own preference.

Yield: Serves 4

10 hot green peppers, cored and caps removed (choice of peppers depends on how hot you want the final product to be), chopped
1 bunch fresh coriander leaves, chopped (about 1 cup)
1 bunch fresh parsley leaves, chopped (about ½ cup)
1 tsp cumin powder
½ tsp coriander seeds
10 garlic cloves, peeled and chopped
1 tsp black pepper, ground
1 tsp salt
½ tsp fenugreek powder
1 Tbsp olive oil

1. Place all ingredients in a blender or food processor. Process to a smooth paste, stopping to scrape down the sides occasionally. Store in an airtight container in the refrigerator. The sauce deteriorates fast, so it is best to make in small batches and renew daily.

Place in center of table for diners to help themselves as a relish.

Appetizers and Side Dishes

Zchug, in contrast to red *'arissa*, is bright green, the color provided by fresh coriander and fenugreek leaves. It is made by grinding together hot green chilies, fenugreek seeds, fenugreek leaves, coriander leaves, olive oil, and salt. The sauce may have originated in the Indian subcontinent, where a similar green sauce—*saag*—is popular. In Israel, it has become an iconic hot sauce, which, if it does not take the roof off one's mouth, is not considered worth eating.

'Arissa

'Arissa (not to be confused with *harees*, a meat and grain dish popular from the Arabian Gulf down to Tanzania) is a hot red sauce originating from Morocco and popularized in Israel by Moroccan immigrants. For

---

'Arissa

Yield: Serves 4

- 1 large sweet (bell) pepper
- 2 medium hot chili peppers (bishop's mitre or similar) and same quantity hot red chili peppers (bird's eye, scotch bonnet, or similar)
- 1 tsp coriander powder
- 1 tsp cumin powder
- 2 Tbsp olive oil
- 4 cloves garlic, peeled and chopped
- 1 Tbsp lemon juice
- 1 tsp salt

1. Place peppers under a hot grill and allow to roast. Removed hot peppers while slightly browned, but allow bell pepper to blacken on all sides.
2. Remove peppers and drop into a bowl of cold water.
3. Rub off all burned spots on the chili peppers. Peel the papery black skin off the bell pepper, core, cut into strips, and rinse off seeds.
4. Place salt, coriander, and cumin into a hot wok and toast for a minute or two until fragrant but not burned. Remove and add to peppers.
5. Place all ingredients in a blender or food processor and blitz until a smooth paste (the traditional way is to use a mortar and pestle).

Store in a sealed sterilized glass jar in the refrigerator. The heat lessens daily, but the sauce will keep for a week if it is well refrigerated.

many Israeli households (whether originating in Morocco or not), a saucer of *'arissa* is a necessary table condiment for virtually any meal. In "Oriental" (i.e., Arab-style) restaurants, a small dish of *'arissa* may be put on the table as a matter of course. A dab of the sauce is used to flavor meat or vegetable dishes. Most housewives know to put their hottest *'arissa* on the table as a covert war will be raged between males present about who can eat the most *'arissa*, and her prowess as a hot sauce maker will come up in later conversation.

CHAPTER FOUR

Main Dishes

Israelis tend to eat two "light" meals and one main meal a day. The difference is largely between meat and nonmeat meals on the one hand, and a main dish (or succession of them on special events) versus a table selection on the other. The distinction between meat and nonmeat dishes derives for Jewish Israelis from the *kashrut* proscriptions (whether adhered to or not). A main meal will thus be characterized by the presence of a meat centerpiece, whether this is a roast, grill, a baked dish, or something similar. Behaviorally, this is also dealt with in a specific way: the meat/fish/fowl will be cut and distributed by the host/ess or a member of the presiding couple or individual (parents, housewife, husband: differing according to family tradition rather than fixed). Light meals, on the other hand, lack the formality in that there is no centerpiece: generally speaking, foods are placed in dishes and bowls on the table and people help themselves to what they please. Main meals, notably those on Friday evening, may also have several courses served one after the other: starter, soup, fish, meat, dessert. Light meals are served in a Middle Eastern fashion: all dishes are placed on the table at the same time (except, perhaps, dessert). While non-Jewish Israelis tend to use the "light" meal format almost exclusively, even in that demographic special meals that include meat are often served as courses, with the meat featuring as a separate course.

Second generation immigrants tend to seek to emulate the majority and accustom themselves to doing things the majority way. In Israel, this was visible immediately after the mass immigrations in the 1950s. Mizrachi and Sephardi immigrants, under the influences of secularization and the Ashkenazi majority at the time of mass immigrations, adopted "standard," that is, European-style foods modified by Levantine food practices as preached by the ideological heads of the country. By the third generation, more and more of these immigrants, whose culture was seen as inappropriate and backward by the elite and had established themselves and their food culture more suitable to the climate and circumstances, re-emerged in force. By the fourth generation—roughly from 1990 onward—intermarriage between Jews of most communities had become commonplace, and these families chose, or did not, to pick one set of food choices over another or blend several traditions. In most cases, the results were a mixture of styles and foods, leaning toward a mix of vegetarian and meat dishes appropriate to the climate and enabled by local agriculture. Thus a "mixed" Ashkenazi–Sephardi couple might eat a mix of foods from different community traditions. On the weekend, meals might be taken with parents/in-laws who preferred one particular food culture, and on another weekend, with the other set of parents who preferred something different. The end result, for most households, is a mix of Sephardi, Mizrahi, Ashkenazi, and others, with exotic foods such as sushi (but without raw fish) or Chinese food thrown in occasionally. To some degree, this has happened within the Arab-Israeli community as well.

Arab-Israelis are not a monolithic ethnic group either. Urbanites, villagers, and Bedouins differ markedly in their way of life and even in their food culture. And the geographical location of the community, as well as its origin; some Israeli-Arab families are descendants of families that have lived in the same community for centuries, others arrived in the nineteenth and twentieth centuries from southern Syria, Egypt, Libya, and Sudan. Moreover, there are internal differences due to place of residence. Bedouins in the Galilee are generally sedentary, and many are well integrated into Israeli society. Negev Bedouin are still nomadic when possible, and some tribespeople are barely integrated into Israeli society. Arabs from "mixed" cities with Arab and Jewish populations emulate one another's way of life; those in homogeneous Arab communities, much less so. All this means that a "standard" Israeli meal, or even a standard "Arab-Israeli" meal is more a fantasy and external construct than a reality.

One community—the ultra-orthodox—are far less permeable to the food culture of other groups. The Ashkenazi sects tend to stick to Ashkenazi food and meal cultures, the Sephardi to theirs. Even so, due to the high rate of ultra-orthodox leaving the fold and becoming less, even nonreligious, and the penetration—through simple interaction with other Israelis—of nonreligious behaviors that do not impact directly on the religious core behaviors, changes occur, albeit more slowly and with greater resistance than among other groups. Main meals for this community remain as they had been in whichever the place of origin of the sect or Hassidic court, attaining the status of religious ordinance.

Breakfast

Breakfast is eaten before work, and it varies according to age, background, and class. The kibbutz breakfast is a well-known Israeli institution that has spread beyond the kibbutzim. It consists of an array of salads, fresh vegetables, pickled fish, cheeses, eggs, fruit, yogurts, and breads, washed down with coffee, tea, fruit juice, or milk. In most kibbutzim, this is commonly available from around 6 a.m. to around 8 a.m. When one eats breakfast depends on the particular tasks assigned the individual by the work coordinator. For example, those assigned to a harvest will eat early, whereas assignment to administrative tasks allow an individual more leisure for breakfast since the work day in a kibbutz is the same as for the rest of the country.

The most common form of breakfast can be considered an abbreviated form of the kibbutz breakfast. A standard breakfast table will be set with knives, forks, and spoons. Fresh vegetables, sometimes cut into a salad, are made available: tomatoes, cucumbers, peppers, onions, kohlrabi, radish, whatever is in season. A dish(es) of olives is a must, and sometimes some other form of pickles. Cheeses, particularly soft cheeses—cream cheese and cottage cheese, as well as salty hard Bulgarian-style sheep's cheese and yellow Turkish-style *kashkaval*—as well as Israeli-made yellow cheeses in European styles are usually available. Other foods include pickled herring, various spreads, and butter or margarine. Variations depend on the family's orientation. Some have *hummus beTehina* as a regular meal occurrence, hot sauces are common as well. Eggs run the gamut from simple boiled eggs to elaborate *shakshouka*. Breads range from white breads through rye, bagels (a recent commercial addition, although homemade bagels were prepared by many grannies), and various types of pita. Food is placed centrally on the table and diners help themselves from the various dishes. Drinks include yogurts, milk, tea, cocoa, and of course coffee. In the right seasons, fresh orange juice is also made available. Obviously, the precise makeup of breakfast is subject to many variables, from class and community preferences, to individual choice and finances.

In the non-kibbutz population, unlike lunch or dinner, which are eminently social affairs, breakfast may be solitary, depending on the individual's work or school schedule and the different timetables of family members. Some people, out of preference or necessity, consume little more than bread with jam and tea or coffee. Others with more funds, leisure, or from habit consume a more extensive early meal. Nevertheless, most breakfasts conform to the pattern described here.

Some special dishes are either made for special occasions, or are considered "ethnic" breakfast foods available at homes or in specialist restaurants. Many of these, such as *malawach* and *shakshouka,* have become so fashionable that they are now a part of general Israeli cuisine, and eaten by all, either occasionally or as a regular daily food.

Jahnoon

The Jewish population of Yemen was, generally speaking, a poor one. High carbohydrate foods and oils were a central part of the cuisine, and Yemenite Jewish cooking has a large variety of doughy foods to be eaten with a vegetable sauce or plain oil. Jahnoon is one of those dishes that became popular in the 1980s and makes a simple, satisfying breakfast, which people eat at home or in cafés that are influenced by Yemenite cooking.

Malawach

Another Yemenite introduction is *malawach*. For several centuries, Yemen was the nominal vassal of the Ottoman Empire. Some food practices, heavily modified, became a part of Yemenite Jewish cooking, and eventually, that of Israel. *Malawach* is a Yemenite version of a Turkish meat stuffed dough roulade. Among poor Yemenites, which generally included most Jews, the dish lost its expensive meat filling, and only the dough roll remained, which is served with grated tomato and onion relish and olive oil.

Malawach is a popular and cheap breakfast dish, which is available fresh at Yemenite cafés. It is easy to make at home, and can be eaten hot or cold.

Malawach

Yield: Serves 4

4 cups all-purpose flour
1 ½ cups warm water
1 tsp salt
½ cup oil, normally clarified butter or olive oil
1 tsp nigella seeds
4 peeled hard-boiled eggs

4 medium-small tomatoes, grated
Zchug to taste

1. Combine water, flour, and salt in a large bowl and mix well.
2. Knead dough for 15 minutes until you have a smooth, solid dough.
3. Divide dough into six or eight pieces and form into balls. Cover with plastic wrap and allow to stand for 30 minutes.
4. On an oiled smooth surface, roll out one ball at a time into a rectangular shape, making the dough as thin as possible. Pull out the corners of the sheet to make it even thinner (a few holes are no problem).
5. Oil both sides of the dough sheet.
6. Now comes the tricky part. Fold one of the long edges of the rectangle, about a quarter or one-sixth the width, over the sheet. Fold again, then again, until the sheet has become a long fat ribbon. Working quickly, tie the ribbon into a knot, and, if long enough, add another knot. Tuck the ends of the ribbon between the strands of the knots so they are hidden.
7. Allow the dough to rest 15 minutes while you make the remaining dough balls.
8. Squash the knots to about ¼" thick or a trifle more with your palm.
9. Heat the oven to 500°F.
10. Place one flattened *malawach,* or more if they fit, on an oiled cookie tray and bake for about 5–6 minutes until well browned.

Serve hot with sliced boiled eggs, grated tomato, and zchug *for dipping.*

Shakshouka

Perhaps the most popular dish brought by Moroccan Jews to Israel is *shakshouka*—eggs cooked in tomatoes—of which there are many variants. For many households, *shakshouka* is a standard breakfast, since preparation can be divided into two: preparing the tomato sauce the evening before, and adding the eggs just before consumption. It is also available in many small cafés as a midmorning snack. Israelis, notably men, pride themselves on how hot the *shakshouka* is, so like chili con carne in the United States, there are recipes that go to great extremes in the chili department.

Shakshouka is best eaten with soft bread, preferably a pita or some equivalent. Mint tea is traditionally drunk with the dish. Fresh vegetables or a vegetable salad, and pickles, including cucumber, turnip, cabbage, or whatever one fancies, are eaten as well. Since the dish is *parve* (neither meat nor milk), some people eat buttered bread with the eggs, others a serving of sausages, notably North African *merguez*.

Shakshouka

Yield: Serves 4

1 Tbsp oil for frying
1 medium onion, minced fine
4 cloves garlic, crushed and peeled, minced fine
1 fresh bell pepper (green color preferred for visual appeal), cored, seeded, and cut into strips
1 large very ripe tomato minced fine, or one can crushed tomatoes with pulp
1 tsp *'arissa* (see *'arissa* recipe in Chapter 3)
½ tsp smoked paprika
1 tsp cumin powder
1 small bunch fresh coriander leaves, rinsed, minced fine
1 or 2 eggs per person
Salt and pepper to taste

1. Heat oil in a pan until shivering.
2. Fry onions until golden, being careful not to brown.
3. Add garlic and stir fry for 30 seconds.
4. Add pepper strips and stir fry until peppers are softened.
5. Add *'arissa*, paprika, and cumin and stir fry for 30 seconds. Add one half the coriander leaves.
6. Add tomatoes, lower heat, and cook gently until tomatoes are cooked through and juice is well-blended but not dry. Season to taste.
    (All this can be prepared the evening before, and stored until breakfast, when it must be reheated to boiling point.)
7. Stir eggs into simmering vegetables without breaking the yolks. With a wooden spoon or fork, whip the egg *whites* for a short while into the vegetables. Do not break the yolks.
8. When the yolks are at desired consistency, slide one or two egg yolks and the blended whites and vegetables onto each plate. Scatter additional fresh coriander leaf if desired.

Serve with chermoulah, *fresh flat bread and butter,* pickles, *cooked* merguez sausages, *and mint tea.*

Main Dishes

Porridge

Porridges of semolina (solet), or oats (*kvaker*, from Quaker) are a common breakfast dish in the colder months of the year. Since it is easy to prepare, considered nutritious, and easy to digest, *daysat solet* is also one of the first foods given to weaning infants. A variation adds cocoa powder to the basic porridge, which makes it attractive to the young. Whether or not milk is added to the porridge depends, of course, in observant households, on whether there are meat dishes in the breakfast as well. Some older Israelis will not use sugar in their porridge, preferring salt only.

Ful

Many Israelis, notably those with roots in Egypt (Muslim and Jews alike), eat *ful* (broadbeans) for breakfast as a standard. In many cases, this is a dish of long-cooked broadbeans called *ful medames* (q.v.). A plate of hummus is sometimes garnished with a ladle of cooked *ful* beans for a hearty warm breakfast.

Daysat Solet

Yield: Serves 4

2 cups semolina
2 cups water
½ tsp salt
2 Tbsp cocoa powder (optional)
Warm milk to serve (optional)
Sugar or honey to serve (optional)
Butter to serve (optional)
Raisins to serve (optional)

1. Heat water in a pot to boiling, then immediately lower heat to a simmer.
2. Pour semolina (or oats) in a steady, slow stream into the simmering water, stirring constantly.
3. Stir in salt.
4. Stir in cocoa powder if using.
5. Allow the porridge to cook on a low heat, stirring constantly, until all water is absorbed and the porridge is thickened.

Serve in bowls, adding milk, sweetener, butter, and raisins to taste.

Sephardi Israelis will often, notably on Saturdays, eat a traditional *desayuno* of three pastries, which will have been prepared Friday morning. Bourekas are an Israeli institution, with every café and small bakery serving a variety of vegetable, meat, or cheese stuffed puff pastries. *Boyos* are a form of small doughnuts: dough bits fried in deep oil. The third pastry is *bulemas*. The latter two are common among Sephardi families in the Balkans and Turkey, less well-known among other Israelis. The pastries are accompanied by side dishes, mainly vegetarian, which include *haminados* (long-cooked eggs), stuffed grape leaves and other vegetables, fried eggplant, hummus, and so on. This is normally eaten in a traditional household after the men return from early prayers at the synagogue. A similar breakfast will be eaten among many Iraqi Israelis, called *sabich,* which gave rise to the popular Israeli sandwich of the same name.

Haminados (Long-Cooked Eggs)

Yield: Serves 4

4 large fresh eggs
Water to cover
Dry brown husks from at least two onions
1 tsp salt

1. Place eggs in a pot and cover with water. Bring to a slow boil. Allow to cook gently for 10 minutes.
2. Remove eggs from pot and add onion and salt to water.
3. Crack each egg all over, then replace in the pot. Alternatively, peel and add to any *hamin* to cook overnight.
4. Allow to simmer as slowly as possible for at least 5 hours and preferably overnight. Replace water if necessary to keep eggs covered.
5. Peel the eggs carefully so as not to mar the marbled appearance of the surface.

Alternatively, if you have a fireplace, once the eggs are cooked, do not crack. Instead, place them overnight in the ashes of the fire. Make sure the eggs are well covered with ashes and not close to any embers. Rake off the ashes in the morning, peel the eggs (the volume of the egg within the shell will have decreased).

Serve with ful, *in a* hamin, *with* tahina *in a* salad, *in a* sabich.

Main Dishes

Light Meal

Before Israel became an industrial and mercantile capitalist society, it was common for offices and workplaces to close down for lunch and have a siesta between 1 p.m. and 4 p.m. Workers would often go home to have a main meal in comfort. With the growing pace of work, as well as longer school days and working couples, it became less practical to have the main meal at lunch. As a consequence, while a heavy meal is still eaten in some households and institutions (e.g., kibbutzim, the army), in others the evening dinner is the one time when all family members can assemble for a joint meal, and it has thus sometimes become the main meal, characterized by a protein centerpiece.

The second light meal of the day can thus be eaten at midday or in the evening. This light meal rarely includes both meat or milk products (in Muslim, Christian, and nonreligious households this does not apply, of course). The second light meal is a kind of expanded *mezze* with whatever dishes the household fancies being offered and consumed. Eggs may be made, but may be replaced by some form of protein such as sausages or cold cuts. The meal tends to be less heavy on carbohydrates than breakfast—no cereals or porridge—although bread is included as a matter of course, and occasionally a rice dish such as *majadarah*, or burgul in the form of a salad, a *pashtida* (casserole, baked dish), or *kugel*. Adults may drink wine or beer with this meal. The meal will end with coffee or tea, and in some households with an eau-de-vie such as brandy or *'arak*.

Kaved Katzuz (Chopped Liver)

Chicken livers are relatively cheaply available, and are well liked by Israelis, Ashkenazi, Sephardi, and others. While this is originally an Ashkenazi dish, it has become common among many Israelis. There are two chopped liver schools. Some prefer it to be as smooth as possible. Others prefer it dryer and crumbly. In any case, a generous use of chicken fat is the only way to ensure a really good chopped chicken liver dish.

Yield: Serves 4

3 Tbsp oil for frying, preferably rendered chicken fat (schmalz)
Around 1 lb chicken livers (hearts included if possible), rinsed and dried, uncut

1 Tbsp water
1 large onion, minced fine
2 cloves garlic, crushed and skinned, then minced fine
2 hard-boiled eggs, peeled and (yolk and whites separated, optional) minced fine
Freshly ground black pepper
Salt to taste

1. Heat half the oil or fat in a lidded saucepan.
2. When oil is shivering, place cleaned, but not cut, livers into the hot oil and brown lightly on all sides.
3. Add water, lower heat to minimum, and allow to cook until well-cooked inside, about 10 minutes or more.
4. In a separate lidded saucepan, heat remaining oil or fat.
5. Add onions and brown carefully so onions do not burn.
6. Add garlic while stirring, and as onions turn color.
7. When both onions and liver are cooked, remove from fire and allow to cool.
8. Add onions and their fat to the liver, mix thoroughly, turn out onto a large chopping board, and using a heavy sharp knife or mezzalune, chop liver as fine as liked. Season with black pepper and some salt (kosher chicken livers will be salty and will not need additional).
9. Place liver in a bowl. Spread a layer of the finely minced egg whites on top. Use the minced yolks to add a decorative pattern on top of the whites.

Alternatively, for the creamy school of chopped liver, instead of mincing with a knife, run the liver through a meat grinder, or whizz in a food processor. You may also add the eggs (all or a part) to blend into the liver.

Serve with plenty of bread, and some horseradish or 'amba on the side.

Main Meal

The main meal of the day, as noted, differs from light meals in two ways. First, there is generally a central protein dish—meat, fowl, fish—which is usually placed on the table as a centerpiece, and then carved or cut and distributed by the head of the table (usually a male) or the housewife/cook (usually a female). The main meal is also very often arranged in courses: basically, before and after the centerpiece. Obviously, daily main meals will tend to be less elaborate and with fewer course than, for example, a meal with nonfamily guests. Whether served at midday or evening, such meals are more formal than the light meals of the day and snacks. The choice of the centerpiece is partly economic (wealthier families might have beef, poorer ones, chicken, for example) and partly a matter of preference, association, and so on. The number of courses is affected by economic circumstances, but even more by the nature of the event—even poorer families will make an effort for special occasions—and "ethnic" standards.

Lunch, eaten between 12:30 p.m. and 2:00 p.m. approximately, tends to be the main meal for most Israelis. With a more intense modern lifestyle for many, this is changing, notably in the cities. Excepting quick work-break meals, a main meal usually consists of a starter, a main course, and often dessert as a third. Meat or fish may be the centerpiece, but the place of vegetables is rarely neglected. Main and light meals usually include a salad, which is not served as a starter as in Europe, but which accompanies the main dish. In addition, there will be other side dishes of cooked vegetables, which vary according to the season. Green peas, carrots, eggplant, zucchini, *bamiah*, and fennel are very characteristic of what is offered.

The main meal tends to have a prepared dessert (rather than merely fruit), whether cooked or not. It may be extended, notably in ritual meals, for example Friday night, when several courses—starter, soup, fish, meat, and dessert—are served sequentially, many with accompanying vegetable side dishes. Bread is made available more for reasons of ceremony (and sopping) than as a carbohydrate source. The starch in main meals tends to be cooked—rice, potatoes in different forms, pastas, couscous—and they accompany the centerpiece dish on the same plate. The salad may be placed on the diner's main plate, or on a small separate plate.

Memulaim (Stuffed Vegetables)

In both the Middle East and Eastern Europe, various forms of stuffed vegetables were a common meal centerpiece. For the poor, this allowed one to stretch meat or other expensive foods, for the rich, an array of stuffed vegetables and dough products were evidence of the wealth and leisure to create multiple dishes on a theme. The rich would have many kinds of stuffed items and many kinds of stuffing, the poor would have one, which kept warm, would serve for more than one meal.

Memulaim are featured as a Saturday dish, which can be cooked slowly from Friday onward. Other *memulaim* might be eaten immediately. Almost any vegetable can be stuffed, although the easiest to stuff are the most common. Cabbage rolls and vine leaf *dolmades* can be made at home or bought from a grocery. The most common form of cooking stuffed vegetables is in a stock or other liquid. However, many *memulaim* are baked.

Common fillings range from ground or minced meat, through simple vegetarian stuffings composed of flavored rice, *burgul*, or other grain or indeed grain mixed with vegetables. Older Israeli women will still talk of the times in which women would gather together, usually late on Thursday, to prepare shared dishes of *memulaim*, since the dish is usually labor intensive and time consuming. Younger Israelis make fewer *memulaim* for that very reason.

Baked Tomatoes

Yield: Serves 4

4 large ripe but firm tomatoes
1 Tbsp oil
1 medium onion, minced fine
2 cloves garlic, peeled and minced fine
2 cups cooked rice or burgul
1 tsp *baharat*
¼ tsp ground cinnamon
½ cup finely minced parsley and coriander leaf (proportion depending on taste)
Salt and ground black pepper to taste
1 bay leaf
2 cups vegetable stock

1. Cut off and reserve the cap of each tomato. Core the tomato liquid, seeds, and pith without piercing the outer flesh and skin. Reserve the insides.
2. Heat the oil and fry the onions until golden. Add the garlic and fry, stirring, until fragrant but not burned.
3. Mix rice (or burgul), *baharat*, cinnamon, parsley and coriander, a small quantity of the tomato pulp, and a Tbsp of the stock until the mixture is moist but not soaking. Season to taste.
4. Place the tomatoes in a baking pan, along with the bay leaf.

Main Dishes

5. Fill tomatoes with as much stuffing as possible.
6. Replace cap on tomatoes.
7. Pack left over stuffing around the tomatoes, then pour over remaining stock.
8. Place pan in medium-low oven (about 250°F) for 15 minutes. If tomatoes are soft and caps are cooked, remove from oven and serve. If not, leave for an additional 5 minutes until done.

Serve as a main dish or with salatim.

Chicken

Chicken, roasted in an oven, is a staple of many Israeli main meals. In some households, the chicken boiled for Friday night soup is then also roasted as the main dish. Roast chicken also features as the main dish during the Seder, for those families that cannot afford lamb or a turkey.

Chicken dishes feature prominently in meat meals, inasmuch as the birds are easily available, relatively cheap, and easy to prepare. Stewed, roasted or baked, fried, and grilled are the most common ways of preparation.

Tebit (Stuffed Chicken)

The slow cooking of *tebit* lends itself well to a *hamin*, a dish prepared on Friday for the Saturday meal. *Tebit* was standard fare in many Iraqi-Jewish households for the weekend.

Yield: Serves 4

A heavy, ovenproof pot with a close-fitting lid
1 whole chicken, wing tips clipped
Olive oil for browning
2–3 cups chicken stock

1. Using the tips of one's fingers and a small, very sharp knife, extract the chicken skeleton from the carcass. Detach the long bones (legs and wings) and neck if necessary at the joint from the skeleton, using a sharp, short knife, and leave meat in the skin. You should end up with a boneless carcass, except for wings, legs, and neck.

This is fiddly work, and many people prefer to remove the skin, rather than the skeleton, separate the meat and replace it, and reserve the remaining bones for the stock. Try not to pierce the skin.

Filling
1 onion minced fine
5 cloves of garlic, crushed
2 cups rice or burgul
2 large grated tomatoes or small can tomato paste
½ tsp turmeric
1 flat tsp salt
1–2 tsp *baharat*
The chicken's giblets, chopped
Chicken stock for moistening

1. Mix all stuffing ingredients together.
2. Brown the chicken in olive oil (if using the skin, brown after stuffing).
3. Stuff the cavity loosely with the filling. Seal cavity with metal skewers. If using only skin, stuff more tightly, then brown the stuffed chicken in olive oil.
4. Place browned chicken in middle of pot.
5. Pack the rest of the filling mixture around the chicken.
6. Pour on enough stock to barely cover the meat.
7. Bring to the boil, lower heat, and simmer until the liquid looks absorbed, about 10 minutes.
8. Cover tightly and place in 200°F oven overnight, or for 8 hours.

Serve with salads, relishes, and cooked vegetables.

Vegetable Dishes

Vegetarian and vegan lifestyles are becoming more mainstream in Israel, with restaurants, cookbooks, and events catering to these growing segments of the population. However, as noted earlier, vegetarian dishes have been staples in Israel for an extended time, due largely to economic history, and partly to preference due to the choices available and the weather. Raw vegetables are of course virtually a staple for most Israelis, but in addition there are a large number of vegetarian dishes, most commonly cooked at home, that people are partial to, whether because of ideology or the weather.

Main Dishes

Sheouit Yeruka (Green Beans with Tomatoes)

Yield: Serves 4

1 Tbsp olive oil
1 large yellow onion, chopped
1 large carrot, cubed
2 to 3 cloves garlic, finely minced
1 lb green beans, topped and tailed
1 cup finely minced ripe tomato flesh
1 tsp sugar
Salt and black pepper to taste
½ cup chopped fennel root (*finoccio/shumar*)
2 bird's eye or other small hot chili pepper
1 Tbsp lemon juice

1. Heat the oil in a large pan over medium heat.
2. Fry the onions until translucent, while stirring.
3. Add garlic and stir for 30 seconds.
4. Add carrots and stir for additional 3–5 minutes until carrots are cooked but still firm.
5. Add green beans and stir until well coated for 2 minutes. The beans should still be crisp and not fully cooked.
6. Add tomatoes, sugar, fennel, chilies, and lemon juice. If too dry, add 1 Tbsp of water.
7. Over a very low flame, cook until beans are cooked to your taste. Correct seasoning.

Serve with a meat dish or rice for a vegetarian or milchik *meal.*

Kibbeh

Kibbeh, generally speaking a mix of burgul and meat, comes in a number of forms. In Lebanon, *kibbeh nayeh,* is a mixture of cooked burgul and minced, spiced, raw meat. For most Israelis, however, *kibbeh* are spindle-shaped burgul patties stuffed with meat or other fillings. *Kibbeh* is a favorite food in Kurdistan, and Kurdish *kibbeh* is considered by many to be the peak of the art. Various types are found in the cooking of Syrian, Iraqi, and Kurdish Jews, and for most Israelis, *kibbeh* are considered part of a full *mezze.*

Pashtida

Originally derived from a Ladino (Spanish Jewish) word for a pie (*pastide*) with a dough lid and base, in Israel today it has come to mean any kind of baked good in a deep dish, including noodle dishes, most often vegetarian or cheese-based. A *pashtidat itriyot* is a well-known Ashkenazi dish—*lokshen kugel*—adapted to Israeli tastes, and both *pashtidat kishuim* (zucchini) and *pashtidat hatzilim* are common main dishes adapted from Mizrachi origins. These are rarely if ever made with a crust, instead the filling of beaten eggs, possibly cheese, and a vegetable makes up the entire dish. *Pashtidot* (plural) are made for daily meals as well as special ones, and many households have their own favorite recipes.

Pashtidot are also sold readymade and even frozen and they are considered a very homely dish, one that can be whipped up very quickly. They may be made *parve* (to be eaten with meat), milky, or meaty, depending on preference. They are also made by families from widely different backgrounds, Mizrahim and Ashkenazim and others.

One *pashtida* that has achieved legendary status is *kugel yerushalmi*. A *kugel* is an Ashkenazic dish in which noodles are combined with a binder (eggs, cheese), and often sweetened, served as a main dish for milk meals (if using cheese). Historically, the kugel was developed by the Jewish community "within the walls" of the Old City of Jerusalem in the nineteenth century. It is still a favorite throughout Jerusalem's Jewish population, orthodox and not, and often served as part of the Sabbath meal on Friday evening.

Kugel Yerushalmi (Jerusalem Noodle Pudding)

The mix of sugar and pepper is unusual, and there is little indication of its origin, although sugar was, for the poor Jerusalem community in the late nineteenth and early twentieth century, a major luxury, as was pepper. Kugel was a celebratory, not daily dish, thus the use of expensive condiments.

Yield: Serves 4

10 oz thin egg noodles
½ cup vegetable oil
1 ½ cup sugar
2 tsp ground black pepper
5 eggs, well beaten
Salt to taste

1. Cook noodles in a heavy pan until soft (past *al dente*), drain, and reserve in a heavy casserole or oven-proof pan.
2. Heat the oil and sugar together in another pan, caramelize mixture, stirring occasionally to mix ingredients (they will *not* merge completely). Allow the caramel to darken considerably, just before burning, then pour immediately over the drained noodles. Mix thoroughly.
3. Add beaten eggs, pepper, and salt.
4. Place in a 400°F oven and bake 45 minutes to 1 hour until top is dark.
5. Allow to cool slightly, run a knife around the edges, then invert onto a plate to serve. Can be eaten hot or cold.

Loof

At times, Israeli army food has been simply terrible. One foreign visitor commented during a meal with an army patrol, after hearing a repeat of the old saw, "The worse the food, the better the army" that "No army in the world could possibly be this good." In the opinion of many, the worst of the worst has been a canned meat named *loof* (a Hebraicization of the English "meat*loaf*"). The can was a heavy mix of ground fat and meat. The simplest way to extract and prepare it was to open both ends of the can, push the bottom lid through the can, and as the meat emerged, cut a slice off with the other lid on to a slice of plain bread.

In the field, *loof* was eaten cold or simply warmed. In the mess-hall, attempts to disguise it were legendary—boiling in tomato sauce and served on noodles, battered and fried, grilled, or whatever else the mess chief could come up with. Universally abhorred, there are nevertheless generations of Israeli veterans who still turn misty eyed thinking or dreaming of *loof*.

Schnitzel

European immigrants brought versions of the Central European schnitzel—thin meat slices dredged in flour, eggs, and breadcrumbs, then fried—to add to local cuisine. In the absence of ovens, shallow frying meat was an excellent way to preserve freshness and taste. In the *tsena* years, the government seized on this idea to promote thrifty ways of using meat, which was in short supply. However, again due to costs, instead of veal or beef, schnitzel made of chicken, and later, turkey breast, became the norm.

Turkey Schnitzel

Yield: Serves 4

4 turkey breast slices, about 160 g each
1 cup flour (or fine matza meal if during Passover), plus 1 Tbsp corn starch
2 eggs, beaten
1 scant tsp salt
1 scant tsp black pepper
2 cups stale bread crumbs (or equivalent coarse matza meal if during Passover)
Vegetable oil for shallow frying
Lemon wedges, mustard, *tahina* sauce for garnish

1. Place each piece of meat between two layers of kitchen wrap. Smack with a meat mallet or bottom of heavy pan until meat slice is flattened evenly between wrap sheets. Remove from wrapping.
2. Mix flour, cornstarch, salt, and pepper thoroughly.
3. Heat oil until it shivers, but not smoking hot.
4. Dredge each turkey slice in flour mixture, then in beaten egg, then in crumbs. Slip immediately into hot oil.
5. Allow to cook without burning (if necessary, lower or raise heat) until cooking side is brown and it comes away easily from the pan. You can cook more than one at a time, provided they do not touch.
6. Flip schnitzel over and cook uncooked side until golden brown.
7. Remove from oil and place on paper towel to absorb excess oil.

Place on plate and serve together with chips (French fries) or rice, and an Israeli salad. Place lemon wedges, mustard, and tahina *for diners to help themselves.*

This has persisted to this day, and turkey schnitzel has become a major way of preparing meat, both for the home and in the form of a pita sandwich, which, like falafel and *sabich*, is also loaded with a salad and pickles. Few Israelis have never tasted turkey schnitzel, and its popularity as a sandwich rivals, perhaps eclipses, falafel. Schnitzel may also be served at formal events, ranging from weddings through political dinners. Even Arab restaurants in the Galilee have bowed to popular demand and have schnitzel on the menu.

CHAPTER FIVE

Desserts

Most Israelis have a sweet tooth. This is satisfied by fruit in various ways, by sweet dessert dishes, by baked goods, and by snacks. While fruits hold a place of pride, baked goods run a close second. There is a great degree of choice available. Baked goods in various traditions are available in the home as well as specialist bakeries. Fruits, obviously given the climate, are available in great variety throughout the year.

A sweet at the end of the meal was a common feature of European (both Ashkenazi and Sephardi) Jewish meals, although care was needed to ensure no milk-based desserts were served after meat meals. North African, Middle Eastern, and Asian Jewish communities rarely ate a special sweet dish as a dessert. Instead, sweet dishes were sometimes incorporated into the rest of the meal, or were eaten on their own with tea, coffee, or soda water in the late morning, afternoon, or nighttime.

Israelis have generally adopted the European practice of offering a sweet dessert after a meal, although the choice of dishes varies quite considerably. Fresh fruit in assorted forms are probably the most common. Baked goods, puddings of some sorts, flavored yogurts, and ice cream are also well-liked. Cooked desserts are almost always associated with more formal and special meals.

Cooked fruit are a feature of both Sephardi and Ashkenazi cuisine, the difference being that due to the climate of Eastern Europe, Ashkenazi fruit desserts tend to be based on dry or preserved fruit, whereas Sephardi and Mizrachi Jews lived in countries in which fruit of some sort were available the year round, and thus, although they ate dried fruit, fresh fruit are far more common as desserts. Middle Easterners, Arab and Jew alike, often incorporated cooked fruit into their baked goods.

The most common desserts in Israel, in both summer and winter, are *salat perot* (fruit salad) and its winter counterpart, *marak perot* (fruit soup). Both are considered slightly old-fashioned in many households, but are a safe and well-liked fallback from more elaborate cooking.

Bananot Berotev Tapuzim (Bananas in Orange Sauce)

Israel raises enough bananas for satisfying local demand, and citrus for home consumption and export. Unsurprisingly, these are often brought together.

Yield: Serves 4

4 ripe but firm bananas, peeled and cut lengthwise
½ cup butter
Zest and juice of one large orange
Zest of one lemon and juice of ½ lemon
¼ tsp vanilla essence
1 Tbsp sugar
1 Tbsp citrus flower honey
½ fresh orange from refrigerator, cut lengthwise, then into 4 slices, peel loosened and pips removed cleanly (for garnish)

1. Melt butter in a non-aluminum large pan.
2. Fry banana halves together in butter, turning gently when brown on one side. Remove with slotted spoon when both sides of a slice are done.
3. Add juices and zest to butter, stirring with a fork to blend, then add sugar, honey, and vanilla. When sauce is well blended, return bananas gently to pan. Allow to warm while ladling sauce over them.
4. Divide onto four plates and garnish with orange eighths.

Serve with a scoop of vanilla ice cream.

Varieties of dried-fruit soup were common throughout Jewish communities and their non-Jewish neighbors in Eastern Europe. In Israel, the choice of dried fruit is much greater and cheaper than it would have been in Europe, and fruit soups became a quick dessert fix, sometimes eaten at the end of festivals that celebrate harvest or growth: Rosh Hashana (New Year), Succoth (Booths), Tu Bishvat (New Year of the Trees), Pesach, and Shavuot. The advantage of fruit soup is that it is neither meat nor milk, and thus can as easily be served (for the observant) with either a milk or a meat meal. The same is true of fruit salad.

Dried Fruit

Dried fruits have been a feature of Mediterranean cooking for millennia. Dried dates are still a major food item for Bedouin nomads, as well as for

Desserts

their sedentary descendants in places such as Saudi Arabia and the Persian Gulf. In Israel, dried fruits are eaten as they are for snacks, are used for filling for baked goods, and are made into candies and preserves. Stores that sell *pitzuchim* also usually sell a range of dried fruit.

Several Jewish communities have settled in India over the centuries, including the Bene Israel, who settled in Southwestern India, south of Mumbai, the Bene Menashe who settled in eastern Bengal, Cochinese Jews and the Bagdadi Jews in Mumbai, descendants of eighteenth century Iraqi Jewish traders, and some others. Bene Israel were classified low-caste *kshatriyah* (soldier/administrators) in the Indian caste system and many worked as mercenary guards and soldiers. Bene Israel celebrate happy events with the preparation of a sweet rice food called *maleeda*, which is based on *poha* (flaked rice, common in many parts of India and Nepal as a breakfast dish), sugar, and dried fruit.

Marak Perot (Fruit Soup)

Not many fresh fruits retain their shape while being cooked, so *marak perot*, whose origins are before the current affluent Israel, relies heavily on dried fruit.

Yield: Serves 4

1 ½ cups mixed dried fruit, including sultanas, figs, apricots, prunes, apples
1 ½ cups mixed fresh fruit of the season, or substitute same quantity of dried fruit: strawberries, cherries, currants, cut into halves and preferably de-stoned. No melons, citrus, bananas, which do not cook well.
3 cups cold water
1 stick cinnamon
1 Tbsp honey or sugar (optional)
1 cup fruit juice of choice (apple, pear) (optional)
Juice of ½ lemon

1. Place fruit, cinnamon, and water in pot. Simmer covered for 1 hour until all fruit have cooked through and liquid is infused with fruit flavor.
2. Adjust flavor with sweetener (honey or sugar), fruit juice, and lemon juice to taste.
3. Serve warm or cold with sour cream if desired.

> ## Maleeda
>
> *Yield:* Serves 4
>
> 3 cups *poha* flaked rice (available at Indian stores)
> 2 ½ cups grated coconut (fresh preferred)
> 1 cup sugar
> 10 cardamom pods, seeds crushed
> 1 cup sultana raisins
> 1 cup almond flakes
> 1 cup lightly crushed pistachios
> ¼ cup coconut cream
>
> 1. Soak the *poha* in water to cover until soft. Drain.
> 2. Combine all ingredients and stir to mix.
> 3. Store covered in refrigerator until cool.
>
> *Before serving, drizzle with coconut cream.*

Cooked Puddings

Soft puddings are commonly eaten as desserts, although some may be eaten as snacks, or even as street food. Some of these have a Mediterranean origin, others come from further north. Cornstarch tends to be the basis of most puddings, although sticky rice and rice flour run it a close second. A simple artificially flavored and sweetened cornstarch has been a staple of childhood and infant food for decades, and still serves as one of the first solid foods for infants (and a staple dessert for poor students).

Traditional puddings such as *malabi* and *sahlab* have made a comeback, although because of the protected status and scarcity of the original ingredients, this is replaced by rice, cornstarch, and other starches. *Sahlab*, meaning orchid in both Hebrew and Arabic, is a flour ground from rhizomes of wild orchids, *Orchis mascula* or *Orchis militaris*, once common throughout the Middle East. Due to depletion in nature, most *sahlab* today is made from other starches, including cheap cornstarch. The starch is mixed with hot water or milk, flavored with rose water, and drunk as a hot winter drink. Puddings are made by baking the *sahlab* mixture, then scattering a few ground pistachios and cinnamon over the top. Both drink and pudding are a common street food in Israeli cities. *Malabi* is similar, except made with rice flour.

Desserts

Students' Pudding

2 heaped Tbsp cornstarch
Tap water
4 Tbsp sugar
2 cups boiling water
1 tsp lemon juice
1 cup any of the following: fresh orange juice, pureed uncooked soft fruit (plums, peaches, grapes, ripe bananas), apple juice, lemon juice, bottled fruit syrup, raisins, crushed nuts, grated coconut optional for garnish

1. Mix teaspoon of tap water with starch until absorbed. Add another teaspoon and repeat until all water is absorbed and all starch has become a slurry.
2. Stirring the slurry constantly, pour gently into boiling water.
3. While stirring, add sugar.
4. When sugar is dissolved, keep stirring until mixture coats back of spoon. Remove from heat.
5. Stir in fruit juice or pulp.
6. Pour into serving bowl and place in refrigerator.

Serve when pudding is semisolid, garnishing top if possible.

Malabi (Almond Starch Pudding)

Yield: Serves 4

4 cups milk or almond milk
About ½ cup sugar
Pinch of salt
8 Tbsp cornstarch (called pudding in Israel) or rice flour
2 Tbsp rose water
½ cup toasted and coarsely chopped pistachios, almonds, or coconut curls for garnish

For Syrup
1 cup sugar
½ cup water

1 tsp rose water + 1 tsp red food coloring, or
1 tsp almond extract + 1 tsp green coloring, or
1 tsp orange water + 1 tsp yellow food coloring

1. Combine sugar and water and bring to a simmer while stirring until sugar has all dissolved.
2. Allow to cool slightly, then stir in chosen flavoring and food color.
3. Reserve cool.

Pudding
1. Reserve 1 cup milk.
2. Place other three cups, sugar, and salt into a pan and simmer, stirring, until sugar is dissolved.
3. While whisking, blend reserved milk with cornstarch in a mixing bowl.
4. Pour resulting liquid slowly in a steady stream into the hot milk mixture while whisking continuously.
5. Reduce heat, then whisk continuously until mixture coats the whisk or spoon.
6. Add rose water and cook over very low heat until mixture is thick.
7. Divide result into four glass bowls. Place in refrigerator to cool.

Serve with syrup poured over pudding, and some of the garnishing nuts.

Baked Goods

Several baking traditions contest and merge in Israeli food. On the one hand, one finds European baking traditions at local bakeries and made at home. On the other, one finds Middle Eastern and North African traditions, which differ quite substantially from the European ones. New Israeli chefs have also adopted the principles of modern food, blending the two traditions as well as importing new ideas from abroad.

Generally speaking, since Israelis have a sweet tooth and bakeries, bakers, and traditional sweet-makers do good business, Israelis have two competing standards in providing treats for guests. On the one hand, a housewife who is known for her baking will proudly prepare special cakes or other baked goods for guests. On the other hand, one who is well-off (or wishes to appear to be so) will provide a special cake from a special source. And every Israeli knows a little shop down a narrow alley in an otherwise unremarkable neighborhood where the best cookies/cake/confection can be found.

Ma'amoul are small filled cookies popular all over the Middle East. The filling varies according to location. Some *ma'amoul* are traditionally topped with confectioners' sugar. *Ma'amoul* are traditionally made with a special handled wooden mold—a *tabi*—available in markets in Israel, whose bowl is carved in geometric shapes that are impressed on each cookie. Unfortunately, the art of making *ma'amoul* at home has become rare, so *tabi*-made *ma'amoul* are rather rarer than they ought to be.

Ma'amoul, which keep well, are often kept to offer unexpected guests. They are also a special treat for events such as parties and holidays. *Ma'amoul* are eaten by all sometimes, and by some whenever possible. The quality of *ma'amoul* depends on the dough used (a richer dough, made with butter, but cannot be eaten with a meat meal).

A commercial product that became immensely popular, *argaliyot* were filled cookies that tried to capture the essence of *ma'amoul* for those who could not bake the original. The *argaliyot* dough is buttery and richer than most *ma'amoul*, and packets are available in grocery stores. They are served as a snack, or with coffee for guests. The most common fillings are rose water, dates, and chocolate creams, replicating in two instances common *ma'amoul* fillings.

Pastries and Cakes

Artisanal bakeries, suffering as they do from competition by commercial baked goods, nevertheless proliferate. Depending on the tradition and preference of the baker, the goods offered can vary extensively from American cupcakes to Indian *jalabis*. Many bakeries also serve as cafés, catering to everyone from Ladies Who Lunch to retirees who come for cake and a cup of coffee. Israelis have maintained a great variety of baking traditions, and people often have a favorite bakery, baking goods, or style. Or several. This includes everything from a backstreet bakery that bakes trays of chocolate or cinnamon-flavored croissant or cheese pockets, which disappear so fast customers line up at the serving window as soon as the scent of baking starts wafting out (that the backstreet is also behind the city police-station, with a built in clientele of both cops and robbers is no coincidence) to a German-style coffeehouse favored by the glitterati where customers line up for *dobosh* (chocolate layer cake) and other delicacies. New trends include decorated cupcakes (an American innovation), American-style doughnuts, and gelatin cheesecake.

Lekach Honey Cake

Yield: 8 slices

½ lb honey
¾ cup sugar
½ cup boiling water
¼ cup vegetable oil
2 eggs, beaten
2 cups flour
½ tsp baking powder
½ tsp baking soda
¼ tsp salt
1 tsp ground cinnamon
½ tsp grated nutmeg
½ jigger brandy
½ cup mixed seedless raisins and lightly crushed almonds

1. Mix honey and sugar.
2. Pour boiling water over mixture to dissolve the sugar. Stir and cool.
3. Add oil and eggs and mix well.
4. Mix all dry ingredients together.
5. Mix brandy into dry ingredients.
6. Add mixture to honey mixture and blend in well.
7. Add dry fruit and mix.
8. Pour into well-greased 9" baking pan.
9. Heat oven to 350°F.
10. Place pan in middle of oven. Bake for 45–60 minutes. Test with wooden skewer if done inside at 45 minutes. Remove when inside is cooked.

Serve sliced, with whipped cream and a glass of tea.

Candies

Various forms of children's candies are consumed and compete with other sweets such as fruit. Even more so than bakeries, industrial manufacture of sweets tends to predominate. As in the United States and Europe, a vast range of chocolates in bars and candies can be found throughout the country.

Good quality chocolate arrived in Israel relatively late, and most chocolate available early on was imported. In 1933, the Elite factory opened in

Ramat Gan (the junction where the factory stood is still known as "Elite"), part of the Tel Aviv conurbation, by a Russian immigrant. For decades, Elite supplied the country with its only domestic chocolate. The most commonly known was a flat chocolate bar of milk chocolate known colloquially as "Red Cow" for the image on the front (a blue cow represented bitter chocolate). Later, more manufacturers started operating, and the chocolate market diversified. Every few years, a manufacturer would hit on a new form, which, for a while, became a sensation. Filled individual bars with nut, sugar sponge, or other fillings had their turn in the limelight. Israelis eat a great deal of chocolate, and chocolate bars are a common food supplement of new army recruits until they learn (sometimes never) to appreciate the food in the mess. Red Cow is no longer the only milk chocolate available, but nevertheless, mothers who send boxes of goodies to their sons and daughters in an army camp will almost always include a chocolate bar (which allows sharing) or two, often still Red Cow.

Rahat lokum, a Turkish delight invented in the nineteenth century by an Istanbul chef, is often known colloquially as *rahat*. The best is still imported from Turkey. It is available in many *pitzuchim* shops, and for those from the Balkans or Turkey, is an almost inevitable accompaniment to the morning coffee. There is huge variety, and individually wrapped bite-size *rahat* are sold from barrows. These may be eaten with coffee or soda water, or they are thrown somewhat like rice during weddings as a blessing by some people.

Sugared almonds—toasted almonds with a hard sugary coating—were invented in Spain soon after the production of sugar started in the Iberian Peninsula. Normally white, or dyed pink, they are ubiquitous throughout the Middle East at weddings and other happy occasions. They often feature as nibbles for guests.

Walnuts, almonds, and domestically grown pecans are glazed and are also served, or eaten, alongside or instead of seeds such as sunflower seeds. They fall into the general category of *pitzuchim*.

Ice Cream

Unsurprisingly, ice cream is extremely popular in Israel, both in summer, and in the relatively mild winters, which are often as warm as a Northern European summer. Arabs in the pre-State era had traditionally made mastic-based ice creams. The extract from the plant was blended with fruit juices or cream and chilled. Mastic is the dried resin of a relative of the pistachio tree. Mastic tree-gum crystals, also known as "tears of Chios" from the Greek island where the best grow, were chewed to freshen the breath, and the name *mastic* still means chewing gum in Israel today. The ice cream is reputed to have originated in the Turkish city of Maraç. Mastic ice cream is still available, notably in Jaffa. It has a consistency somewhat like cold salt-water taffy, and is made in much the same way: by pulling thick strands over and over.

In the 1940s, some manufacturers started the production of ice cream which, initially, since few people had reliable refrigerators, was sold in shops that cared to invest in chilling technology (more often than not, ice blocks). Commercial ice creams were very restricted in the 1950s. Ice cream shops were virtually unknown, unlike today, although a few artisanal shops such as the decades-gone Brooklyn Bar made American-style parfaits and banana splits. However, by the end of the 1950s, Israelis were able to purchase ice cream in cartons (usually long bars of $30 \times 5 \times 10$ cm, which fit small refrigerators) in three flavors—vanilla, chocolate, and strawberry—made more with vegetable fats than cream. Ice cream sticks came in three varieties: *Kartiv* (ice lollies in two flavors: lemon and raspberry, both artificial), *Artik* (chocolate covered ice cream, chocolate, vanilla, or banana flavors), and *Luxe* (chocolate-covered vanilla ice cream with candied fruit bits). The variety and quality were both limited. Non-dairy ice creams were also created for consumption with after meat meals, as were "winter" ice creams with higher fat content so they need not be so cold.

The rise of affluence brought about a revolution as more manufacturers entered the market, and the quality, as well as variety of flavors, improved exponentially. In the 1970s, dedicated ice cream parlors began proliferating, offering their own brands of innovative self-made ice creams, sold in scoops, cones, and plastic cups. Some, such as "Doctor Leck" and "Glidah Beersheva," became synonymous with quality ice cream and founded branch stores around the country. By the new millennium, quality ice cream shops could be found around the country, and, as is usual in Israel, are the subject of enduring debate about the "best" ice cream to be had. Many of these new producers specialize in original recipes, as well as in using local fruit and flavors (e.g., *sabra* [Cactus fruit] and fig flavors).

Ice cream may be eaten as a snack, a beach or walking treat, or as desert at home or at a restaurant. Cafés almost always offer scoops of ice cream, and many serve iced coffee.

CHAPTER SIX

Beverages

Unsurprisingly for a hot country, the variety and quantity of drinks served is very large. Like baked goods and ice creams, each type of drink has varieties ranging from industrially made through artisanal to home production. The drink that is most ubiquitous for adults, and is to be found in hundreds of variations, is coffee, which can be had anywhere and everywhere. Tea is somewhat less popular, and when drunk, is usually black tea with sugar and possibly lemon or some other infusion, and not English style, with milk. Sparkling drinks are very popular, and as in the rest of the world (except, perhaps, Scotland and Japan), Coca-Cola and similar international companies have made inroads into popular demand, sometimes at the expense of local drinks, a few of which are making a comeback.

Alcoholic drinks are also common, notably wine and beer, locally produced and imported. Strong liquor, consumption of which was limited in the early years of the State, is growing, partly from the influence of prosperity, partly because younger people and those who immigrated from the Soviet Union have fewer problems with public drunkenness: something reflected in growing traffic casualties due to drinking under the influence. Until three decades ago, the attitude toward alcoholic drinks was relaxed. Children could buy alcoholic drinks—beer, wine, and even liquors—ostensibly, at least for their parents, and stores on army bases would allow the purchase of beer throughout the day. All this has changed with the increase in alcohol use.

There are also specific drinks, mostly fruit-derived, which are common to most Levantine countries, and which are still available, sometimes at home, sometimes in public.

Coffee

Coffee has been a feature of Israeli food since very early on. Middle Eastern Jews drank coffee as a norm for centuries, as did the rest of the Middle

East. The German Jews who started immigrating to Israel before World War II brought with them the custom of cafés, and urban areas, notably those with large Yekke populations such as Tel Aviv, Netanya, and Nahariya, had places for the civilized custom of "kaffe und kuche" to while away the hot hours of the day. For the Arab and notably the Bedouin population, coffee was an essential element in hospitality. The army, to which the vast majority of Israelis are exposed, provides coffee as a matter of course for morning meals and during the day. Thus coffee, in various forms, is an essential part of Israeli life. Many Israelis will drink five or six cups of coffee during the day, whether at home, at work, or at a kiosk or café. Some will drink more.

The two most common versions of coffee are *kafé turki*—most often served in small espresso-type cups, bitter and thick, with a side of heaping sugar—and *kafé hafuch*—milky coffee often served in a glass. Within that broad division are manifold subdivisions, depending on individual taste and pocket. A common variation on *kafé turki* is *kafé im hel*, which is brewed with cardamom seeds. Arguments about "the best" coffee abound. It is possible to hear within the span of ten minutes two people holding forth about the best way to make coffee, one arguing that the only way was to boil the grounds in fresh water so the froth rises seven times before pouring, and the other arguing just as heatedly that the coffee should be poured as soon as the first froth appears.

Some coffee rituals are maintained as a matter of course by individuals or by particular ethnic groups. Ethiopian Israelis make and observe the tradition of *buna* service: a formal presentation of three cups of coffee of gradually growing strength, well-spaced, and accompanied by the scent of burning incense. A cup of coffee is a matter of required ritual for visitors to Israeli Arab houses. And virtually every cohesive small army squad has a (self) appointed coffee master who is responsible for providing, maintaining, and jealously guarding the squad's coffee (bought privately, not the army-provided stuff), sugar, coffee kettle, and kerosene burner, usually lovingly stored in an old ammunition box. Tank crews are reputed to be favored in that regard, since there is always room to store the coffee gear in a tank, and the hot engine serves as the burner, saving on effort.

Coffee drinking has entered the language as a synonym for relaxed or heated discussion, and "Let's have a coffee" can mean anything from an invitation to a break, to a private intense discussion. Traditional Arab households ensure a proper supply of green coffee beans, which are roasted in the house for guests, then pounded in a special mortar and pestle. The sound of pounding meant to indicate that the guest is being

Beverages

Turkish Coffee

Yield: Serves 4

8 heaped tsp green (untoasted) coffee beans
4 cups water
4 pods cardamom
Sugar to taste, optional

1. Toast coffee beans in a dry wok or similar until dark brown but not black. Make sure to toss the beans constantly to avoid burning.
2. Pour beans into a mortar and pound to a rough powder. Alternatively use a coffee mill set to rough mill.
3. Place milled coffee into a steel pot. Add water.
4. Bring to a boil. Add cardamom.
5. If you prefer sweet coffee, add sugar.
6. When coffee froths, allow to come nearly to top, then remove from heat until froth subsides.
7. If you want stronger coffee, repeat frothing process once or twice.
8. For bitter coffee, pour a small amount into each of four small coffee cups. For sweet coffee, fill thick-walled glasses or mugs.

Drink with cookies such as ma'amoul.

---

honored by fresh coffee, and, in Bedouin nomadic communities, an invitation to neighbors to come and meet the guest.

Tea

Next to coffee, tea is the most commonly available hot drink. Tea may be drunk at any time of the day, although less as a breakfast drink. Bedouin hospitality often requires a small cup of bitter coffee followed by numerous cups of very sweet sage-flavored tea to be offered a guest. Tea—usually with sugar and lemon, served the Russian way in a glass with a wire holder—was considered the quintessential drink of the bureaucratic classes, whether in government or trade union service, and the office tea-server was the core of many a comedian's routine commenting on the general gormlessness of government clerks, whose tea server actually ran the office. The ultra-orthodox community often eschews coffee in favor of the traditional tea-drinking habits of Eastern Europe, some drinking it with a spoonful of jam, others drinking the liquid through a sugar cube held between their teeth.

The forms of tea are different according to taste and sometimes place of origin. Sweet tea is normally consumed. English-style tea with milk is less common. East Asian green teas are popular with stylistas. A common variant is mint tea, which is drunk in huge quantities not only by Moroccan Israelis who first popularized this beverage, but by other Israelis as well. This also provides an income to small gardeners, who can always find space in even the smallest garden for a patch of mint, which can be harvested early every morning and sold in the market in bunches. Luxury and designer teas have also arrived on the scene, and Israeli tea-houses in the large cities cater to glitterati and would-be fashionistas, as they do elsewhere in the developed world.

Cocoa is a common drink, largely for children. Since it is made with milk, it is suitable for the two generally meat-free lesser meals of the day. The major consumers are children, and, surprisingly, the military. Chocolate milk is available in stores, either in individual bags or 1-liter cartons. The army provides individual bags of chocolate milk to soldiers as a quick energy pick-up and a treat. Most cafés will also serve hot cocoa, at least in the winter.

Té im Na'ana (Moroccan Mint Tea)

Yield: Serves 4

4 cups water for tea
Tea leaves
1 large handful of fresh mint leaves with no blackened or drooping leaves or stems
4 Tbsp sugar

1. Brew a mild tea (the color should not be dark brown. Chinese tea preferred) for four.
2. In each of four tumblers place 1 Tbsp sugar, then fill the glass with mint leaves.
3. Pour hot tea into glass over mint leaves and sugar.

Serve with any Middle Eastern sweet or cookie such as ma'amoul.

Wine

Wine is one of the most ancient drinks known, and has been a feature of the Middle East for millennia. Modern wine production was restarted in Israel by the Rothschild Foundation, which established two wineries, one each in Zichron Ya'akov on the southern slopes of Mt Carmel, and the other in Rishon Letzion, south of Tel Aviv. The wineries produced much of Israel's wine output for many decades.

The growing affluence of the Israeli public led to a growing taste for wines, and better oenology throughout the country. Local boutique vineyards started competing with imports as the range of quality wines grow. Israeli wines have an inbuilt advantage in the Jewish world, as the presumption is that they are kosher, which, of course, many are.

Israeli wine consumption is at about 9 liters per person and rising. Wine is rarely drunk at every meal, but is virtually a requirement for the Friday and Sabbath meals (not only in religiously adherent households), in which wine is an essential part of the Sabbath rituals. Wine is also a requirement in most Jewish festivals; in particular, everyone is abjured to drink four glasses of wine during the Passover Seder. During the Purim carnival, one is exhorted to drink so much that one would not know the difference between right and left, blessing Mordechai (the hero-protagonist of the tale) and cursing Haman (the villain of the piece). Children in Orthodox communities are also indulgently allowed to steal a drink of wine during Purim. Nevertheless, the consumption of wine in Israel is not very high.

Wine is available in supermarkets and grocery stores, and a few dedicated wine merchants have also set up shop. Both whites and reds are made locally, some of very good quality. Wine is sometimes used in cooking. Households within the French and continental tradition, including Moroccans and Tunisians, generally allow children watered-down glasses of wine during Friday night meals.

While Muslims do not, as a rule, drink wine (nonobservant Muslims will drink beer in preference to wine, since wine is expressly prohibited in Islam, whereas beer is implied), Christian Israelis, notably the Orthodox sects, consume wine during festivals, in addition, of course, to Communion wine.

Malt Beer

Malt/black beer is a well-known drink that is being replaced by more common American-derived soda drinks. *Bira schora/Bira malt* is not a beer at all, it is a variety of *kvass*, a small-beer commonly found all over Eastern Europe with an alcohol content of less than 2 percent. Originally (and still) manufactured by the Tempo drinks company, it is a deep brown color, somewhat like stout. It is an acquired taste, familiar to older Israelis, less so to younger ones. The flavor is sweet, and somewhat, some people say, reminiscent of rusty nails. It was considered very beneficial for lactating mothers and sometimes advertised as such. Since it is less sweet than other pop drinks, many people prefer it, if available, to lemonades and cola drinks.

Beer

Beer has been made in the Middle East since the days of the Sumerians and ancient Egyptians. Beer was made from wheat, barley, and other grains. With the development of the wine industry in the early Iron Age, beer lost its prominent position, and beer-making in the Middle East ceased almost entirely until revived in the early twentieth century. Under the influence of German brewers, the Nesher company (now owned by Tempo) started brewing beer in Israel, and was the sole major beer brewer until the entry of other firms into the market in the late 1960s. Today, the beer market in Israel has diversified, with large Israeli commercial brewers competing with artisanal breweries, some of good quality, and imported brands ranging from Carlsberg to U.S. brands.

Beer is generally drunk as a social drink. Many nontraditional Muslim Israelis drink beer. On the whole, beer drinking in Israel is relatively moderate, although over the past decades there has been a rise in consumption quantities, alcoholism, and public drunkenness. Most beer brewed and sold is of the lager style: other styles of beer, such as true ales, wheat beers, fruits, and lambics, are less common. A large range of imported beers is available, mainly from major manufacturers.

Soft Drinks and Juices

Soft drinks are popular in Israel with all age groups and classes. Like most foods sold publicly, they are manufactured under the supervision of the Rabbinate. Plastic bottles and cans are recyclable and return a deposit. As in other countries, drinks are available in both sugary and diet forms. Soft drinks may be purely artificially flavored, although there are plenty of fruit-based soft drinks to choose from as well.

Bottled commercial soft drinks were made by domestic manufacturers but had to compete with *gazoz* (q.v.), both homemade and store-bought. Due to Arab boycott pressures, the major international manufacturers such as Coca-Cola and PepsiCo avoided selling in Israel until the 1970s, when plants were constructed in Israel and an aggressive program of destroying locally-produced soft drinks was initiated. Today, many bottled soft drinks are the standardized product of one or another international companies. There are, however, a number of small local soft drink companies struggling for market share and offering consumers a wider range of choice.

Fruit juices are very common drinks. Freshly squeezed orange juice is available in many kiosks in winter. In the fall, many kiosks sell freshly squeezed, red-purple sour-sweet pomegranate juices. Apple juice, freshly squeezed lemonade, and a number of other fresh fruit juices are also available. For many Israelis who care to, there are locally made implements for squeezing the juice by hand, ready for a family's breakfast or snack.

Suss

A licorice-flavored drink called *suss* has been sold by professional ambulant drink salesmen in most urban areas with an Arab population, notably to this day in the Old City of Jerusalem. The seller carries a large tin jug on his back with a long spout arching over the shoulder. Dressed in traditional Ottoman clothes in many cases, he clinks cups together to indicate

---

Suss

Yield: Serves 4

Approximately 4 oz dried licorice root
1 scant tsp baking soda
6 cups water

1. Grind roots in a mortar as fine as possible.
2. Add baking soda and mix well.
3. Put in bowl and pour on water.
4. Allow to soak overnight.
5. Place in a sieve lined with clean cheesecloth and collect liquid. Discard solids.
6. Cool in refrigerator for a hot day.

Note: Suss is not recommended for those suffering from either diabetes or hypertension, as it can raise blood pressure quite significantly.

his wares. These days, *suss* is delivered in disposable cups, as the traditional rinsed glass or metal cups are considered unsanitary.

Licorice sticks (dried roots of the plant *Glycyrrhiza glabra*) are sometimes sold in markets in Israel, and they can be chewed for a sweet juice that is several times sweeter than sugar, although the concentration in the root is low.

Tamarhindi

Like the suss seller, the *tamarhindi* (tamarind) seller dressed in Ottoman clothes is a feature of the market of the Old City in Jerusalem. *Tamarhindi* is a sour-sweet, slightly musty, but very refreshing drink that can also be bought bottled in some groceries. The *suss* and *tamarhindi* seller may

---

Tamarhindi Drink

Tamarind is a large, brown fragile pod about 5″ long containing many hard, inedible seeds in a sticky, brown, fibrous pulp. In the United States, it can be bought as compressed cakes or dried pods at Asian groceries. Drinking in excess can cause strong diarrhea, but one glass on a hot day is very refreshing.

Yield: Serves 4

About ¼ lb from a cake of compressed tamarind
6 cups hot water
2 Tbsp brown sugar (optional)

1. Soak tamarind cake in hot water. After 1 hour, break up cake into small pieces, using your fingers or a fork.
2. After another hour, when the pulp is starting to loosen, repeat the breakup. This time, extract the hard, black seeds and discard. Make sure *all* seeds have been discarded.
3. Place liquid and pulp in a blender or food processor and process until you get a brown liquid with no discernible bits.
4. Place in refrigerator overnight.

The drink can be drunk as is. Alternatively, place in a sieve and allow to filter, discarding the semisolid sludge. If too sour, add as much of the sugar as you like and stir well.

Beverages

often be the same person, using a double-nozzled container, one for each drink.

Gazoz

Gazoz is Israel's quintessential nostalgic drink. Starting in the early 1930s, and sold in most small kiosks that peppered the cities, the essential *gazoz* was composed of a fruit syrup—*petel* (raspberry) and lemon predominated—that was diluted with cold soda water (seltzer). It was cheap and refreshing, and sold by the glass was an excellent rehydrator in the summer, drunk as a brief break in the day. Most households would keep a bottle or two of the commercial syrup and bottles, or siphons, of soda water to mix their own. With the emergence of commercial sweet sodas—the Tempo company, now an affiliate of PepsiCo, had been producing a lemon-flavored soda since the early 1950s—and notably the introduction of Coca-Cola into Israel, *gazoz* fountains in kiosks and shops disappeared, although some households with a home soda fountain (SodaStream) will still buy the commercial syrups to offer guests as people have been doing since the 1950s.

As Israel entered the period of international food, *gazoz* has become more popular again, although under new guises. Today, artisanal *gazoz* is made and served in high-end restaurants, and in specialist shops in markets and other public areas. Unlike the original, *gazoz* now comes in many flavors, some of them exotic, boosted by herbs and tropical fruit pulps. Nevertheless, the principle is the same: about ¼ to ⅓ quantity of fruit-flavored syrup, the rest cold soda water.

The importance of sparkling water in Israeli life is evidenced by the commercial success of SodaStream, a company now owned by PepsiCo, which manufactures a device for making soda water at home. The firm, which has a mixed Arab–Jewish workforce, has dedicated itself to building bridges between people in the Middle East. A shared love of soda water would seem to be a strange, but nevertheless successful bridge.

Milk and Milk Products

Fresh milk products have been a staple of Israeli food from early on. Among the products are a large variety of fermented milk drinks, which were a breakfast and supper staple in many working-class homes. One of the earliest that was commercially available under several brand names was *lebeniyah*—drinking yogurt—which was consumed by many as a breakfast drink. The market has since diversified, and in addition to the

> ### Homemade Lemon/Lemon-Honey Gazoz
>
> *Yield:* Serves 4
>
> Juice and zest of 4–5 lemons
> Heavy sugar syrup, ⅓ or more of the juice quantity, or equivalent liquid honey
> 1 Tbsp finely grated ginger root (optional)
> ¼ tsp finely grated chili pepper (optional)
> Cold soda water
> Mint leaves for garnish
>
> Note: You can use any strong flavored fruit juice (apple, raspberry, mulberry, pomegranate, peach, grape, . . .) or blend of juices to your taste. Experiment! Make sure to add some lemon juice to give sparkle to very sweet fruit juices.
>
> *To make syrup:*
> 1. Mix juice and zest with sugar syrup or honey to taste in a pitcher. Stir well until completely mixed.
> 2. Add optional ingredients if desired.
> 3. Cool in refrigerator. Can last for three to four days if kept chilled.
>
> *To make gazoz:*
> 1. Pour desired amount of *gazoz* syrup onto ice cubes in glass.
> 2. Top with soda water.
> 3. Garnish with mint leaves.

classical *lebeniyah*, *rivyon* (buttermilk), and a number of flavored yogurt drinks, including some imported from international brands, are popular drinks at home. This also includes a large number of fruit-flavored yogurts, particularly popular among the young, but something of a contributor to obesity and diabetes in the population.

Liquor

"Burned wines" (brandywine, brandy) have been available in the Middle East since distillation—brought by the Arabs, who also invented the word alcohol, from India to Europe—was introduced. Israelis, depending on their preferences and sometimes place of origin, exhibit a varied preference for distilled alcohol.

Lebeniyah

Yield: Serves 4

2 cups *leben* (may be available at Middle Eastern stores) or plain Greek yogurt
2 cups soda water/seltzer
Salt to taste, or
4 tsp sugar and 1 cup very ripe strawberries, watermelon (seeded), peaches (pitted), or pulp of other soft fruit
4 sprigs mint to garnish

1. Place all ingredients in a blender. Blend until well mixed.
2. Share between 4 glasses, adding ice if desired and garnished with mint.

The most common Levantine alcoholic drink is *'arak*, distilled of grape must and flavored with anise. A shot is always served with a side of water. Dropping a few drops of the water into the alcohol (or tipping the shot glass into the water) causes the liquid to turn from transparent to milky white (due to chemical changes in the aniseed). It is popular as an after-dinner drink, as well as an afternoon pickup in cafés across the country. The best comes from the town of Zahle in Lebanon. Known as *zahlawi*, it is almost universally available notwithstanding the lack of peaceful relations between the two countries. Locally made brandies are also available, and drunk at the same occasions by those who dislike the taste of anise. Whiskey is imported (the one attempt to manufacture "Scotch-style whiskey" in the 1950s did not go well, as the manufacturer was taken to court for using the term). Vodka, both flavored and neat, has become increasingly popular, notably as there are some 700,000 Israelis with roots in the former Soviet Union.

Many people, while not habitual drinkers, will nevertheless "raise a glass" on special occasions, whether these are family events (*brit milah*, wedding) or more public within a company or office. While the most common drink is wine, brandy or *slivovitz* (Eastern European fruit brandy) are often used for a toast.

CHAPTER SEVEN

Holidays and Special Occasions

Virtually every holiday in Israel (and there are many of them) has characteristic foods that are either religiously mandated, or traditionally served. For Passover, there is a long list of foods that are required to be present, eaten, and displayed publicly. Other holidays may have specific foods that are highly recommended. To a lesser degree, this is also true of Israel's non-Jewish citizens, although they have fewer religious proscriptions and prescriptions concerning food.

Yom Ha'atzmaut

The State of Israel was officially founded on May 5, 1948 (the fifth day of the Jewish month of Iyar, the fifth month of the Jewish calendar: the holiday is celebrated according to the lunar-based Hebrew calendar, and thus moves around the Gregorian date). Devoid of religious connotations, it remains a popular holiday with ultra-orthodox and non-religious alike, since none of the normal Jewish religious restrictions on travel, work, or food are present. In the past three decades at least, as the Israeli population has become more affluent, it has been able to afford two consumers goods that were out of reach during the first decades of the state: automobiles and meat. During Yom Ha'atzmaut, families pack themselves in a car and travel to some favored spot where they unship a charcoal grill and (usually the male of the household) grill meat, rest, talk, and otherwise entertain themselves. The most popular locations are the beaches of the Sea of Galilee/Lake Kinneret and the Mediterranean. National parks are full of visitors, and some, exhausted by the slow travel on overburdened highways, stop and park on the side of a road and barbecue there.

There are no specifics for what is to eaten and how. Grilled meat, and sometimes vegetables (Israel has growing vegetarian and vegan movements), cold drinks from iceboxes, and homemade or bought snacks and nibbles are common. Extended families, or groups of friends, will meet as well, creating large crowds.

The most prominent grilled items are kababs (minced meat formed on a skewer), *shashlik* (chunks of meat, often turkey, sometimes beef or mutton on a skewer), steaks (most often small by U.S. standards, beef, more rarely mutton or for some, "white meat," such as pork) and mixed vegetables (eggplant, zucchini, onions, peppers, tomatoes).

Picnic locations may be chosen in advance, and some prime locations (for example, Sacher Park in Jerusalem, the beaches around Lake Kinneret, Achziv beach) may be occupied the day before to ensure a prime family spot. Families may equip themselves with one or more charcoal grills, charcoal, plastic chairs, containers of food and iceboxes for drinks and salads. There is a distinct gender distinction. Men establish the family's perimeter, unload the heavy items from the car, prepare and tend the barbecue fire, and grill the meat. The women of the family do everything else, including providing snacks to the "cook," keeping children in line, preparing salads, and dishing out drinks and desserts. While the meat is the center of the meal, properly speaking most of the food consists of salads and pitot brought from and prepared at home.

Independence Day Grill

Israeli grills vary by family, season, and location, although four products seem to predominate: meat cubes (*shashlik*), chicken, meat patties (*kabab*), and grilled vegetables, all on skewers.

Yield: Serves 4

Shashlik
1 lb roasting meat, beef, mutton, or red turkey meat
2 medium onions, peeled and quartered
1 tsp cumin powder
1 tsp coriander seed powder
1 tsp garlic powder
½ tsp turmeric
2 Tbsp lemon juice
2 Tbsp olive oil
Salt and black pepper to taste

1. Cut meat into 1" cubes
2. Place meat and onions in a bowl.
3. Beat all other ingredients together, then pour over meat and onions.
4. Marinade for at least half an hour.
5. Thread two meat cubes on a skewer. Thread a portion of onion. Repeat until skewer is full.
6. Grill over hot glowing charcoal.

Chicken pieces
1 chicken cut into eight portions, skin removed, joints pierced
1 large sweet bell pepper, cored and cleaned of all seeds, and cut into 1" squares
Juice of 1 lemon
1 tsp sweet paprika
1 tsp cumin powder
1 tsp hot chili powder of your choice
1 tsp tomato ketchup
Salt and black pepper to taste

1. Blend lemon juice and all spices and condiments.
2. Rub mix into chicken parts and allow to marinade for at least half an hour. (You may wish to bake chicken until only slightly bloody in your home oven to speed up barbecuing.)
3. Thread chicken on skewer, alternating with sweet pepper squares.
4. Grill over hot glowing charcoal.

Kabab
1 lb minced meat (beef, mutton)
1 Tbsp fresh parsley leaves, minced fine
½ garlic bulb, cloves peeled and minced fine
1 tsp sumac powder
1 tsp cumin powder
½ tsp chili powder
Salt and black pepper to taste

1. Place all ingredients in a bowl and mix and knead well with your hands.
2. Form into either balls or 1–3" long sausages on a *flat* skewer.
3. Allow to chill in the refrigerator for 1 hour or overnight.

Grilled mixed vegetables
1 onion cut into eights
2 semi-ripe tomatoes, cut in half at the equator

> 1 eggplant cut into cubes
> 2 sweet bell peppers cored and seeded and cut into quarters lengthwise, or 4 thick rings
> Juice of 1 lemon
> ¼ cup olive oil
> Rough sea or kosher salt
>
> 1. Sweat the eggplant cubes by salting heavily and laying on an inclined board or griddle to drain the brown bitter juice for ½ hour.
> 2. Pat the cubes dry with a paper towel.
> 3. Place all vegetables in a large bowl.
> 4. Mix lemon juice, olive oil, and salt, and mix well so all vegetable pieces are well coated, notably the eggplant.
> 5. Thread a mix of vegetables onto flat skewers, making them as decorative as you like.
>
> *Cooking*
> 1. Prepare a hot charcoal grill.
> 2. Grill meat and vegetables until done, basting with additional olive oil and lemon juice as necessary. The chicken will be slowest to cook, so if you want all to be ready simultaneously, start with the precooked chicken, then raw *shashlik*, then raw kababs, and finally vegetables. Spray some water on coals if a flame appears or it will scorch the meat.
>
> *Serve in pitot, or on a plate with hummus, vegetable salad, and pickles.*

The Jewish Religious Year

The Jewish religious year consists of a series of holidays and fasts, almost all of which have specific foods associated with them. A large minority of Israeli Jews observe the strictures on food lightly, if at all. But even the most secular Israelis do make an effort to have a family meal, sometimes the entire extended family, or, in kibbutzim, the entire community. This meal is generally festive in nature, with decorated tables, wine, and several courses. The more religiously orthodox a family is, the more it will adhere to very specific requirements in terms of purification, presentation of foods or avoidances, and the "proper" rituals that each holiday requires.

In addition to the annual roster of holidays, Saturday—Shabbat—is also celebrated on a weekly basis. For secular Jewish Israelis, the Sabbath meal is also often a special, formal one, with courses and a serving of wine, even if the religious rituals are not adhered to. The more religious a family is, the more formality and the greater adherence to specific requirements in terms of foods chosen, order, and rituals.

Shabbat

The commandment "Six days shall thou work, but on the seventh day, thou shall rest, thou and your servants, your donkey . . ." (Exodus 20:8) has been elaborated upon to an enormous degree throughout the past three millennia, to the point that many Jews do not fulfill all of the rabbinic requirements. The ordinances concerning Shabbat practices include many concerning food.

The most important prohibition concerns a prohibition on work. This generalization that appears in the Ten Commandments was elaborated by the rabbis over the centuries so that there is now a prohibition on lighting fires or, for that matter, turning electric devices (including lights) on or off (housewife labors such as serving and clearing the table were clearly not considered work by the rabbis, all of them men). This means that all food and other preparations must be accomplished before the evening on Friday. Fires that are already lit may not be turned off, which leads to the reparation of long-cooked stews, called *hamin*, which have specific local variations.

Prescriptive obligations contain three that are relevant here. First, commandments and religious obligations are to be obeyed joyously and elaborately: more and better are the watchwords for this holy day. Second, wine and bread, at the least, must be consumed and blessed. Third, a portion of the bread dough prepared for the Shabbat must be separated and offered to God (during Temple times [until 70 CE], the priests). This led to the elaboration of a special bread—*challah*—which in European tradition was elaborated by white flour, and decorations such as braiding the dough.

According to religious law, it is forbidden to cook from sundown on Friday to sundown on Saturday. Jewish housewives all over the world were therefore forced to look for ingenious ways to prepare food on Friday and keep it warm for the Saturday meal that was eaten after return from synagogue for Saturday prayers.

The result was an endless variety of slow-cooked stews that could mature under gentle heat (since fires lit before the Sabbath could be used for cooking if the food was already on the hob before the Sabbath. Thus, the emergence of *hamin* (from the Hebrew word *ham*: hot), a general word to describe such stews that generally varied a great deal from one Jewish community to another. Traditional Jews of all stripes will eat *hamin* on Saturday in order to ensure the commandment against work is kept.

Hamin is prepared on Friday, then set on a low fire until consumed at midday on the Shabbat. The precise makeup of the *hamin* varied from one community to another. Beans were almost universal, since the Talmud suggests that the longer they are cooked, the better they taste. Most *hamin* also include garlic, greens, and since the discovery of the Americas, potatoes in Eastern and Northern Europe where they became a staple, and chilies and sweet potatoes in North Africa and the Middle East.

The secret to all *hamin* is slow cooking, preferably in an oven. The two major versions are Sephardic *adafina* (from the Moorish "to bury" in the ashes) and Ashkenazi *cholent* (possibly from the Provençal *chaud* "hot"). There are even vegetarian versions such as Bokharan *dimlama*. Traditionally, the stew was placed in an ovenproof dish in the oven after baking bread and left overnight in the ashes.

In modern Israel, which suffers from a hectic lifestyle, slow cooking in an oven is difficult (and expensive). Nevertheless, traditional families will almost always have some version of *hamin* for Saturday lunch. Instead of an oven, use of a slow-cooker is common, unless the *hamin* is left on the low heat of a *platat Shabbat* (Saturday plate): a timer-controlled low-temperature electric hotplate with which most traditional homes are equipped. Another change in Israel is that traditions are melded and few except the elderly and ultra-orthodox stick to their community's version of the dish.

Adafina (Sephardi Hamin)

Yield: Serves 4

2 Tbsp olive oil
2 onions, peeled and halved
8 cloves garlic, crushed and peeled
½ chicken, cut into 4 pieces
1 lb stewing beef cut into 2" cubes
4 pieces beef marrow bone
1 lamb shank
1 sweet potato, peeled and cut into 4 pieces
4 small white potatoes, peeled
2 carrots, peeled and cut in half
1 cup canned/cooked chickpeas, drained
½ cup parsley, rinsed well and roughly chopped
½ cup cilantro, washed well and roughly chopped

1 tsp cumin powder
2 allspice berries, crushed
½ tsp cinnamon
1 tsp coriander seed powder
Water to cover
Salt and black pepper to taste
4 *haminados*, shelled
4 *merguez* sausages (optional)
'*Arissa* to taste (optional)

1. Heat oil in a pot, and fry onions until golden.
2. Add garlic and fry additional minute.
3. Add meat, vegetables, spices and herbs. Stir well.
4. Cover with water. Cover pot and bring to a simmer. Allow to cook for half an hour, covered.
5. Season to taste.
6. Transfer to a slow cooker on low.
7. Add *haminados* and *merguez* if using.
8. Seal pot and allow to cook overnight on very low heat.
9. Remove lamb shank, separate meat from bone, and cut into 4 pieces. Correct seasoning.

Note: Instead of a slow cooker, you can place all ingredients into an oven-proof, close-lidded casserole dish. Heat the oven to 450°F. Lower heat to 200°F and leave the casserole dish in the oven overnight until noon.

Serve in bowls, with each diner receiving a piece of every element with 'arissa on the side.

Cholent (Ashkenazi Hamin)

Yield: Serves 4

2 Tbsp chicken or melted goose fat, or vegetable oil (*not* olive oil)
4 small waxy potatoes, peeled
2 onions, peeled and quartered
6 cloves garlic, peeled and slivered
2 carrots, peeled and quartered
½ cup beans of your choice (white navy beans are traditional but any bean will do) soaked overnight, then drained

¼ cup barley
1 lb stewing beef, cut into cubes
Salt and black pepper to taste
2 cups chicken or beef stock
Water to add
4 eggs, well rinsed (optional)

1. Heat oven to 450°F if using.
2. Pour the oil into an ovenproof casserole with a well-fitted lid, or in a slow cooker and swirl around so bottom and sides are coated.
3. Mix potatoes, onions, carrots, and layer at bottom.
4. Add a layer of beans and barley.
5. Add beef cubes.
6. Add eggs in shell gently, if using.
7. Pour in stock, and top with water so all ingredients are covered. Season to taste.
8. Place casserole in oven and immediately lower heat to 200°F. Otherwise, turn slow cooker to high for 1 hour, then to lowest. Allow to cook for 20–24 hours. One hour before serving, correct seasoning if necessary. If *cholent* is too dry, add ½ cup boiling water. If there is too much liquid (the consistency should be porridge-like, not soupy) raise heat for remaining hour.

Divide ingredients among diners.

Sabzavot Dimlama (Bokharan Vegetarian Hamin)

Yield: Serves 4

½ cup vegetable oil, or, if other meat is prepared, mutton fat, called *dumba*
1 onion, peeled and chopped
2 carrots peeled and cut in 1 cm pieces
½ lb pumpkin, chopped roughly
2 tomatoes, peeled and chopped
2 sweet bell peppers, any color, cored, seeded, and sliced into strips lengthwise
2 quinces, peeled, cored, and cut into eighths
2 crisp, slightly sour apples, peeled, cored, and cut into eighths
1 medium eggplant cut in cubes, salted, and drained for half an hour, then patted dry

2 turnips, peeled, topped, and quartered
1 small cabbage cut in medium pieces
8 cloves of garlic (minced for stronger garlic flavor)
2 potatoes peeled and quartered
2 bay leaves
Salt and ground black pepper
½ tsp cumin seeds
½ tsp coriander seeds, whole (or crushed for stronger flavor)
1 cup water
Minced dill and minced fresh coriander leaves for garnish

1. Heat oil in large pot with a well-fitting lid. Salt lightly.
2. Fry onions to light brown.
3. Remove pot from heat and layer vegetables and fruit on top of onions in pot, alternating with garlic: carrots, turnips, eggplant, then the others, with potato and bay leaf topmost. Season each layer with some cumin, coriander, salt, and black pepper.
4. Add water to barely cover.
5. Cook, covered and well-sealed (traditionally, a strip of dough would seal the pot) on lowest heat overnight or in the oven at 200°F.
6. 15 minutes before serving, open lid, correct seasoning if necessary, and scatter garnish over.
7. Close pot and allow to sit for 10 minutes or more.

Serve with additional minced dill and/or coriander, and fresh flatbread.

Pesach/Passover

Pesach/Passover is one of the major Jewish rituals and festivals. It places obligatory requirements on all Jews in the realm of food. Central to Pesach is the opening dinner, called Seder (from the Hebrew word meaning "order" or "protocol"), which is probably one of the world's first multimedia scripts. It involves a text, the *Haggadah* ("Telling"), which includes texts read out loud, songs, specific actions, and particular foods and drink consumed in specific and determined ways. All of these actions are aimed at ensuring that the idea of freedom from oppression is maintained.

In terms of food, Pesach has some very strict requirements that extend throughout the week of the festival. These requirements, notably the prohibition on using or even owning *hametz* ("fermentable") foods made of the five grains, extend throughout the festival.

Seder

The festival of Passover is marked by a week's holiday, of which the first night is the most important. Officially, this night, celebrated in Temple times (i.e., before 70 CE) in the form of public sacrifices at the Temple in Jerusalem, is the night of the Seder, a domestic ritual expected to be performed by every Jewish household. The Seder centers around a set of foodstuffs detailed in a written text, the *Haggadah*, which was codified in its final form in the tenth century. As Judaism has evolved in the twentieth century, new variants of the *Haggadah* have emerged: for *kibbutzim*, for women, for world peace, which have been bowdlerized/modified to fit particular constituencies.

The Seder is a celebratory meal wrapped in a fixed liturgy. The celebratory meal varies from one liturgical community and family to another, within certain fixed parameters. Some of the foodstuffs are defined and prescribed in detail. Ritually important foods are placed on the table, and the *Haggadah* specifies how the ritual foodstuffs—three pieces of *matza* (unleavened bread), a piece of roast bone, two kinds of *maror* (bitter herbs), a *charoset*, a mixture of fruit, honey, and wine, and a hard-boiled egg in salt water for each person—are to be arranged on the table. This, the Seder plate, is the centerpiece of the table, and the ritual actions make continuous references to, and use of, the ritually prescribed foods that are visual, olfactory, and finally, edible, parts of the ritual. Four full cups of wine are to be consumed ("enough to make your head swim" as one formal legal interpretation has it).

The dinner that follows the reading of the *Haggadah* varies from one family (and liturgical community or locale of origin) to another. In Israel, more often than not, for those who "do" a Seder, there is usually a series of dishes, running through a starter, soup, fish (gefilte fish or *khreime*), roast meat (turkey, beef, chicken, and sometimes mutton) with sides, and a nondairy dessert. Wine will be drunk in addition to the required four cups. (Many nonreligious families absent themselves by taking an overseas vacation. Many orthodox simply book a place for the family in an appropriately kosher hotel, leaving the administrative and cooking effort to others.) Collective institutions—the army and kibbutzim—generally hold the Seder as well, and there are special rations for soldiers on duty.

Passover Foods

The avoidance of *hametz* (leavened bread) throughout the week of Pesach caused Jewish communities to come up with a number of ways of exploiting the ever-present matza. In addition, many communities

Matziya for Pesach

Yield: Serves 4

4 matzot
2 Tbsp milk for soaking + 2 for the egg
4 eggs
Salt to taste
1 Tbsp butter or oil for dry frying

1. Break up the matzot into 2" pieces.
2. Place matzot into a flat soup plate, then pour over 3 Tbsp milk beaten with a little water. Allow to soak until soft but not soggy and the milk is absorbed.
3. Beat the eggs with the remaining milk (and any not absorbed by the matza) in another soup plate. Season.
4. Once the eggs are well beaten and seasoned, add the soaked matza to the beaten egg and mix well.
5. Heat a medium frying pan. Add oil/butter. When the oil is hot, slide in the matza and egg mixture. Fry until golden brown on one side. Carefully turn over and cook the other side.
6. Slide onto plates.

Eat with a salad, meat products, cheese for a savory dish, or chocolate spread, honey, jelly, or jam for a sweet one.

Sephardi Pastel de Pesach

Yield: Serves 4

3 matzot
1 soup plate warm water
1 Tbsp olive oil
3 cups Sephardic minced meat filling. Alternatively, nonmeat filling
2 eggs, lightly beaten and salted

1. Soak the whole matzot briefly in warm water until semi-soft for no more than 30 seconds.
2. Remove and drain on towel.
3. Preheat the oven to 350°F.
4. Oil a deep square baking pan large enough for matza. Heat oiled pan in oven.

5. Place one matza on the bottom of the pan. Use another to line the sides, filling in any large cracks.
6. Place filling evenly on bottom matza, spreading evenly to the sides.
7. Cover the filling with remaining matza.
8. Pour egg over top matza.
9. Bake until light brown, 30–40 minutes.

Serve warm.

Meat filling
1 Tbsp olive or argan oil
½ tsp salt
½ cup finely minced onion
1 Tbsp finely minced garlic
Pepper to taste
1 tsp cumin powder
¼ tsp cinnamon powder
2 ½ cup mince meat
½ cup fresh coriander leaves, minced fine

1. Heat oil and when rippling, add salt.
2. Add onions and fry over medium heat until golden brown.
3. Add garlic and fry for additional 30 seconds.
4. Add spices and stir for 15 seconds until fragrant.
5. Add meat, raise heat slightly, and stir fry until cooked.
6. Mix in coriander leaves, adjust seasoning, and store until needed, no more than 1 day.

Nonmeat filling
Replace meat with a mix of white cheese such as brinza and chopped spinach, or boiled waxy potato fried with onions until brown.

developed foods that would remind them of the Seder just passed, and extend the joy of the season.

Mimouna

The Mimouna, a festival on its own, takes place after the seven days of Pesach, but is not directly connected to it. In Morocco, it was an opportunity for internal solidarity, overcoming class differences (to a degree) as well as intercommunity solidarity, as Muslim neighbors were invited to

Holidays and Special Occasions

join the "open house" festivities. The Mimouna almost disappeared publicly under the desire of the early leaders of the State (almost all secular Ashkenazi Jews) to restrict or sweep away ethnic differences and religious practices. It was revived in Jerusalem in 1971 by Israeli politicians who had been born in Morocco, and participation increased to such a degree that it is now, in effect, a national holiday. Although religious symbols abound, it is a celebration of the life of Moshe ben Maimon (Maimonides), famous Jewish sage and philosopher, on the anniversary of his father's death in Morocco, after having been expelled from Spain by the Almowahids, a North African Muslim sect. Participation in the main Mimouna tent in Sacher Park in Jerusalem is almost de rigueur for secular and non-orthodox politicians at the national level. Other cities also have "official" Mimouna tents, as do private individuals and some institutions. As a matter of course, as in Morocco, the tents (reminders of the fact that Jacob son of Isaac was a "tent dweller") are open house, and anyone who cares to may drop in and is expected to taste the Moroccan-style sweets on offer.

Moufleta Honey Wraps

Yield: Serves 4

1 packet dry yeast (about 1 tsp)
¼ tsp sugar
4 cups flour
1 Tbsp sugar
1 tsp salt
1 egg
3–4 cups lukewarm water
About 1 cup vegetable oil
Liquid honey and soft butter for topping

1. Dissolve sugar in ¼ cup of the water. Add yeast, stir once, then allow to freshen, 5 minutes.
2. In a bowl, mix flour, sugar, salt, egg, and water. Mix well. Add yeast mixture, and mix well. Turn out onto an oiled surface.
3. Knead for at least 10 minutes until dough is smooth and elastic.
4. Divide dough into 15–20 equal pieces (depending on your flour and the size of your pan).

5. Form dough pieces into balls, with oiled hands, then allow to rest 30 minutes.
6. Heat a heavy frying pan or shallow skillet over a low flame until hot but not sizzling.
7. Flatten a dough ball as much as possible with the palms of your oiled hands. Slip the flattened dough onto the hot pan.
8. Allow one side to cook until lightly browned. Meanwhile, flatten another dough ball. Once cooked, flip over the cake in the pan, place the uncooked cake on top of the one cooking, then flip over both together.
9. While the second cake is cooking, flatten the third dough ball. Slip the cake onto the stack, and turn the stack over.
10. Repeat until you have a stack of seven to ten cakes and as soon as it is awkward to handle (it will become heavy), move them onto a plate and cover with a damp towel.
11. Start another stack and repeat.

Serve with honey and soft/liquid butter for diners to help themselves.

Lag Ba'omer

The thirty-third day after the *omer*, the offering of newly harvested grain on the second day after the Seder, is a commemoration of the final unsuccessful revolt of the Jewish population of Judea (132–135 CE) led by Shimon Bar Kochva (or Bar Kosiva) and Rabbi Akiva. In a very real sense, this event was the start of the 2,000-year Diaspora period in Jewish history, and the destruction of both the land and the Jewish people in Judea (the Romans destroyed over 500 Jewish communities during the revolt, all the palm groves, and most other agricultural resources). Among other things, the Romans, in an effort to obliterate Jewish presence, renamed the area of Judea "Palaestina" after the coastal cities of the non-Jewish Philistines; which eventually became Palestine, a name adopted by early Jewish immigrants to the Holy Land between 1880 and the 1940s, and subsequently by the Arab residents of the area.

Ultra-orthodox Jews assemble at the grave of Rabbi Shimon bar Yochai, another stalwart of the rebellion and a student of Rabbi Akiva in Meiron, near Tsfat in the Upper Galilee. Three-year-old boys receive their first haircut at the celebration. Bonfires are lit and men dance around them to commemorate the sage, who is also the apocryphal author of the *Kabbalah*, a Jewish mystical work probably written in the thirteenth century.

Lag Ba'omer is a public holiday in Israel and is traditionally celebrated by the general public by lighting bonfires, and making and attempting to use homemade bows and arrows to commemorate Bar Kochva's attempts to revive the fighting arts among the youth of that generation. Children and adults roast potatoes in the coals. Those of Moroccan origin often serve *ka'ab el ghazal*, cookies in the shape of antelope horns. Although this is a minor religious festival, it is hugely popular among children due to the bonfires (and much less popular among their parents for the same reason). A garland or individual potatoes roasted in the coals of a fire and eaten with little but salt are a common outdoor food, known as *kartofelim*, from the German *kartoffel*.

Kartofelim

Yield: Serves 4

As many medium-sized potatoes as desired, normally equal to the number of guests
A length of clean galvanized wire. This helps in cooking the potatoes inside, as well as avoiding the problem of losing potatoes in the coals.
One campfire, well-lit, preferably with lots of coals and a low fire, and a long branch or piece of metal for use as a rake
Salt for sprinkling on potatoes
Aluminum foil (optional)

1. Thread the raw potatoes on the wire and twist the wire ends loosely together. You may wrap each potato in aluminum foil.
2. Place the garland carefully in the fire, raking coals over and ensuring each potato is covered.
3. Allow to bake for about 30–40 minutes. Once potatoes are soft inside (the outside will be hard and ash covered if not wrapped in foil), rake garland out of fire.
4. Unlink and uncurl garland ends carefully and slip off potatoes.
5. Hold potato (this will require some juggling to avoid overheated hands) and crack open.
6. Sprinkle as much salt as desired and eat.

Shavuot

Shavuot is the second of the three pilgrimage dates in ancient Israel. It is essentially a celebration of the beginning of the spring harvest of barley and wheat, and the first fruit after winter. The holiday is celebrated publicly in Israel, and is particularly noted in schools, where younger children get to know the harvest and its meaning. The food most associated with Shavuot is cheese and cheese confections: cheesecake, cheese turnovers, and so on.

Rosh Hashana

The New Year is celebrated in late summer, which traditionally would have been the end of the summer harvest: a time in all agricultural societies for merrymaking. Rosh Hashana is the first of three proximate holidays. It is followed by Yom Kippur, ten days later, and then by Succoth (The Feast of Booths). The essential nature of Rosh Hashana is the wish for a better new year, which is often symbolized by the consumption of sweet things, multiplications of blessings and good things, and good wishes for the year.

By-and-large, with the exception of synagogue prayers, which some people attend and others not, Rosh Hashana is a family event, with extended families generally meeting on the day for a festive family meal. Generally, most households adhere to the custom of eating an apple (or other fruit) dipped into honey to symbolize a sweet new year. Other food customs vary, depending heavily on family preference and background. Some form of honey cake is almost de rigueur.

Yom Kippur

Yom Kippur is a twenty-four-hour fast, from sundown before the fast day, to its end at the next sundown. During this time, all adults except those in danger of death or severe ill-health, must refrain from food or drink. Thus, the meal before the fast, as well as how to break the fast, attain extraordinary importance. Generally speaking, most foods eaten immediately after the fast are made of sweet foods. That having been said, there are vast differences in the way that families and individuals fulfill this preference. Both Sephardi and Ashkenazi rite Jews break the fast with a sweet drink—coffee, tea, almond milk, fruit juice—and often a cake or some other small snack before the *maftir* ("finished") dinner takes place.

Succoth

The Feast of Booths is the third and final pilgrimage festival of the ritual calendar. The holiday, which is eight days long, combines the Feast of Booths in the beginning, and *Simchat Torah*, celebrating the giving of the tablets of the Law (and their subsequent elaborations, the Talmud and Commentaries) directly from God. Succoth is principally the celebration of the end of the summer harvest. Fruit such as pomegranates are in evidence as decorations for the *succah* (booth) and as foods.

Traditionally, Jewish families would construct a booth roofed with branches and leaves (although even plain wooden planks are ritually acceptable), and the tradition is to decorate these booths insofar as possible. Fruit or images of them such as figs, pomegranates, and other fall fruit, as well as lights, mobiles, and so on, are used to decorate the *Succoth*. Inasmuch as most Israeli families live in large apartment buildings, most of which have verandahs, the booths are often constructed on those verandas, rendering entire structures festive. More observant and religious families eat all their dinners in the *succah*, and some even sleep in them for the eight days of the festival.

The foods associated with Succoth are those of the end of the harvest: fruit dishes predominate.

Sigd

Virtually the entire Jewish community of Ethiopia was brought to Israel in two major secret operations by the Israeli military and special agencies in the 1980s. Numbering about 40,000 in Israel today, their Judaism and practices are restricted to pre-Talmudic observances. They have, however, added a holiday—the Sigd—which is now celebrated in public, with many non-Ethiopian Israelis attending. The Sigd is a unique festival celebrated fifty days after Yom Kippur, on the 29th of Cheshvan of the Jewish calendar (late fall). The first half of the day is a solemn fast, followed by a reading of the Torah by the priests. The second half of the day includes feasting, dancing, and displays of Ethiopian Israeli crafts and practices. In Israel, it has become an opportunity for the entire community to assemble and celebrate their heritage and rituals. As with other ethnic celebrations such as the Mimouna, this has become to some extent an Israeli celebration, with politicians, in particular, anxious to establish their credentials appearing at the large public gathering.

Foods offered include a mix of Ethiopian traditional foods, and more and more mixes of common Israeli foods with Ethiopian ones (e.g., falafel, which has become popular in the Ethiopian community). While the Ethiopian community is still struggling with identity problems and prejudice, they are slowly becoming an unremarkable part of Israeli society. Ethiopian food is now served in a number of Ethiopian restaurants around the country, and there is something of a cachet in eating (very peppery) Ethiopian food.

Dabo (Spiced Honey Bread)

Dabo can be eaten at any time as a snack or addition to a cup of tea or coffee. However, it is specially made for the Sabbath and other festive events, an Ethiopian version of *challah*. Traditionally, dabo was made by souring dough for 24 or 48 hours. It was then steamed. In Israel today, housewives usually add dried yeast to the wheat flour, and the bread is baked in home ovens.

Yield: Serves 4

1 ½ tsp dried yeast grains
½ cup lukewarm water
¼ tsp sugar
6 cups flour
1 Tbsp ground coriander
½ Tbsp of any combination of the following ground spices (optional):
    Cinnamon
    Fenugreek
    Cloves
1 tsp salt
1 cup liquid honey
½ cup vegetable oil
2 cups warm water

1. Heat oven to 420°F.
2. Mix yeast, ½ cup water and sugar and allow to bubble (10–15 minutes).
3. Mix flour, salt, and spices in large bowl. Crater the top.
4. Pour in yeast mixture, oil, and about one half the water. Mix well. If necessary, add water to make a pliable soft dough with your fingers.
5. Knead in the honey.
6. Knead dough to a soft pliable dough.
7. Place in an oiled bowl, and rotate so dough is oiled all over, then allow to rest until dough almost doubles in size.

> 8. Punch down dough, cut into 6 pieces, roll into balls. Place dough balls in a single layer in a circular pan and allow to rise again for 30–45 minutes.
> 9. Place in oven until top is golden, about 45 minutes. Check doneness with wooden skewer.
> 10. Remove from oven, allow to cool. Remove from pan and serve with additional honey and tea, or coffee.
>
> *Note*: Instead of baking, you can place dough pan in a steamer and steam for 1 hour.

The revival of the festivals of *edot* (origin groups) in Israel restored a number of festivals that were the custom in one Jewish community or another, but not Judaism wide, such as the Moroccan-origin Mimouna. The Sahrana, celebrated by Kurdish Jews, has become a quasi-national festival almost as popular as the Mimouna (cynics might say that since Kurdish and Iraqi Jews have less political power, their festival is of less interest to the political elite, thus a more subdued festival).

The Bene Israel, Jews who settled in India, possibly before European Middle Ages, maintain a celebration named for the Prophet Elijah, the most important biblical figure for this south Indian Jewish community. *Maleeda* (q.v.) is prepared and eaten for the annual pilgrimage that members of the community make to Elijah's cave on the slopes of Mt Carmel (now in the Haifa suburb of Bat Galim). Both the thanksgiving rituals and the pilgrimage are known as Eliyahu Hanabi.

Hanukkah

Many Americans will be familiar with Hanukkah, largely, perhaps, because this Jewish holiday falls in proximity to Christmas, although the two events have no liturgical or historical connection. The eight-day holiday celebrates the relief of Jerusalem and particularly the Temple from control of the Seleucid Syrio-Greek Empire in the second century BCE. The Temple had been deliberately polluted by the Seleucids. A small jug of pure oil was found that sufficed to keep the lamps of the temple burning for eight days, during which more purified oil was procured. Hanukkah is celebrated by the lighting of candles in a succession, starting with one and adding one each day. The candelabra are expected to be placed in a window where they can be seen by passers-by.

The association with the miracle means that foods during Hanukkah are often oil-based. Thus, in Ashkenazi tradition (and currently in the United States), jelly doughnuts and fried potato fritters (*latkes*), similar to German *reibkuchen*, are available throughout the holiday. In Israel, both appear several weeks before the holiday, and most bakeries and groceries offer a wide selection of doughnuts. For many years, these were of poor

---

Levivot

Levivot are an essential item for celebrating Hanukkah, which features oily foods. *Levivot*, which are essentially a German winter treat, have become ubiquitous and are eaten by everyone in Israel during the holiday. In Germany, they are served with applesauce, but the Jewish custom is to serve them with sour cream, which some in Israel still do.

Yield: Serves 4

4 large potatoes, peeled, and shredded
Oil for ½″ deep frying
½ tsp salt
Pepper to taste (optional)
4 Tbsp finely grated onion (optional)
Sour cream or applesauce for dipping (optional)

1. Make sure *not* to rinse the shredded potato, to keep the starch.
2. Mix potatoes and salt. Add onions if using. Add pepper if using. Mix ingredients well. Allow mixture to rest for half an hour.
3. Heat oil to a shimmer, but not smoking.
4. Take a handful of the mixture and flatten between the moistened flats of your palms. The ideal latke is about ½″ thick at most, and the size of one's palm or a little larger.
5. Place each latke gently into the hot oil, cooking no more than a few at a time.
6. When the latke is golden brown on one side, gently turn over with a spatula until brown on the other. Monitor the heat carefully so the latkes do not burn.
7. Remove and drain on paper towels. While still hot, transfer to individual plates.

Eat with sour cream (*as snack or for a nonmeat meal*) or with applesauce for any meal.

quality; more recently, with a greater demand for food quality and gourmet items, gourmet doughnuts have started raising the bar, and the quality has improved.

Tu Bishvat "New Year of the Trees"

Tu Bishvat (the 15th of the month of Shvat in the Hebrew calendar) celebrates the start of the planting season and the end of winter. It is a thanksgiving for the life-giving properties of trees, which are crucial for human existence. In Israel, the holiday became a civil ritual, within an early effort to change the nature of the environment from arid to more verdant. Schoolchildren and politicians are exhorted to plant trees, and under the direction of the Jewish National Fund, a nongovernmental organization (NGO) charged with reforestation, new tree plantations are started in urban and rural areas.

Dried fruit are traditionally eaten for Tu Bishvat. Many households and politicians prepare presentation plates of dried fruit to symbolize the renewal of the agricultural year. There is a certain amount of competition in terms of lavishness and artistic presentation.

Purim

Purim is a Jewish carnival celebrated in early spring. Children, and often adults, put on fancy dress, and there are often carnival parades called *Adeloyada,* from a phrase exhorting the people to drink until they do not know their right from their left. While it has a lengthy history, the emphasis on the holiday may well be a reaction to European Carnival (between Christmas and Lent), to which it has many similarities. The background story is the relief from threat of a pogrom planned by Haman, a minister of the Persian king Ahasuerus (possibly identified with Artaxerxes). Under the influence of the Jewish leader Mordechai, who had his niece Esther inducted into the King's harem where she influenced him against the scheme, tables were turned, and Haman and his sons were hanged.

During Purim, the story of Esther's success is read from the Scroll of Esther (a noncanonical book of the Bible). The festival is celebrated with dressing up, often a carnival parade, eating, and drinking so much wine one "cannot differentiate between blessing Mordecai and excoriating Haman." While not legal, in the Orthodox community many children are indulged with wine and even smoking. Costumes vary depending on the fashion that year. Adults and children indulge in parties and joint meals.

One religious commandment that is observed by religious Jewish families as well as secular, is that of *mishloakh manot* ("sending portions"). Neighbors will send one another gifts of sweets, dried fruit, and cakes, most often *oznei haman*. Almonds, nuts, and dried fruit are associated with the Purim festival because, according to tradition, Queen Esther, one protagonist of the story, ate nothing but fruit and nuts during her stay in King Ahasuerus's palace for fear of violating *kashrut*. Given the festival is celebrated in late winter, it is also possible that dried fruit and nuts were the most common sweet things available. The sweet-fillings of the *oznei haman* presumably indicate that the story ended well after all.

Oznei Haman

The triangular, stuffed shortbread confections are a favorite food for most children. In Israel, they are available from about a week before the festival to a week after, and are consumed in large quantities. Many households still make their own, although it is possible to buy many varieties from bakeries. *Oznei haman* originate in Germany as *maultasche*, which can be filled with savory or sweet fillings and are often steamed rather than baked. Traditionally, and often today in Israel, they are filled with poppy seed (*mohn* is German for poppy seed, and the word may be homonymous with "Haman"). The pastries are almost required in *mishloakh manot*, although fillings now may include dates, fruit confections, prunes, raisins, and even marshmallows.

Yield: Serves 4

½ cup softened unsalted butter
½ cup sugar
2 eggs
2 cups all-purpose flour
1 flat tsp baking powder
¼ tsp salt

1. Using an electric mixer, beat butter and sugar together until pale and fluffy.
2. Add eggs, one after the other until completely incorporated.
3. Mix flour, salt, and baking powder in another bowl.
4. While continuing to whisk slowly, add flour mixture to sugar mixture, a third at a time, allowing the flour to mix completely before adding more.

5. Allow dough to come together. Remove from mixer and chill in refrigerator for 15 minutes.
6. Heat oven to 360°F.
7. Cover a cookie sheet with baking paper.
8. Roll out chilled dough (dough should be chilled, not cold, else it will crack) on a lightly floured surface to about ¼" thick.
9. Using a glass or cookie cutter, cut out 4" disks of the dough and place each on the cookie sheet.
10. Place a teaspoon of filling—traditional poppy seed (see below), thick fruit preserve, finely minced dates, and any other nonliquid sweet filling of your choice—in the middle of each dough disk.
11. Fold up the three sides of the disk and pinch the corners together to about halfway or more up the seam toward the center. Some of the filling may show. The result should look like a tricorn hat.
12. Bake until tops are light tan and bottoms light brown.

For traditional poppy seed filling
1 cup poppy seeds, rinsed and drained
1 cup milk
½ cup liquid honey (or more to taste)
1 heaping Tbsp small seedless raisins, or preserved citrus peel
1 Tbsp roughly chopped nuts (walnuts, pecans, and so on), optional

1. Combine milk and poppy seeds in a small pot and bring to a low simmer (do not allow to boil).
2. Simmer 10 minutes, stirring.
3. Transfer to a food processor or food mill and grind to a paste.
4. Mix in honey, dried fruit, and nuts if using.
5. Store in a sealed jar in the refrigerator until use.

The Muslim Religious Year

The Muslim religious calendar is based on the appearance of the moon, and in the absence of leap years, the festivals precess in relation to the Gregorian calendar. This means that a given festival or fast will appear at different times in the solar year, and is not fixed.

The Muslim calendar has two festivals and one lengthy fast prescribed in the Koran and *Hadith* (Sayings of the Prophet Muhammad). 'Id al 'Adha (Feast of the Sacrifice) celebrates Abraham's attempted sacrifice of his son, Ishmael (in the Bible, this story figures Isaac) and his replacement by a sacrificial goat. This also coincides with the end of the Hajj (greater pilgrimage season). The entire month of Ramadan is dedicated to fasting during daylight hours, with special foods consumed during the nighttime. 'Id al Fitr celebrates the end of Ramadan and is traditionally a family feast.

While the Koran does not specify what foods are to be eaten during these three events, except for the need to sacrifice a beast for al 'Adha, the sayings of the Prophet indicate that the Prophet himself was fond of certain foods to break his fast during Ramadan, and some Muslims attempt to emulate his preferences. Crucially, a day of fasting in a hot Middle Eastern summer is problematic, and thus fasts tend to end with consumption of "energy drinks"; that is, drinks that provide both liquid and immediate energy support. Since Ramadan is considered a joyous season, meals during Ramadan tend to be heavy on sweet foods and delicacies that are otherwise not consumed often.

'Id al 'Adha

The preferred animal for sacrifice is a sheep or goat. Families that can afford to do so will procure a live animal and slaughter it for the holiday. Those that cannot may receive *zakat* (charity) from their wealthier neighbors, in the form of raw or cooked meat from the wealthier family's beast or else roast a chicken, pigeons, or some other affordable meat.

Ramadan

For observant Muslims in Israel, the (lunar) month of Ramadan is both the most solemn and most joyous of the year. Muslims are required to fast from sunrise to sunset. Most Muslims reduce their workload accordingly, wherever possible. In the evening and before dawn during Ramadan, people indulge in foods, some of them traditional (e.g., because the Prophet Muhammad was reputed to like those foods to break his fast), some local. The consumption of sweets, ranging from dried fruit through elaborate baked dishes, increases, and the morning meal, which is eaten before dawn, must provide enough energy to get through the day.

It is common to break the fast with an energy drink of some sort, and a simple snack such as sweetened cooked barley, which the Prophet favored. Later in the evening, when everyone has recovered and there is time to cook, a full meal will be served, accompanied by a choice of sweet dishes, notably *atayef* (cheese wrapped in thin crisp noodles or pancakes soaked in rose-flavored syrup) and sweet drinks. Dishes during Ramadan are expected to be rich and flavorful to encourage diners to eat a great deal. An Israeli favorite is *siniya*, spiced minced meat balls baked in *tahina* sauce.

Holidays and Special Occasions

Roast Chicken for 'Id al 'Adha

Roasting is the preferred way of preparing celebratory dishes, whenever possible. Urban Israeli Arabs, unless they have rural kin, usually make do without a sheep, and may use chicken instead.

Yield: Serves 4

1 large chicken, cut into eight
1 tsp cumin seeds
2 tsp sumac
4–5 grated garlic cloves
1 Tbsp *silan* (date honey), available from Middle Eastern stores
1 scant tsp salt or to taste
2 ripe tomatoes, sliced thickly
¼ cup olive oil
1 tsp sumac additional (optional) or juice of ½ lemon

1. Blend cumin seeds, sumac, garlic, *silan*, and salt. Allow to sit for 5 minutes.
2. Marinade chicken 2–4 hours in mixture, taking care to cover all surfaces of chicken.
3. Lay sliced tomatoes in base of roasting pan and pack marinated chicken on top.
4. Beat remaining marinade with olive oil, and pour on top of chicken.
5. Add lemon juice or additional sumac if a sourer dish is preferred.
6. Bake in 400°F oven until juice from chicken joints runs clear.

Serve with flavored rice and fresh vegetable salad.

Bamardan/Kaer al din

Yield: Serves 4

2 cups dried apricots, minced
3 cups cold water
Soda water/seltzer to taste
4 sprigs mint
Ice optional

1. Mince apricots with a heavy knife.
3. Place minced apricots with cold water into a blender, and blend until you have as smooth a paste as possible (this might take 5 minutes).
4. Keep in the refrigerator until needed.
5. Fill four large tumblers ¾ full with the apricot drink (and ice if desired) and top up with soda water to taste, garnish with mint.

Serve with or before a meal.

Haroof Mahshi: Baked Stuffed Lamb

Since Ramadan moves about the year, sometimes the "lamb" is really mutton, which means it is larger and more flavorful. Traditionally, the meat would be brought to the table as is, and diners help themselves with their hands.

Yield: Serves 4

1 breast of boneless lamb, rinsed and patted dry. Allow ½ lb per person.
3 tsp cumin powder mixed with 1 tsp coriander powder, 2 tsp sumac, and salt and black pepper to taste
½ cup beef stock
4–5 onions, peeled, whole or cut in halves

For stuffing
1 cup rice
2 cups water
About ½ lb mince meat, mutton, or mix of mutton and beef
½ cup yogurt and ½ cup water or ½ cup beef stock well mixed
3 Tbsp fresh parsley leaf, finely minced
1 tsp turmeric
½ cup sultanas
4 garlic cloves according to taste, grated or mashed fine
Handful pine nuts

First prepare the stuffing
1. Cook rice in 2 cups of water until it is half cooked and still firm, about 4–5 minutes. Drain.

Holidays and Special Occasions

2. Soak the rice about 1 hour in the yogurt and stock. Drain.
3. Mix mince meat, parsley leaf, turmeric, sultanas, mashed garlic, and pine nuts into the rice. Allow to rest for ½ hour or more.
4. Salt and pepper to taste.

Prepare the meat
1. Mix spices and seasoning together.
2. Rub the outer side of the meat with spice mix and allow to rest.

Assembly and cooking
1. Lay mutton skin side down. Layer the stuffing along the center of the meat.
2. Using a baking needle and thread, fold one long edge of the meat toward the other, and sew together with 4–5 stitches. Fold the short ends over and sew the flaps to close off the ends, making a package.
3. Place meat in a lidded roasting pan, stitched side down. Surround with onions. Add stock to pan. Close lid.
4. Place in preheated oven at 350°F.
5. Roast 1 hour covered. Meat should be near done. Remove lid. Raise temperature to 390°F and allow to brown on the outside. Meat should be falling off the bone. Allow to rest 10 minutes before serving.

Serve with additional rice and a full mezze. Offer plenty of soft drinks.

'Id al Fitr

The solemn month of Ramadan ends with the holiday of 'Id al Fitr, when life resumes its normal course. Roast mutton is consumed in great quantities, and households that can afford a sheep ensure that there is sufficient meat to entertain guests, and to provide for poorer individuals and households that cannot afford to do so themselves. Israeli Arabs can (sometimes) get away with traveling in Palestinian areas, where Israeli Jews fear to go. Some go to market in Palestine, or to visit relatives. Palestinian foods, notably *atayef*, which, reputedly, is best made in the city of Nablus in Palestine, are a common item on the shopping list during Ramadan, and notably for the holiday, which ends the fasting month. Other sweets include Ka'ak al Eid (date-stuffed cookies), *ma'amoul* (another form of stuffed cookies), and sweet drinks such as *bamardan* (q.v.), *tamarhindi* (q.v.), and *karkade* (hibiscus tea).

Atayef (also Kadayef) (Stuffed Pancakes)

These are popular during Ramadan and at 'Id al Fitr too, throughout the Levant. The most common filling is white cheese, so that the slightly salty cheese contrasts with the syrup. An alternative using walnuts is also common.

Yield: Serves 4

For the syrup:
1 cup sugar
1 cup water
1 Tbsp orange flower water

For the fillings:
Cheese filling
1 cup lightly salted white cheese (available at most Middle Eastern stores) or ricotta (or homemade *labaneh*)
1 heaped Tbsp seedless raisins
1 Tbsp sugar
1 tsp lemon juice
Mix all ingredients well just before filling.

Walnut filling
1 cup roughly chopped walnuts
2 Tbsp sugar
¼ tsp salt
1 tsp cinnamon
Mix all ingredients a few hours before filling.

For the cakes:
1 tsp yeast (dried or fresh)
½ tsp sugar to liven yeast
¼ cup lukewarm water
2 cups all-purpose flour
About 2 cups lukewarm water
1 tsp vegetable oil
Oil for pan
Crushed pistachios for garnish (optional)

Prepare syrup the day before:
1. Warm water and dissolve sugar.
2. Allow to simmer, while stirring, to make a light syrup.

Holidays and Special Occasions

> 3. Allow to cool, then stir in orange blossom water.
> 4. Store overnight in refrigerator.
> 5. Take out just before using (the colder the syrup and the hotter the cakes, the crisper the result).
> 6. Mix yeast, ½ tsp sugar, and ¼ cup water in a bowl and allow yeast to liven for about 10 minutes.
> 7. Heat oven to 360°F.
> 8. Mound flour in a large bowl.
> 9. Make a crater in flour and mix in the bubbling yeast.
> 10. Beat in one half of the water and 1 tsp oil.
> 11. Keep beating, adding more water until you have a smooth pancake batter (this may take less or more water).
> 12. Cover with a damp towel and allow to rise for about 30–50 minutes.
> 13. Heat a lightly oiled, heavy pan over medium-high heat.
> 14. Pour in a quarter or one-sixth of the batter, starting from middle of pan, and keeping the cake as round as possible. The cake should be about ¼" thick.
> 15. Allow to cook until top surface is bubbly and all wet surfaces have dried out.
> 16. Remove from pan and transfer to a clean kitchen towel. Do not flip cakes over!
> 17. Repeat until all cakes are done.
> 18. Divide filling into a number of cakes. Place filling in middle of cake's upper surface. Fold over, and pinch edges together.
> 19. Place folded cakes onto a warm baking pan, and bake for 10–15 minutes until cakes are golden brown on top.
> 20. Just before removing pan from oven, take syrup from refrigerator.
> 21. Remove pan from oven, and transfer cakes to heatproof ceramic or metal serving dish (not glass, which may crack).
>
> *Immediately pour cold syrup over hot stuffed cakes and serve. Garnish with crushed pistachios if desired.*

Life-Cycle Events

Almost all people around the world mark life-cycle events in some way. The marking may be religious or secular, public or private. Specific foods are often either recommended or prescribed (or sometimes, proscribed). Jewish religious law has specific ritual activities that are prescribed for the celebrant and the family or community. In Israel, these have often been modified for secular consumption. Many families, however, retain rituals and foods that were used by their predecessors, notably in the use of foods. Muslim life-cycle events are similar in some ways to Jewish ones, not surprising considering near half the Jewish population have antecedents in Muslim lands.

Rites of Passage

Since aside from specific blessings, there are no prescribed foods for a birth, traditions of one's family/ethnic group tend to be upheld. In addition, the birth of a son means that the *brit milah* ceremony will take place eight days later, and therefore birth ceremonies tend to be subsumed in the ritually more-significant circumcision celebration. The eighth day after the birth of a Jewish boy is celebrated by the trimming of the newborn's prepuce. A specialist—*mohel*—performs the circumcision and the necessary actions, tools, and blessings are specified very carefully in Jewish religious tradition. Sweet cookies, or *ma'amoul*, as well as honey-flavored cakes and dishes are common. Muslims too (and Druze) circumcise their sons. This is however done at a later age, as was done by Abraham to Ishmael. In Muslim communities, this is more a communal than a family affair. The young boys (anything from age four to prepubescent age) are richly dressed and paraded through town. They are given strengthening foods and drinks, as well as sweet treats to support them for the ordeal.

At the age of twelve (for girls, marking menarche) or thirteen (for boys), children are considered responsible for themselves, and notably, responsible for all religious obligations, in traditional Jewish thought. In Israel, as in many Jewish communities elsewhere, a bar-mitzvah is a major event for the family. The choice of celebratory foods is wide, and there are few prescriptions. Many families will have a catered affair, largely for the parents' associates and families.

While Jewish wedding rules are very specific, the foods associated with the festivities are not specified. Most weddings (Jewish and Arab alike) are catered dinners and few people marry in their homes. The choice of food depends largely on the event location and caterer. Every Arab village and most Jewish towns are likely to have an events hall catering to weddings in particular. Men and women are often separated (although this is becoming less common with the younger and more urbanized generation). While wine is not offered in Muslim weddings, it is available in Christian Arab ones. Sweet foods—*rahat, ma'amoul, atayef,* and so on—are commonly offered.

After a funeral, the deceased family in Judaism are abjured from working, including cooking. Instead, they are expected to sit *shiva* (seven) for seven days, during which food is prepared by outsiders. Food is brought by neighbors; thus, the choice of food depends largely on the family's location and socioeconomic status. Immediately after the funeral, there is normally a meal that may be catered or arranged by the family, usually of cold cuts and other finger foods. During the week of the *shiva*, neighbors tend to bring in food, normally vegetarian casseroles of various sorts. Muslim funerals have few prescribed foods beyond coffee and nibbles. More orthodox Muslim families will bury the remains in a modest grave, following traditions emanating recently from Saudi Arabia. Less orthodox and those less affected by the rise of Wahabi orthodoxy within Islam, tend to hold to standards of hospitality throughout the mourning period as well.

CHAPTER EIGHT

Street Food and Snacks

Street foods in Israel come in several categories. The most popular and iconic are snacks (sometimes substantial enough to be called meals) stuffed into pita pocket bread, and *pitzuchim* "crackables," that is, seeds and nuts that need to be cracked before or while eating. Both are sold in kiosks or street-side shops specializing in this type of food, which may be eaten on the spot or taken away. Other snacks that are commonly indulged in include commercial and "children's" fruit, pastries and cakes (European and Middle Eastern), and commercial snacks.

The market for snacks is very large and constitutes, as in most industrialized societies, a large economic segment. The consumption of some snacks has major health consequences. Two such issues are the growing problem of child obesity and high rates of diabetes among some populations in Israel. Child obesity is not as much of an epidemic as it is in some Western countries, but the prevalence of snacks with little more than flavors and empty calories contributes to a growing trend.

Pita-Based Street Foods

The ubiquitous pita has been adopted by Israelis from every walk of life and every possible social position. The pocket bread is in as much demand as an edible container for fast-food in frenetic Tel Aviv, as it is in relaxed, laid-back Eilat. In short, Israeli food life would be inconceivable without this simple bread. Unsurprisingly, the pita comes into its own as the conveyor of a large variety of fast-foods. So popular is this bakery good that nontraditional items—hamburgers, schnitzel, stews—are now served in pita, sometimes in preference to their original serving forms.

Hummus

Hummus is both a street food and a staple of many meals, part of a *mezze*, starter, and a sandwich. It varies according to taste, pocket, and ethnic choice. While political controversy about origins and authorship has clouded the hummus horizon, the real origins are lost in the mists of time, and there are hints in very old sources (e.g., the Bible's Book of Ruth and Nasrallah's *A Fourteenth-Century Egyptian Cookbook*) that it has been eaten in the Middle East from antiquity. In Israel, hummus has achieved iconic status, and many Israeli's first thought after a long absence from the country is to "wipe some hummus."

For most Israelis, hummus is a more or less fine paste made by crushing boiled chickpeas mixed with salt, some garlic, olive oil, lemon, and *tahina* (sesame) paste. The proportions can be varied according to taste, and spices—cumin, cardamom powder—may be incorporated as well. A proper hummus serving is spread in a circular motion on a plate to make a steep-walled crater. The crater is then splashed with all or some olive oil, additional *tahina* sauce, minced parsley, whole boiled chickpeas, pine nuts, cumin powder, hot paprika, hot red *'arissa*, or green *zchug* sauces. This means that there are almost as many variations as there are cooks.

Hummus is eaten by hand. Either by tearing off a piece of flatbread and collecting the hummus in a wiping motion (thus "wiping a hummus"), or spread in a pita pocket bread, mainly with salads and pickles or some other filling. Traditional accompaniments to hummus are vegetable salads, pickles, and olives. There are numerous restaurants specializing in hummus (known as *humussiyah*) throughout the country, with many people having a favorite that they will swear is the best.

Industrially made hummus is available in all food stores as well. Some brands have been marketing overseas for several decades, and these have served as pioneers in introducing Middle Eastern and Israeli foods overseas. Few families except in Arab communities still make their own hummus, although it was a feature of childhood in the 1960s and before to set children to peeling the cooked beans from the translucent coats. While less popular than overseas, flavored hummus spread is also available, although most Israelis are purists when it comes to this food.

Falafel

Falafel is one of the two Israeli signature dishes, hummus being the other. Political polemics aside, the idea of deep frying balls of ground pulses must have occurred well before the first time the food was mentioned in medieval

Egypt. Whatever its origin, historical circumstances have made of this simple dish, variations of which can be found in most Middle Eastern countries, a quintessential marker of Israeli food.

In Israel, falafel may be eaten from a plate with other salads or dishes, or it may be eaten in the way most people think of it: as a sandwich. Specialized falafel places, ranging from simple barrows to large kiosks, have been in existence since at least the 1920s.

A proper falafel sandwich is a construct limited by the imagination and expansiveness of the establishment and the preference of the customer. The sandwich has three crucial components. The falafel balls must not be too small or large (very large *ta'amiya* made Egyptian-style with a mixture of *ful* [broad] beans and chickpeas are largely a feature of Jerusalem) and leave little room for the salad. The best falafel balls are served hot from the cooking oil, which must be clear and first-use, not recycled. The falafel balls are the heart of the dish: crisp on the outside, hot and crumbly inside, they are flavored with spices of which turmeric and cumin predominate. The pita's quality, whose pocket makes the sandwich, is crucial. The best falafel places either bake their own or buy fresh from a local pita bakery. The pita must be thick and its insides fluffy, to keep the sandwich and sauces together. The pita is filled with several falafel balls, then comes the turn of the salads. In some establishments, salads are dished out by the

Falafel and Ta'amiya

Yemenite Jews started returning to Israel in the 1880s, at about the same time the First Aliya took place in a mass movement triggered by discrimination and persecution-derived poverty, and by a messianic belief in the resurrection of the Jewish people in the Land of Israel. Although unknown in Yemen, Yemenite-born entrepreneurs could, with a small investment, get a pot of oil boiling over a kerosene burner, bags of pita, a container of mixed salad, another of German-style sauerkraut (pickled cabbage), another of liquid sesame paste (*tahina*), and a hot chili sauce, and start a small business. As time went by, many of these operators prospered, and falafel became associated with Yemenites. In the 1960s, perhaps due to competition from the grilled meat business and the growing prosperity of the country, the falafel trade added another twist: free salads. Israelis stood around with bulging pitot (plural of pita) stuffed to overflowing with salads, which, in many cases, completely overwhelmed the core of the sandwich: the falafel balls.

staff. In others, there is an array of trays from which customers can help themselves. The salads may include a plain vegetable salad (chopped tomatoes, cucumbers, and peppers) sauerkraut or white cabbage salad, pickles (peppers, radish, cucumber, beets, or other root vegetables), sliced fresh vegetables, fried eggplant, and sliced onions. Once the pita is filled to the customer's satisfaction (and often overflowing) is the turn of the sauces. Three sauces are common: *tahina* sauce (of ground sesame seeds), *'amba* (a Jewish Iraqi condiment made of green mangoes and chilies), and chili sauces: red Moroccan-origin *'arissa* or green Yemenite-origin *zchug* of cilantro and chilies.

Ful

While *ful* (broadbeans) are eaten all over the Middle East, Egypt prides itself on its version, which is the basic food for peasant and rich man alike. Jewish immigrants from Egypt brought the love of *ful* with them, and it is a staple in many households. In some cities—Beersheva and Jerusalem in particular—*ful* is second to falafel as a street food. In Jerusalem, *ful* is served in the form of *ta'amiya* (fried *ful* and chickpea disks) served just as falafel is served elsewhere, in a pita with a choice of salads. In Beersheva and some other locations, in the form of *ful medames*, a traditional Egyptian peasant dish of long-simmered beans with garlic, onion, tomatoes, and olive oil, spiced with cumin and coriander powders, are placed in a pita.

A good *ful medames* kiosk provides a *full* show. After cutting open a "mouth" in the pita, *ful* is ladled from the simmering pot and spread inside the pita. The customer is then asked whether they want *tahina* and an egg. The eggs have been cooking overnight, and are brown in color. The egg and *tahina* are then mashed with a circular motion onto one wall of the pocket bread. A salad is then added. Mixed Middle Eastern pickles too, and, if one is eating on the spot, a small saucer of olives. Like hummus, *ful* too can be placed on a plate and "wiped," if the kiosk has some tables and chairs outside.

Shawarma

Shawarma was and is a product of Israel's growing affluence. It is a contradictory dish in some ways. On the one hand, a large spindle of meat about 2″ long and 1″ wide rotating before an (electric) fire indicating affluence. On the other hand, the meat is more often than not turkey meat rather than lamb, and only a thin slab of mutton fat at the top of the spindle shows its origins and barely flavors the turkey, a commonly cheap food.

Ful Be'ersheva

Yield: Serves 4

1 onion, minced fine
2 cups dried broad beans, soaked for 6 hours, and the tough outer skin removed. To remove the skins, make a small cut in each soaked bean's edge, resoak, then pop the kernel out by squeezing the skin.
1 tsp ground cumin
1 tsp ground coriander seed, or 2 Tbsp fresh coriander leaf (cilantro)
1 medium ripe tomato, chopped
¼ cup + 1 Tbsp virgin olive oil
2–4 cloves garlic, crushed and minced
Salt and pepper to taste

To serve:
4 fresh pitot
4 *haminado* eggs (q.v.)
4 Tbsp prepared *tahina* sauce
A small vegetable salad (*salat yerakot*)

1. Fry the onions in plenty of oil in a heavy pot with a heavy lid, until golden brown.
2. Add the garlic and fry for 30 seconds, making sure the garlic does not burn.
3. Add the spices, stir for 30 seconds, then the tomatoes. Cook for 1 minute.
4. Add the beans, water to cover, and bring uncovered to a simmer.
5. Once the beans are smiling, season to taste (less is better than more, as the liquid will boil down). Add the remaining olive oil except for 1 Tbsp.
6. Close the pot and make sure the lid is well seated. Place pot on lowest flame and simmer for at least four hours, and preferably overnight. Do not open the lid: the flavor is better if the beans are allowed to mature slowly, and the flavors are well blended.
7. Once the beans are done, open the lid and check. If the liquid has evaporated and the result is dry, the beans are not soft, add some boiling water. Reseal and cook another 2 hours or less.
8. Mash the beans roughly (a potato masher works wonders). Season if necessary, and add 1 Tbsp olive oil, mixing it in well.

To serve:
1. Slit one side of each pita near one edge to make a pocket.
2. Place two or three Tbsp of the *ful* mixture (which should now be a rich reddish-brown) into each pita, and mash with the back of a spoon gently against one of the pita's inner sides.

> 3. Mash a *haminado* egg roughly into the beans.
> 4. Add some *tahina* sauce for those who want.
> 5. Add some salad to complete.
>
> Eat on its own, or with some pickles and olives.

Shawarma originated in Turkey, and was adapted to Israeli preferences. Served in a pita, like falafel, the meat sandwich may incorporate hummus, as well as the rest of the *salatim* and *pickles* that characterize a hummus or falafel sandwich. For most Israelis, *shawarma* is preferred to falafel, which is sometimes considered a dish attractive mainly to tourists.

Thin, wide, slices of meat are layered on top of one another with a large skewer pushed through the meats. A spitted *shawarma* may be up to 31" tall and 12" wide. The spit is placed vertically in a turnspit. A charcoal fire kept in a basket, these days, alas, replaced by gas burners, is placed alongside. As the spit turns, the outer layer of the meat spindle sears, and the juices and fat run down the spindle, moistening the meat. A long sharp knife is used to shave slivers of meat off the entire length of the spindle. As with all pita-filled foods, most *shawarma* places will offer a menu of *salatim* for the customer to choose and fill the pita with.

Sabich

A traditional breakfast for Iraqi Jews, notably on Saturday morning, was a *mezze* of foods prepared the previous day. The centerpiece of this breakfast was fried eggplant slices, *haminados* (long-boiled eggs), vegetable salads, *'amba*, and bread. In the 1960s, a born-in-Iraq entrepreneur from Ramat Gan, a satellite town of Tel Aviv, hungry for the old-time breakfast he grew up with, reinvented the dish in an Israeli guise. The new pita sandwich, named *sabich* (*sabah* means morning in Arabic) was at first a Ramat Gan specialty, but soon took off as a competitor to falafel and hummus. A *sabich*, traditionally served in a flat Iraqi *lafa* wrap, but now more and more often in a pita, consists of a mix of grilled or fried eggplant slices, Israeli salad, boiled egg slices, and then a choice of *salatim* with *'amba* and *tahina* sauces, pickles, and *zchug* or *'arissa*. It is now available throughout the country, with connoisseurs (or would be connoisseurs) arguing which is the best in the country.

Sabich Sandwich

1 large eggplant, sliced into ¼″ thick disks, salted and drained
Olive oil for frying
4 pitot, tops sliced to open the pocket
4 Tbsp prepared hummus (optional)
4 *haminados* (q.v.), peeled and sliced lengthwise into quarters
8 Tbsp Israeli salad (q.v.)
4 Tbsp prepared *tahina* (q.v.)
4 Tbsp *'amba* (q.v.) (Or less, to individual taste)
A bowl of olives for garnish
4 Tbsp finely minced parsley for garnish

1. Heat oil until hazy. Fry slices of eggplant a few at a time until soft, then turn over and fry other side until both sides are golden brown (eggplants "drink" oil so you may need to add some between batches). Remove, drain.
2. If using hummus, place 1 tbsp in each pita, then spread over one inner side of pocket with back of spoon.
3. Slide one quarter of the fried eggplant, spreading evenly over the side of the pita with the hummus.
4. Layer 4 *haminados* slices on top of the eggplant.
5. Layer salad on top of the *haminados*.
6. Raise pita upright, and lade in 1 Tbsp *tahina* along with as much *'amba* as desired, in any order.
7. Garnish mouth of sandwich with parsley.

Eat with olives on the side. Wash down with tea, coffee, or fruit juice.

Jerusalem Mixed Grill

Like *sabich* in Israel, and American chop suey, *meorav yerushalmi* was born of ingenuity and hungry customers. *Meorav yerushalmi* (Jerusalem mix) came about as a stall owner in Jerusalem's Mahane Yehuda market wondered what to do with chicken innards: heart, liver, spleen. As an experiment, he dry-fried bits and pieces on a griddle, flavored the mix with plenty of cardamom, cumin, and particularly turmeric, and served it in a pocket pita with the usual garnishing of salad, pickles, and relishes. A classic was born, which is now available throughout the country.

Meorav Yerushalmi (Jerusalem Mix)

Yield: Serves 4

2 chicken livers, cut into 1" pieces
4 chicken hearts, cut in half
4 chicken spleens
2 chicken breasts, cut into 1" cubes
1 Tbsp oil for dry frying
A spice mix of:
½ tsp ground cardamom
1 tsp cumin powder
1 tsp coriander powder
1 tsp turmeric powder
Salt and black pepper to taste
Eight thin slices of leek (optional)

1. Heat a skillet to medium hot and add the oil, spreading it to cover the skillet. Fry the meat pieces, liver first for 5 minutes, then the rest.
2. Once the meat is starting to cook, scatter the spice mix on the meat while continuously stirring. If desired, add slices of leek to cook with the meat.
3. Once the meat is cooked thoroughly, place in a pita pocket, and offer any of the following garnishes for people to help themselves:

    Vegetable salad (q.v.)

    Pickled lemons (q.v.)

    Fairly liquid *tahina* sauce

    'Amba (q.v.)

    Zchug (q.v.)

Serve with coffee, tea, or orange juice to drink. Have additional hot sauces available.

Risen Bread Sandwiches

Sandwiches are popular both as snacks and for school lunches (there are no catered school lunches in Israeli schools). The variety of sandwiches of course depends on the family or individual concerned, and there is no standard or normal loaf bread sandwich. Sandwich fillings range from charcuterie, through cheese to vegetables and spreads. Religious families will make a distinction between meat and milk-based sandwiches, secular families and non-Jews will not. By-and-large, the role of sandwiches has been usurped by the various filled pita. One exception is the popular Tunisian sandwich, which is made with a French baguette, and owes its existence to the pervasive French influence on Tunisian life. Tunisian immigrants brought this popular snack with them, and it is served at home as an easy hand meal, as well as at kiosks and cafés.

Sandwich Tunisai

There are no hard and fast rules for *sandwich Tunisai*, so long as it has tuna, *'arissa*, and some vegetable. Additional fillings are optional.

Yield: Serves 4

1 fresh long French loaf, or *batôn*
'Arissa to taste
1 cup canned tuna, or fresh fried tuna steaks, flaked and drained of oil
4 heaping Tbsp *salata mechoui* (see the next recipe) or Israeli vegetable salad of whatever is in season
2 boiled eggs, peeled and sliced into thin slices
4 slices pickled lemon (q.v.)
10 pitted olives, sliced thin

1. Slice the loaf horizontally and spread open.
2. Rub *'arissa* on the lower half.
3. Spread tuna evenly over the *'arissa*.
4. Follow with egg slices, then salad, sliced lemon, and pitted olive slices.
5. Place upper half of loaf on top, then with an extra-sharp knife cut sandwich into four.
6. Arrange each quarter on a plate together with additional lemon and olives on the side.

Salata Mechoui

A "proper" *sandwich Tunisai* is made with a salad of grilled vegetables, called *salata mechoui*. This can also be offered as a side dish, part of the ubiquitous *salatim*.

Yield: Serves 4

1 ripe large tomato
1 large sweet pepper, any color
1 small onion, peeled
2 whole garlic cloves, unpeeled
1 Tbsp virgin olive oil
Salt and black pepper
Pinch of coriander powder

1. Wash all vegetables and dry, then place in a bowl.
2. Add olive oil and shake the bowl to ensure all vegetables have been coated.
3. Place vegetables on a baking tray and under the grill. Make sure to turn the pepper as the skin chars. Turn other vegetables as necessary.
4. Remove all vegetables from grill once pepper is charred on all sides. Place peppers in bowl of cold water. Peel off whatever papery dry skin you can. Remove pepper cores and all loose seeds.
5. Peel garlic and mince.
6. Chop tomato, onion, and peppers roughly. Add garlic, salt and pepper to taste, coriander, and mix well.
7. Add to *sandwich Tunisai* or as side dish for fish or meat. Keeps well in refrigerator in a sealed jar for a few days.

Pitzuchim

Pitzuchim, eaten at home and on the street, are seeds that are cracked in the teeth. The most common are sunflower seeds, which come in several varieties: black and white striped, white, unsalted, salted, heavily salted, extra large, and so on. The individual seed is held pointy end forward between the front teeth and cracked gently, the internal seed extracted with the tongue, and the shell discarded. Experts can do the entire operation in their mouths without holding on to the seed with their fingers. Other seeds, the most popular being melon, pumpkin, and watermelon are also available. True aficionados buy from specialist shops that offer bins of freshly roasted seeds for all tastes. One-half- and 1-kilogram bags are sold in supermarkets or other stores. *Pitzuchim* are served at almost all social gatherings in the home. By extension, *pitzuchim* has come to mean any nut or seed that needs cracking and shelling, and can be offered as a snack.

Street Pastries

Many pastries are available for casual snacking, often sold by vendors carrying baskets or trays on their arms or heads. These pastries include both baked and fried goods, some savory, others sweet. They are often bought with a small twist of paper containing a condiment for scattering on the pastry or dipping pieces.

Ka'ak are the Israeli and Palestinian equivalent of bagels or Philadelphia pretzels, inasmuch as they are baked tire-shaped savory cakes with a semi-hard exterior. *Ka'ak* are topped with sesame seeds that are added before baking. Vendors, particularly in Jerusalem, will carry a tray or stick of *ka'ak* for the hungry. Accompanying the *ka'ak* will be a twist of paper filled with *za'atar*, a spice compound of hyssop, salt, and sesame, into which pieces of the *ka'ak* are dipped.

Bourekas are a popular party and snack food throughout Israel. There are few communities in which bourekas, some better some worse, are not made (or brought in) and sold. Bourekas in Israel come in several recognized varieties: onion-and-meat, spinach and white cheese, and cooked and fried mashed potatoes. Other fillings—mushrooms, chickpeas, eggplant—are also available. Commercial ones are almost universally square or oblong, made in large baking pans. They are often eaten with a glass of hot tea or cold yogurt drink. Another popular doughy street food is *sufganiyot*, notably in the weeks before and during the holiday of Hanukkah. Known in Germany as Berliners, and in the United States as jelly doughnuts, these fried dough goodies are sold at kiosks, groceries, and sometimes by vendors on the street. The normal filling is strawberry jelly, and the cakes are dipped into powdered sugar. In recent years, there have been improvements in the qualities of *sufganiyot*, and new flavors have been introduced. After the Hanukkah period, it is still possible to find these doughnuts, although their availability declines a great deal.

Jalabi, a street food originally of Indian origin, are popular throughout the country as a street food. A dough flavored with bright yellow turmeric is piped into hot oil, and then dipped into syrup, to make a crunchy chewy snack. *Jalabi* are particularly common from stalls at markets, although some confectioners make and sell them from shops. They are sticky, crisp on the outside, and have a deep orange color.

Fruit

Fruit are universally consumed by almost all Israelis. These might range from a whole fruit presented and eaten without fuss, to fruit such as pomegranates, which a conscientious housekeeper will empty and offer bowls of pomegranate seeds looking like bowls of shining rubies, to be eaten with a spoon. Fruit will be eaten at any time of the year, and given the variety of landforms and agricultural technology, fresh fruit are available the year-round. Many fruits have become commonplace and what were once seasonal fruit have now become year-round foodstuffs, including watermelons, citrus, and strawberries. Dried fruit are extremely popular and are eaten as is, as part of *pitzuchim* offered to guests, or in homemade and bought confectionary. Exotic dried fruit such as pineapple and cranberries can also be found.

Children's Fruit

As in most countries, there are fruit that have no or little commercial value, and yet are consumed in small or large quantities by opportunistic consumers: largely children, to the greater or lesser concern of their mothers. The consumption of children's fruit, which was relatively high until the end of the 1960s, has declined markedly as attractive commercial snacks and sweets have proliferated, and as urban areas encroach upon rural wastelands and wild areas.

Sycamore (*Ficus sycomorus*) trees, which develop a nutritious fig-like fruit, were once common, and had been planted in some major avenues in Tel Aviv. The fruit need to be opened manually by cutting the apex, but can ripen naturally. Children would climb the trees in search of these fruit, which were available year-round. Carob is another endemic tree that yields brown edible sweet pods at the end of summer. These too are picked largely by children, and often used for pretend travel rations. Another endemic tree is the large *domim* tree (*Ziziphus jujuba*), which gives out a large number of small fruit with thin floury flesh over a large seed. Since the fruit are also useful as slingshot ammunition, it's use is suppressed, when possible, by parents.

Commercial Children's Snacks

Children's' snacks, both sweet and savory, took off in the 1960s once the strictures on sugar were removed, and once there were options for food choice. From time to time, a manufacturer would come up with an innovation that became a cynosure, with appreciative rise in sales. As children grew into adulthood, many still enjoyed an occasional childhood favorite, and of course, sometimes encouraged their own children to enjoy these as well. In addition to the range of chocolate bars, both domestically made and imported, there are a number of local treats (some of which have become popular overseas) that were developed in Israel.

During the *tsena* period, the choice of children's snacks was extremely limited. The ubiquitous sunflower seeds were of course available, often sold in twists of newspaper from barrows. Hard sweets were sold by number of items, although the choice of flavors was limited (lemon and raspberry flavors, both artificial predominated). Savory snacks also included *beigale*: salt-crystal enhanced twiglets. Sweets were often dried fruit: in the early 1950s, it was not uncommon to see children wandering around with "necklaces" of dried figs, imported from Turkey, and fending off their friends begging using elaborate formalized childhood rituals.

Savory

Savory snacks have always been popular in Israel, perhaps because as they tend to be heavily salted, they induce thirst. Two commercial savory snacks intended for children of all ages have become a desired good, particularly for Israelis overseas. The two, *bisli* ("A bite for me") and *bamba* have reached the apex as a single noun "bislibamba" meaning a savory snack. The first is crunchy and dry, somewhat hard, and comes in several flavors including grill, salted, and chili. Bamba is made of puffed maize, very fragile and airy, and the original had a peanut flavor, although today there are several variants. Coated with a yellow vaguely grill-like flavor, it was copied from a European original. Both are popular *nishnushim* for adults, and few children's birthday parties would be found without large bowls of either or both offered to the participants.

Sweets

The range of sweet packaged snacks is of course as large as in most industrialized countries. Some of these such as chocolate bars replicate what can be found elsewhere. Others may be unique to Israel. A sweet treat that has achieved iconic status as a packaged commercial snack are layered wafers—*vaflot* (from "waffles" or "wafers")—that in Israeli parlance has mutated to *bafla*. *Krembo*, another Israeli twist on an import (from Germany), is also still available.

As a relatively cheap, and durable sweet snack, *baflot* are available commercially in Israel in the form of waffle sandwiches, in which thin flour-based wafers were alternated with an artificial "cream" flavored with vanilla, lemon, chocolate, and (more rarely) strawberry. These were also sold in packs at Army stores, and having a "Tempo (a locally manufactured fizzy lemonade drink, now extinct) and *bafla* (Israeli slang for the waffles deriving from a popular comedy act)" became a slang for a short break. *Baflot* are still available in most groceries (including army stores), but are now sold in much more elaborate forms and flavors. They are still favorite treats, and the small packs of six or twelve *bafla* are easily transportable in a pocket, and just as easily shared.

Argaliyot are filled cookies made somewhat like fat lozenges about 1.5″ long. They are filled with a variety of fillings, chocolate being the most common, and will be found in homes, offices, and soldier's snack packs. *Argaliyot* enjoyed a brief fashionable moment several decades ago, and have since settled down into a commonplace treat. *Krembo*, invoking the idea of cream, and based on a German original, are made of a biscuit piled with a fluff of stabilized egg white and sugar, the entire confection coated with chocolate. They are popular with school children, and almost any kiosk near a school will offer a variety. They come in several flavors including vanilla and chocolate.

Individual chocolate bars include *Pesek zman* ("Time Out"), a chocolate snack wafer with a malted syrup filling and covered with milk chocolate. This too was extremely fashionable and popular for a while, and is still commonly available.

Commercial snacks in Israel, as can be seen from the examples given here, often enjoy a period of fashionable demand, with advertising campaigns and public recognition that goes well beyond their intrinsic value. Israeli society is extremely fashion conscious, and fads tend to flow and peak for no discernible reason. Some commercial snacks but not others achieve, for a period at least, iconic status (of course, capitalized upon both by the producing corporation and, wherever possible, by the competition). As the fad dies away, the snack remains in Israeli's consciousness but is superseded by some other fad. Often enough, even when the food originates elsewhere, the Israeli public may be completely convinced that it is an Israeli innovation, which may well help explain the surge of popularity. Another element in the development of the fad may well be the small population size (which means fads easily run from one end of the country to the other) and the presence of cooperative systems, which encourage uniformity, such as the army, where the demand for small, light, energy-filled, and sweet snacks is high and relatively constant, and where fashion—ranging from styles for wearing a beret to pins and badges, combat gear, and of course snacks—percolate very quickly through crowds of teenagers anxious to be a part of "their" community.

CHAPTER NINE

Dining Out

During *tsena* (circa 1948–1970), dining out was a rarity for most Israelis. Men, in particular, might have spent time in a café, lingering over a cup of Turkish coffee and a glass of water, or playing backgammon or dominoes. The average family could not afford eating out except under special circumstances, and the choice was limited. With the post–Yom Kippur War (1973) affluence, dining out became the norm, and the offerings expanded appropriately, from European/American Jewish home cooking (which was new to many Israelis) through traditional "Oriental/Mizrachi" (i.e., restaurants serving Israeli Arab and generally Levantine dishes) to a growing range of exotica: sushi, Chinese, vegan, and South American grilled meat.

Other changes also occurred. Service at restaurants, which had been abysmal through the first days of the state, when waiters felt that service was an onerous burden rather than a job, improved drastically. Many restaurants rejected *kashrut* and so could invest more heavily in their food, ambience, and service. Most importantly, the Israeli public, to whom overseas holidays and trips were the norm rather than the exception, brought home expectations of foods and service they experienced in their overseas travels.

Most urban areas have a selection of restaurants, with the greatest variety to be found in metropolitan areas (Tel Aviv-Yaffo conurbation, Haifa and its satellites, and Jerusalem) and in tourist areas such as Akko and the Galilee. Further afield, the choices narrow to Mizrachi restaurants and cafés with occasional mavericks found in odd corners. Dining locations range from hole-in-the-wall establishments patronized mainly, but not only, by students and bohemians, to ultra-luxurious Michelin-starred restaurants (eleven at the last count).

For most Israelis, a restaurant meal is not something to make a fuss about, and the market is sufficiently diversified to fit every pocket and taste. Middle-class families will choose a pricey French-style restaurant or a seafood place for special occasions. Celebrity chefs abound, as do food blogs and restaurant criticism, so waves of fads in the food business come and go. Service may still be spotty, as the Israeli tendency for intimacy and *chevremaniyut* (roughly, fellowship, but meaning brusque assumptions of equality and intimacy) trumps decorum and serving formality. With the exception of old-school, established European-style restaurants, the waiters are not professionals: students, unemployed performers, and relatives of owners predominate.

More specialized gourmet restaurants are becoming available, notably in areas with heavy interior tourism traffic, such as the Western Galilee, which claims some eighty self-styled gourmet restaurants in a mainly rural area of about 15×20 miles (Yaakobi 2006). Gourmet restaurants, boutique wineries, and cheese manufacturers are a relatively new mass phenomenon and have taken off since the massive industrialization and technologization of the country in the past two decades.

Cafés

The coffeeshop tradition is shared by many of Israel's immigrants, and unsurprisingly, cafés of all sorts abound. They run the gamut from *fashionista* and artists' hangouts, to lowly neighborhood cafés that cater to an *amami* (popular/low-brow) clientele. Whether one wants to dawdle a few hours away (in the heat of the day or cool of the evening) or one merely wants a quick pick-me-up, one is never far from a café in Israel.

The range of food and drinks served at cafés varies as much as the clientele, the decor, and the ambience. Of course, all cafés serve coffee, ranging from Turkish coffee, which is thick and often sweet (and served traditionally with a glass of cold water or seltzer) through *kafé hafuch* (upside-down coffee, made with milk on the bottom and coffee on top) to whatever bean/roast/make is in fashion. Tea, usually served with lemon, sometimes Moroccan-style mint tea, but very rarely English tea with milk, is another staple. Most cafés also offer a range of bottled sweet drinks, ranging from juice to pops. Other drinks depend heavily on location and on the owner's particular skills, marketing, and other. Some cafés embellish their drink offerings with freshly squeezed juices, alcoholic and nonalcoholic drinks ranging from beer (of several kinds if the management is open to, or wants to encourage, a sophisticated clientele) to cocktails and shots of brandy, whiskey, or *'arak*, depending on the customer base.

Food at cafés varies to a much greater degree than drinks. Some cafés offer the barest minimum—buns, perhaps sandwiches, and the inevitable *sufganiyot* (filled doughnuts) in the weeks leading up to Hanukkah. Others offer a wide range of snacks, light meals, and even full dinners, cooked on the spot, and catering to specific tastes.

Geographically, the center of café culture is Tel Aviv, where thousands of cafés thrive. Some of them have devoted clientele going back generations. Others are part of a newly created franchise of chain operations, which to some degree emulate the business practices of the United States and Europe. The further one gets from the centers of Tel Aviv and Jerusalem, which also has a long list of popular cafés, the less one finds so-called sophisticated cafés catering to a globalized and trend-searching crowd, and the more the *amami*-style cafés take over. In smaller towns in the periphery, cafés tend to be local, catering to local taste, which means a standard menu of coffee, tea, sweet, and alcoholic drinks. Virtually every such café will have a backgammon set for customers' use, and many have interminable domino games going on at all hours. Most such cafés cater largely to men. Younger men will arrive, rest, and refresh themselves. Older men will use the café as a locus for a "parliament": an ongoing, never-ending discussion-cum-argument about everything in the world—politics, agriculture, local scandal and gossip, the quality of famous singing stars' bottoms, and again, politics. While they set the world to rights, the parliament members drink coffee or tea, chew sunflower seeds, eat some cakes or olives, and generally pass the time. Women are not discouraged from sitting at cafés (except perhaps in some Muslim and religious communities). But, with the exception

Shesh-Besh/Tabla and Coffee

Tabla (backgammon), better known in Israel as *shesh-besh* (six-five: a winning throw) is commonly played all over the Middle East as a social activity. Almost every *amami* café in Israel will have a backgammon set, and often dominos as well. This is a surprisingly important part of the role of the *café amami* in society. *Shesh-besh* is a social lubricant, allowing participants and kibitzers alike to engage in conversation and social exchange while appearing to be "doing something."

Someone who knows how to play *shesh-besh*—the rules, the strategies, the correct way to slap down counters so the board clacks, the proper use of the wrist in throwing the dice—becomes, ipso facto a member of the discussion and part of the social group. Playing *shesh-besh*, with the occasional orders of coffee or other drinks and chewing sunflower seeds, the conversation around the board allows people to be focused while still being free to speak, exchange opinions, and demonstrate social solidarity.

Jelly Khavushim/Dulce de Membrillo

Sephardim are the most frequent users of quinces, and this sweet is eaten with coffee and a glass of water. Few housekeepers still make it today since it is labor intensive, and membrillo is to be found in some groceries. *Amami* cafés that cater to Bulgarian, Greek, or other Balkan Sephardi customers usually offer this as a standard.

Yield: Serves 4

4 lb quinces, wiped of fuzz, peeled, cored, and inner stem removed. Reserve peelings and core, discarding only those pieces that are clearly damaged or fungal.
About 2 lb white sugar
¼ cup water
Juice of 1 lemon
Grated coconut (optional)

1. Cut fruit quarters into smaller pieces, then place in large, nonaluminum pot. Add peelings and cores, preferably in a muslin bag.
2. Add sugar, lemon juice, and ¼ cup water.
3. Cook covered over a low heat until color changes (this will depend on the variety of quince used) and the fruit is very soft. Add sugar if necessary as the fruit cooks to ensure it is as sweet as you like.
4. Remove from heat. Remove and discard peels and cores after squeezing out all moisture. Return juice of squeezing to pot.
5. Mash fruit thoroughly, first with a potato masher, then with a ricer. Discard all hard, woody grains if possible.
6. Place pulp in a baking tray to about 1.5" deep.
7. Place in a warm, not hot, oven (less than 150°F), and allow to dry (or place in an oven every time you have finished baking, keeping the membrillo in a warm, fly-free, well-ventilated spot to continue drying between oven sessions).
8. Once the pulp has dried completely after a few days (it might turn darker), cut into lozenges and keep in a dry place.
9. Roll in grated coconut if you wish to ensure the lozenges do not stick to one another.

Serve with coffee or tea and a glass of water for a snack.

of "sophisticated" cafés in famous middle- and upper-class locations, their stay at local cafés is functional: a rest from shopping or from a day's work. As in every culture, there are exceptions, with cafés that serve as well-known meet-and-greet locations for upper middle-class and upper-class "Ladies Who Lunch."

Cafés create and sustain a culture all their own, and they are important loci for social and cultural exchanges. To some degree, of course, each type of café (and many individual cafés) can be described as a social island (excluding the passing trade, who, in any case, are usually ignored by all except the staff) of people with some shared interest and a deep investment in social exchanges. However, since people are highly mobile and connected in Israel, patterns from one "island" café soon trickle into others.

This effect of communication islands nonetheless connected to other islands to make a communicative whole is particularly important in politics and economics. Opinions formed in the parliament of an obscure café in the northern town of Shlomi may well heterodyne with similar sentiments in the southern town of Yeruham, and become a social meme. Unsurprisingly, any starting politician who wants to keep their ear to the ground needs to find some way to tap into this vast and irregular network. To a degree, this is also true in economics: trends surge, or are dampened by the reactions to potential changes that café sitters become aware of through, among other channels, their in-café interactions.

Restaurants

With little disposable income, restaurants were, if not rare, barely holding their own in the first two decades of the State. With growing affluence, dining out at restaurants became possible. In the twenty-first century, dining out became a standard way of meeting friends, entertainment, and displaying wealth, power, and discernment.

Restaurants in Israel, crosscutting all the rather rough categories below, can be divided into two large and mutually exclusive groups: kosher restaurants and non-kosher ones. The growing proportion of non-kosher restaurants is evidence of the weakening grip of the Rabbinate as an economic institution, inasmuch as much of the Rabbinate's income derives from the fees they extract from restaurants for kosher certification. Non-kosher restaurants are of course free to plunder any cultural memes that they think will make money. Kosher restaurants, on the other hand, must often sacrifice quality for *kashrut* requirements. Thus, no cream- or butter-based sauces in Cordon Bleu cooking, and no authentic *misoshiru* in would-be Japanese restaurants. Nevertheless, one can find (semi-) authentic Chinese,

Indian, haute cuisine, hamburger, and other styles of cooking that are kosher to some degree of *kashrut*. This ranges from self-certification, through Chief Rabbinate certification, to the most severe *glatt kosher* certification by one of the rabbinical courts that do not recognize the authority of the Chief Rabbinate, believing them to be too permissive.

"Oriental" Restaurants (Mis'adot Mizrahiyot)

Still the most popular and common experience of eating out for most Israelis are Mizrachi ("oriental") restaurants serving Israeli Arab food. These can be found in various forms throughout the country, even in poorer and less well-developed towns. By-and-large, the experience is similar throughout the country, although in recent years, some Arab restaurants have become more sophisticated and discerning, serving Arab Israeli haute cuisine while at the same time attempting to revive and popularize homely dishes of wild herbs and simple home dishes.

Most of the benchmark "oriental" restaurants rely on the standards that Israelis—the Jewish majority and the Arab minority—have negotiated as "authentic" Arab dishes. This generally means a wide selection of *salatim* to start, a restricted list of meat dishes—*kabab* (grilled minced meat), *shashlik* (grilled meat pieces), *siniya* (minced meat cooked in *tahina*), steaks, grilled liver, chicken hearts—and finally a dessert, often baklava, and coffee. Restaurants close to the coast or in coastal towns also offer a range of fish, mainly baked or grilled *buri* and *farida* and others. The average Jewish Israeli accepts these dishes as the standard fare: this is what they ask for, and this is what they get. Some "oriental" restaurants have gone in one of two different directions. Famous restaurants in the Galilee offer a wider range of foods including a range of uncommon salads, stuffed vegetable and meat dishes, and so on. At the other end, some Galilee villagers have started offering traditional home cooking, and eschewing the standard grilled meat and chips.

Oriental restaurants, notably those run in or near Arab villages, have two marketing advantages. First, they have a reputation for quality food. For many Israelis, the best *hummus* (and other Levantine foods, such as *tahina*, salads, pickles, and so on) is that made and served by Arabs. Paradoxically (although not unusually in a worldwide scope), a minority establishes its worth and status by providing "authentic" and highly desirable foodstuffs to cater to the taste of the majority. Second, since most Mizrachi restaurants (and all those run by Israeli Arabs) do not seek a *kashrut* certificate, their expenses tend to be slightly lower, and they can

> ## Cauliflower in Tahina Sauce
>
> A well-loved Lebanese and Syrian dish, Jews from those countries often cook it as a side dish. Arab restaurants often offer it as part of *salatim*.
>
> *Yield:* Serves 4
>
> 1 half medium cauliflower head, cut into medium size florets
> 2 Tbsp virgin olive oil
> Salt and pepper to taste
> 1 cup *thin* prepared *tahina* sauce. As garlicky as you like, slightly more lemon than usual
>
> 1. Place florets in a deep bowl. Season with salt and pepper.
> 2. Sprinkle olive oil on florets and toss in bowl until well coated.
> 3. Place florets in a baking pan in a single layer.
> 4. Bake on relatively high heat (around 350°F) until florets start browning. Do not allow to burn. Approximately 5–20 minutes. Remove from oven.
> 5. Sprinkle ½ the *tahina* sauce on florets, mix in well. Sprinkle rest of *tahina* on top of florets.
> 6. Return to oven and grill on medium for 3–5 minutes until dish is well scented.
>
> *Serve as part of a* mezze/salatim.

freely open on Saturdays and Jewish holidays (Muslim holidays do not require work-free days as Christian and Jewish ones do), and, if run by Christians, might serve pork products. Notably, with the rise of fine dining in Israel as result of affluence, the restaurant business has served for many Arab Israelis as a route into affluence themselves, and even as channels into mainstream Israeli society.

Stekiyot

Many of the roadside grilled steak stands of the 1960s morphed into proper steakhouses as affluence became the norm. The foods served are taken largely from the repertoire of "oriental" restaurants, but the emphasis is largely on grilled meats, notably steaks grilled over charcoal or gas burners.

Squash Soup

This soup, which is easy to make, has both meat and dairy versions, allowing the cook flexibility even if *kashrut* is kept.

Yield: Serves 4

1 Tbsp olive oil or butter (if making a milky version)
1 large onion, peeled and chopped
3 cloves garlic, peeled and minced
About 1 lb flavorful squash of any sort, peeled if necessary and cut into chunks.
3 cups water or vegetable (milky version) or meat/chicken stock (meat version)
1 fresh chili (seeds and all for a spicier soup).
2 very ripe tomatoes, chopped.
2 medium carrots, peeled and chunked
Salt and pepper to taste
Handful of fresh, well-washed parsley, finely minced

1. Heat oil in pot, then stir fry onions and garlic until soft.
2. Add squash and water/stock. Bring to a boil, then lower heat to a simmer. Cover pot and simmer until squash are soft.
3. Add rest of vegetables and simmer until all vegetables are soft.
4. Using a wand mixer, or place in a blender, blend until texture is to your liking.
5. Adjust seasoning and add parsley.

Serve with fresh bread.

Steakhouses were the average Israeli's first introduction to large meat servings, and some steakhouses such as "Hapil" (The Elephant) became famous throughout wide areas, whatever the quality of their food. *Stekiyot* have declined in importance with growing food sophistication among the young, but can still be found at highway petrol stations and elsewhere.

Hummusiyot

A similar although reverse phenomenon is found in *hummusiyot*: restaurant-cafés specializing in hummus prepared in-house with all the trimmings. *Hummusiyot* have now become mainstream, and are found both in the cities and along major traffic arteries. They are intended for a quick plate of hummus, pickles, and fresh pita with a drink. As is often the case in Israel, competition for the top slot is fierce, at least according to aficionados. While stekiyot have morphed into more conventional restaurants, *hummusiyot* compete over the definition of good hummus and the proper way of serving the dish. A few establishments have become synonymous with quality hummus, making and serving a limited quantity of hummus, then closing for the day. Some of these are patronized by the good and the great, and have waiting lines for the enjoyment of a dish of hummus, fresh from the pot, adorned with fresh spices, herbs, and virgin olive oil, and served with pitot straight from the restaurant's oven.

Mis'adot Poalim

Since before the founding of the State of Israel, feeding the general populace has been an issue. One solution was the development, by the large Histadrut trade union, and other workers' organizations, of cheap, accessible cafeterias that could feed working people. Such cafeterias initially largely served Eastern European foods. Since these did not exactly suit the climate nor the economy, various modifications were made to ensure a reasonable diet. Local *leben*-type yogurt, salads, white cheese, eggs, chicken soup, chicken, and later turkey schnitzel with mashed potatoes became the staples. Desserts of fruit salad, jellies, and other simple desserts predominated. Such cafeterias were to be found in both urban and semi-urban settings. Few such cafeterias survive both because of changing tastes and because there were other cheap sources of food. Nevertheless, *mis'adot poalim* helped shape the Israeli food scene by serving as a transitional step between the foods of origin for those who emigrated from Europe and the new foods of Israel, which were in many ways distinctly different.

Ethnic Restaurants

In the early 1960s, a Chinese restaurant opened in Haifa to cheers from the dining public. By repute, the food was not particularly good, but, at least at first, the very Chinese-ness of the place, however inauthentic, drew a large crowd of diners. The intense relationship between Jewish diners and Chinese restaurateurs in the United States is well documented (Tuchman and Levine 1993). Something of the same phenomenon may have been brought about in Israel as well. Certainly, the growing number of post-Army young Israelis touring East Asia brought back a demand for nonstandard Israeli types of food.

> ### Pilpelim Hamutzim (Pickled Peppers)
>
> *Yield:* Serves 4
>
> 3 large sweet peppers, one green, one yellow, one red, or any other color combination
> 2 cloves garlic, peeled and minced fine
> Vinegar to cover (or equal amount fresh lemon juice)
> Virgin olive oil
> Salt and pepper to taste
> 1 finely minced chili pepper of choice (optional)
>
> 1. Under a hot grill, sear the three peppers, turning them so they blacken more or less evenly.
> 2. Meanwhile, mix all other ingredients in a bowl, the amount of olive oil depends on preference. Allow to sit for half an hour to blend properly.
> 3. Once peppers are fully seared, remove from grill and plunge into very cold water.
> 4. Remove as much of the now-papery charred skin as possible.
> 5. Gently pull out core with its attached seeds and discard.
> 6. Slice cooked and deskinned peppers lengthwise into ½" wide strips. Rinse to get rid of any seeds.
> 7. Place in a glass or steel (not aluminum) bowl and pour dressing over the pepper slices, tossing them lightly.
> 8. Allow to rest for 1 hour before consuming. Can be kept in refrigerator for several days.
>
> Eat as a salad or relish with any main dish.

No urban concentration in Israel is absent a foreign food establishment, whether Chinese, Indian, or other. In large conurbations such as Tel Aviv and Jerusalem, there is a widespread demand for "ethnic foods." U.S. food (which Israelis do not seem to consider "ethnic") and Chinese foods predominate. Thai, Japanese, Mexican, Spanish, and of course French, and many other types of dining alternatives are available in both kosher and non-kosher versions. Russian restaurants, which have an inbuilt audience of the hundreds of thousands of immigrants from Russia, are common both in and outside the conurbations.

Some of these ethnic restaurants make no or little concession to local tastes: Russian restaurants which cater to those of Russian origin attempt to adhere to strict standards of authenticity. Others are heavily modified: Chinese food in Israel, as in many other places outside China, is heavily adapted to local tastes and expectations. Globalization, and the intensity with which Israelis have embraced it, means that many restaurants, however they label themselves, introduce features that are trendy (i.e., globalized) into their dishes and what they offer. These changes may be minor (cute names for standard menu items) or serious acceptance of world trends (new coffee varieties).

Ethnic foods, including Chinese, tend to be pricier than others. However, even the simplest of ethnic restaurants, serving food that most Israelis are completely ignorant of, are well patronized. A low-priced Chinese restaurant in the heart of Tel Aviv illustrates both features. The restaurant focuses on *dim sum*, which few Israeli know about or understand. Nevertheless, people queue to get in. Very often, they require an explanation as to what is on offer (the owner speaks fluent Hebrew), and just as often they ask for something familiar: "Why didn't you just say *kreplach?*" exclaimed one diner after an explanation of wonton soup. (*Kreplach* are an Eastern European stuffed dough packet staple in chicken soup, which may well have descended historically from wonton.)

The palates of Israelis, under the influences of familiarity and foreign travel, have also become more sophisticated. When a well-known Israeli restaurateur, after a quick tour of East Asia, opened an "authentic" Chinese restaurant, wealthy and would-be sophisticated Israelis flocked to his establishment, notwithstanding the heavily adapted, inauthentic tastes of his dishes. While this phenomenon still exists, many Israelis today are far choosier, and with better background at sorting out the authentic from the would-be.

Seafood Restaurants

Like other restaurants, seafood restaurants, some of which have lengthy (by Israeli standards) histories, have been a feature of the foodscape for many decades. In this area, as in other realms of food, Arab restaurants took early primacy, with the cities of Jaffa (now part of Tel Aviv) and Akko (north of Haifa) offering freshly caught seafood dishes. The entire coast of Israel, from Nahariya in the north to Ashkelon in the south now boasts an array of seafood restaurants. These can be divided by two cross-cutting lines. As with all restaurants, some are kosher and some not. The non-kosher restaurants offer a range of nonfish seafoods—locally caught and imported crustaceans, shellfish, and even eel—while the kosher ones do not. A second dividing line that crosses the other is between those that serve "traditional" fish dishes (a fishy version of "oriental" restaurants, which include *salatim*, and grilled or baked seafood) and those based on foreign and more sophisticated cuisines, such as French-style sauces and methods, sushi, and so on. All four types are well patronized, and even sushi restaurants have been blossoming throughout the country. For a population that widely considered the consumption of raw fish to be disgusting, this is a remarkable cultural turnabout. In the 1970s, I was told by several Israeli acquaintances visiting Japan that the mere thought of eating raw fish or seafood, as *sashimi* or *sushi*, turned their stomachs.

Seafood is relatively expensive in Israel, as the number of prawns and shrimp have declined due to overfishing (the Israeli government and the fisheries industry are only now getting around to licensing and controlling the fisheries). Nevertheless, seafood restaurants are almost always full, and consuming fish and seafood are a mark of sophistication, and, of course, wealth. On weekends and holidays, these places are filled with Israelis looking for food sensations that their parents' generation would not have dreamed of, let alone afforded.

Yiddishkeit Restaurants

Yiddishkeit is a term that evoked nostalgia for the Yiddish-speaking, insular, slow-paced, oral world of Eastern European Jewry that was brought to an end by the Holocaust. A nostalgia for the old days remains in Israel among elderly former Europeans and some of their descendants. Eastern European foods predominated in Israeli official circles during the first few decades of the State, and the desire to at least taste (or re-taste) these "granny foods" is prevalent in the secular public, at least those of European derivation.

One sector of the populace has retained much of the trappings of *Yiddishkeit*: the ultra-orthodox. Largely, the ultra-orthodox keep to themselves, maintaining their own institutions including food suppliers who provide *glatt* (pure) kosher food and foodstuff. Most of this population is poor to very poor. In the past decades, they have become more and more affluent, as women (who are the major breadwinners) have embraced some opportunities in IT (e.g., computer programming, which can be done remotely at home or in women-only offices). As a result, the demand for (what for Americans more than for Israelis is) "Jewish food" has risen. *Yiddishkeit* restaurants can now be found even in Tel Aviv and Haifa (the major secular bastions of the country). They serve traditional Eastern European foods ranging from chopped liver, through *kishke* (sausage of chicken intestines), kugels, and tzimmes, and keep *glatt* kosher, often supervised by one of the ultra-orthodox rabbinical schools rather than the official Israel Rabbinate.

Yiddishkeit restaurants have, of course, been present in the orthodox sector of the population and in orthodox communities for decades, but they were hardly visible to the average more-or-less traditional or nonreligious Israeli. A new trend combines *yiddishkeit* with vegan or at least vegetarian foods, making *yiddishkeit* restaurants even more fashionable and slightly more trendy. As the Israeli Jewish populace becomes more right wing, religious, and nostalgic, it is possible that more such restaurants will become mainstream and enter the roster of easily available public eating establishments.

Fine Dining

Israel now boasts over ten Michelin-starred restaurants, a feature of societies and economies that are affluent and connected to global trends. Many Israelis have never eaten at a European-style dining establishment of this sort, but many others have, and the demand for fine European dining is on the rise.

Fine dining restaurants tend to be expensive, and they largely cater to a non-kosher crowd. Many have started taking advantage of the many local and field foods available, and pride themselves on "restoring" the demand for traditional herbs and vegetables. A side effect is the presence of fine dining establishments that cater to specific segments of the populace: vegetarian, vegan, orthodox. This adds to the contention that the Israeli public is becoming more sophisticated in its tastes, which correlates with greater disposable income for at least some of the population. This is linked heavily to the evolution in the past two decades of "Innovation Israel," a program driven by the rise in demand for IT products, new devices, and electronic components in virtually everything: something Israeli technology and economy pride themselves on. The employees and entrepreneurs who participate in this economy spend much time conferring with colleagues overseas, for shorter or longer times, and have come to expect fine dining as a norm.

Who Eats Out and When?

As in most countries, dining out frequency and type of restaurant are closely correlated to class and wealth. Very roughly, the population of Israel is divided into three groups when it comes to dining out. One fairly large group rarely dines out. Another smaller group dines out frequently

Marak Avocado (Avocado Soup)

Avocados cannot be cooked, as they become bitter and inedible. However, the flesh can be combined with cooked foods. This soup is a winter dish, when avocados in Israel are at their best.

Yield: Serves 4

One very ripe, unblemished avocado or two smaller Haas, cut in half, stone and skin discarded
4 cups homemade clear chicken stock, sieved to remove all chicken bones, meat, and vegetables. Meat and vegetables reserved if desired.
1 hot pepper of your choice
Juice of ½ lemon or lime, sieved
Leaves of 1 sprig of fresh coriander, well rinsed

1. With a table knife, cut from stem end around the stone back to the stem end, then four parallel cuts parallel to the fruit's equator from the surface of the flesh about ¼″ apart, as if slicing bread. Gently remove the half-moon shaped slices and reserve, drizzle with some of the lemon juice to keep the surface from darkening.
2. Scoop out the remaining pulp, and mash thoroughly with a fork.
3. Add a whole pepper pod to soup (cut into rounds if you want a spicier soup).
4. Heat the soup to a simmer.
5. Remove from heat, remove pepper pod and reserve, add avocado pulp and blend with a wand blender. The soup should be creamy.
6. Return to heat together with pepper, and warm, *making sure soup does not boil.*

To serve, divide soup between four bowls, and garnish with reserved avocado slices and coriander leaves. Drizzle with lemon juice to taste.

(probably more than 3 times weekly). The majority dines out occasionally, and under specific circumstances. If we include stopping at a café for a drink, a rest, and possibly a chat, the number of occasional "diners out" increases substantially. Moreover, in addition to class and culture, we need to keep gender in mind. While in sophisticated café-culture-orientated Tel Aviv, a woman sitting at a café is an unremarkable sight, the same is not true in a traditional rural community, or among orthodox Jews.

Women and Food

The dichotomy between the normative, legal concept of gender equality and the traditional and religious cultural perceptions of women's subordination to men is evident in the realm of food as well. Domestic cooking is largely viewed as the domain of women, and indeed many men—notably in the Muslim and Orthodox communities—never enter the kitchen and are, or claim to be, ignorant of cooking.

Women and men differ as consumers as well. On the average, men or couples predominate as consumers in restaurants, with the exception of cafés in the large conurbations where women alone or in groups may be customers. Middle-class women tend to be more adventurous in trying new and foreign foods, notably when those foods have purported health and/or beauty benefits. In the home, women often eat less meat than men, preferring vegetable dishes and consuming more of those than meat dishes. Whether this is a true preference or a feature of male-dominated society is difficult to tell.

Very generally, to start with gender, women from working class and even many from middle-class backgrounds are unlikely to dine out by themselves. If they do, it will be for a special event, usually with several other women in attendance. Women from all classes and backgrounds may eat at a restaurant together with their families. This normally occurs in special events (birthdays, for example) and an entire family will be present.

Working-class people with less disposable income are less likely to eat at restaurants. On the other hand, since for many Israelis, there is a cultural (and, indeed, political and economic) benefit, men will meet with their (male) friends at cafés to while away some time, drink, and occasionally, eat. Women with children or without, usually after some errand, might stop in a café (selecting it carefully so as not to be caught in a sexually charged atmosphere) but their stay will be limited and functional: having a rest and a drink.

Obviously, for the wealthy, attending, and more importantly, being seen at trendy, popular, and importantly, expansive and exclusive restaurants is a must. Those who can attend such places on a regular basis become regulars, and can call other "important" people by name, or at least recognize them by face: one channel for personal advancement in politics, the economy, and other fields. These are also the most likely to make reference (in their behavior or choice of dishes) to their exclusive and lavish experiences with the original dishes in their origin overseas (e.g., "This is not bad, but not as good as the duck I ate at *Le Bistro* in Paris"). The game of food posturing is not, of course, exclusive to Israeli society, and by participating in it, people affirm publicly their own self-importance and right to be part of the cultural, artistic, political, and economic elites.

The middle group, composed largely of middle-class people, chooses when and where to eat on the basis of a number of criteria. Value for money is probably a major consideration. Family (and most such people dine out as a family or couple) preferences play a major role. Food liking and dislikes play a role as well, as does *kashrut* for that section of the population that is more religious. Younger people from that set may travel long distances to eat at a place that has caught their fancy, whereas most family groups are likely to choose a place closer to home.

Finally, both white and blue-collar workers are likely to eat as individuals or together with colleagues, at some restaurant normally close to their place of work. Blue-collar workers are likely to eat at an oriental or ethnic restaurant they feel comfortable with. White-collar workers (and this depends on their rank in the workplace) will likely choose a place based on value for money (at the lower end), or on the display of seniority, wealth, power, and managerial credentials at the upper end of the work rank scale.

Further Reading

Tuchman, G., and H. Levine. 1993. "New York Jews and Chinese Food: The Social Construction of an Ethnic Pattern." *Journal of Contemporary Ethnography* 22 (3): 382–407.

Yaakobi, Gil. 2006. *Psifas Teamim Bagalil Hamaaravi (Mosaic of Flavors in the Western Galilee)*. Israel: MATI Galil Maaravi.

CHAPTER TEN

Food Issues and Dietary Concerns

A number of specific issues highlighted in this chapter either hovered in the background of earlier chapters, or warrant more focused attention.

Food Security and the Mediterranean

Famine has been a feature of life in the Levant ever since recorded history. Most modern nations make attempts to prepare for such eventuality, by stockpiling, price control, water allocation, and ensuring trade partners. Israel is no different. Although Israel has the *potential* to feed the entire population, modern food culture implies the need to source many different foods from many different countries. Many foods are also uneconomical to raise in Israel, such as beef. Thus, food security is very much a matter of the international as well as the local economy.

Notwithstanding government efforts, and a generous social security policy, some 20 percent of Israelis live below the poverty line due to a variety of factors and need food supplementation. This includes efforts to wean people away from relying strictly on carbohydrates. Much of the populace is not resistant to the idea of eating vegetables as part of their diet, so in a sense this is a battle half won. Nevertheless, price does constitute a problem for some households. The experience of the *tsena* period of rationing (1947–1965 in practice) means that the authorities are conscious of the food issue. Moreover, during the *tsena* period, the government and many nongovernmental organizations (NGOs) made efforts to teach the newcomers from many different countries how to utilize the new foodstuffs they were exposed to, to best effect. These efforts persist today in an attempt to limit dangers of malnutrition.

In Israel in particular, there is another dimension. Notwithstanding peace treaties with two of its neighbors (Egypt and Jordan), Israel is very much an island, economically and politically-speaking, and the peace agreements that are in existence are not as robust as they ought to be. Israel's only untrammeled access to the rest of the world is the Mediterranean Sea (the sea lanes to the southern port of Eilat via a long narrow gulf and the long Red Sea can be even more easily cut). Inasmuch as the country is at the extreme east of the sea, and both sea and air power can threaten its trade lanes, the possibility of a major disruption in food supplies is one the government takes seriously. This means that the Israeli public is well aware that current affluence, and the availability of foodstuffs, are fragile things. The country could no doubt supply sufficient calories and trace elements to its population even if cut off militarily or politically from the rest of the world, but everyone is aware that that would be difficult, and that food security for the average citizen is not a given thing.

Scientific Food and Agriculture

Israel's only access to food from the outside is via insecure sea routes: across the Eastern Mediterranean, or through the Red Sea and the Gulf of Aqaba. As result, the Israeli political, scientific, and agricultural establishment has placed great importance on the scientific development of means to improve crops, make harvest more reliable, and use water, which is a scarce resource, sparingly. Israeli tech, ranging through drip irrigation, biological insect control, and improved varieties of common vegetables and fruit, have become a feature of many agricultural systems outside Israel, after having been developed and demonstrated their utility within the country.

New varieties of agricultural products are an almost annual feature of agriculture in Israel. In the span of 3 years (2015–2017), new and improved varieties of dates, avocados, tomatoes, and other vegetables entered the market. Some of these are intended for export, others for local consumption. All are the result of the need to be marketable, but also as self-reliant as possible and a tight cooperation between agricultural science and farmers.

This latter point is crucial. Farmers in Israel are relatively well-educated. They have access to a well-organized agricultural support system, and they can enjoy the products of world-class agricultural research institutes. Most significantly, perhaps, is the fact that there is a relatively small gulf—culturally and socially—between the producers and the researchers. For various reasons—the small size and relative social homogeneity of the populace, a high ideological conciseness—both producers and researchers share a common concern for national survival (of course this does not override other considerations, but is part of the bundle of motivations that motivates them).

Technological innovation in the food realm also includes manufacturers of mass foods. While here the situation is much murkier, since economics, taste, and advertising have a more prominent role, scientific advances nevertheless permeate the industry, and innovations are generally supported and encouraged. The Israeli food industry does have the normal resistance to innovation as it does elsewhere, but for the past three decades, Israelis have generally welcomed innovation with open arms, which means that even traditional and traditionally made products—*tahina* manufacturing is an example—can benefit from newer practices in storage, packaging, and advertising, increasing both sales and quality.

Israelis have had to be innovative about their cooking for a simple reason: scarcity. Throughout most of the twentieth century, both before and after the establishment of the state in 1948, food was scarce. One common mantra was "*Nistader*," roughly meaning "We'll make do." Another reason was that unlike many immigrant-heavy countries, where immigrants arrived over decades and centuries, Israel was faced with the need to accommodate the different customs, fashions, and preferences of different food cultures in a very brief period of little more than a decade, under difficult economic conditions. Moreover, the limitations imposed by the belief system—the need to avoid non-kosher products or milk-and-meat combinations—made the innovations even more necessary. Some are presented below.

Sir Peleh

The population of Mandatory Palestine was a relatively poor one, in which the foods that European Jews were familiar with were almost unavailable. One of the greatest problems for Jewish housewives of the time was the absence of ovens and large stoves. While in Europe it was possible to cook and bake using wood or coal, neither of these resources was available. Cooking was done on one-flame kerosene burner called *ptiliya* (*Ptiliyot* plural, meaning "that which uses a wick"). In the 1930s, a company came up with a solution to the problem: the *sir peleh* ("wonder pot"). This was a development of the bundt pan found in European and American kitchens: a circular pot with a chimney-like cutout that allowed baking toroidal cakes in an oven. The innovation consisted of adding a perforated lid and a shallow iron cone that fitted between the pan and the flame. This arrangement allowed the *sir peleh* to function as a miniature oven. Virtually everyone who lived in Israel in the 1950s and 1960s has eaten something from a *sir peleh*, and although they are not as easily available today as they were in the past, some cooks still swear by them.

Meat Substitutes: Eggplant

Meat rationing during *tsena* meant that people attempted to innovate around the meat shortage, and a number of foods were developed and encouraged by the government of the time, to substitute for meat. Eggplants—cheap, easily available, and able to absorb other flavors—became the "go-to" vegetable for replacing meat.

One common innovation found in almost all Ashkenazi homes, as well as in many others, was false chopped liver. By hydrolyzing onions and spices together with eggplant flesh, a mass not too unlike finely mashed chopped liver emerged. This was popular at home as well as in *mis'adot poalim*, and is still consumed today in many homes. For those who prefer roughly chopped liver, there was, of course, no comparison, but if one preferred the smooth stuff, the eggplant ersatz variety provided a palliative.

Mimrach Tzimchi

The lack of meat during the *tsena* rationing period brought about a number of solutions to meat hunger, both domestic and commercial. A very successful commercial product is *mimrach tzimkhi* (vegetable spread) sold in small cans. The product is a paste of spices and vegetables in a vegetable fat matrix, tasting vaguely like liver spread (and thus labeled "liver taste"). It was and is cheap, and a staple for many school-age children on their sandwiches. Being nonmeat, it has the advantage of being *parve* (neither milk nor meat) and thus fitting to consume in either milk- or meat-meals for those who care about *kashrut*.

Pork Substitute: Turkey Shawarma and Turkey Ham

Jewish dietary law and the control of religiously orthodox parties in the parliament has meant that pork products are not sold in mainstream supermarkets. Nevertheless, the desire for well-smoked ham and related pork products exists whether one keeps kosher by choice or fiat. To satisfy this niche, meat processors have developed a mock ham that simulates real ham quite closely. Selling under the commercial name *Jambo*, which is a play on words between the Hebrew word for "lots of . . ." and the

Food Issues and Dietary Concerns

Vegetarian Sandwich Spread

An alternative to *mimrach tzimchi* is this vegetarian/nonvegetarian spread that can be made at home (or, in Israel, bought commercially).

Yield: 4 servings

8 slices *lechem achid* or sour rye bread or any sandwich bread
1 Tbsp finely cut carrot cubes, parboiled lightly
1 sour dill cucumber, minced fine
1 Tbsp finely minced radish
1 Tbsp finely minced olives, black or green
1 chili pepper (as hot as you like), cut open, seeds discarded, minced fine. Optional
4 Tbsp mayonnaise
1 tsp mustard (preferably hot mustard powder)
A few drops chili sauce (optional)
1 tsp lemon juice optional

1. Drain all vegetables and mix well.
2. Add mayonnaise 1 Tbsp at a time until vegetables hold together well.
3. Add mustard and blend well.
4. Add chili if using. Add lemon if desired.
5. Mix ingredients well.
6. Spread on one slice of bread and cover with other to make 4 sandwiches.

Serve with a cold drink.

Short and to the Point: Why Israelis Eat What and How They Do

The ecology. A varied, compact ecology has offered opportunities for the domestication of desirable plants such as wheat.

History. The trade routes of the ancient world and modern globalization have meant that the original ecology has been enriched by imports over the years and centuries. Many imports have become so "nativized" that their foreign origin is lost to most people: citrus fruit are a good example.

Religion. Jewish, and to a lesser extent Muslim religious proscriptions, determine what legitimate food is. There are factors in the Jewish majority's choice that affect non-Jews as well.

> *Immigration.* Many people still maintain the food traditions of the county they, or their parents or grandparents, immigrated from.
>
> *Modernization.* The agricultural sector is highly technologized. Selective breeding of plants and animals, and genetic engineering at various levels, have created new culinary opportunities for the average Israeli.
>
> *Globalization.* Israelis are being exposed to foreign cuisines and foodstuffs. The growing popularity of Israeli chefs overseas, who bring with them both the traditions of their homeland (varied and complex as they are) and the desire and skill in innovation and change, which characterizes much of Israeli society.

Spanish word for ham, *jamon,* it tries to appease the desire for a cheap, yet kosher pork-like light meal product.

Prawn-Shaped Surimi

Since Jewish dietary rules forbid the consumption of nonfish seafood, shrimp, which are considered a delicacy, cannot be eaten by observant Jews. The worldwide emergence from Japan of *surimi* fish paste was therefore greeted happily by observant Jewish Israelis. *Surimi* is made by finely mincing white fleshed fish, blending it with a starch, and expressing the resultant mass into a desired shape, then dyeing the result if necessary. *Surimi* has been made in Japan for centuries as an essential part of many Japanese dishes, and it comes in many shapes and colors, but the main interest in *surimi* outside Japan has been in the possibility of emulating expensive shrimp and crab meats with a cheaper substitute. In Israel, the demand for *surimi* derives from the religious stricture on consuming shellfish. One of the kibbutzim acquired a factory for the production of *surimi*, specifically molds for prawn-tail-shaped *surimi*. These are sold in many groceries as mock shrimp. Many observant Israelis, who have never tasted prawns or shrimp in their lives, are nevertheless convinced that the *surimi* reproductions are as good, perhaps better than the real thing.

Vegetarians without Trumpets

While Israelis make a great to-do about the consumption of meat, they are comfortable and indeed, happy, with what amounts to a largely vegetarian diet. The most commonly consumed foods by mass are of vegetable origin, even in those cases—parties, barbecues, eating out—when one would

Kharshaf Memulah (Stuffed Artichokes)

Yield: 4 servings

4 large *young* (the younger and fresher, the more tender) artichokes
2 Tbsp olive oil
1 onion, minced
2 cloves garlic, peeled and minced
1 tsp parsley, minced fine
2 tsp chives, minced fine
1 tsp lemon zest
1 Tbsp dill, minced fine
Juice of 1 lemon
1 cup cooked rice
Salt and freshly ground pepper

1. Using shears or a strong pair of scissors, cut off the tips of all leaves, then snip down the upper leaves to expose the choke. You want to dispose of the hard, inedible part of the leaves.
2. Trim off the artichoke stalks close to the bottom of the artichoke. Reserve the stalks.
3. With a teaspoon, part the leaves exposing the choke, and remove choke carefully, cleaning up the exposed heart. Place each finished artichoke in a bowl of cold water mixed with 1 Tbsp lemon juice.
4. Heat 1 Tbsp of the oil in a pot that will keep the artichokes upright. Place the artichokes upright in the pan and allow to cook briefly. Then carefully add water and ½ tsp salt, cover, and cook over low heat until softened, but not done.
5. Meantime, heat remaining oil in another pot.
6. Stir fry onions until golden.
7. Add garlic and stir fry for 1 minute.
8. Add herbs and lemon zest and fry, stirring constantly, for another 1 minute.
9. Add rice and mix thoroughly with previous ingredients. Ensure all rice is well coated with oil and flavorings. Remove from heat.
10. Stuff each artichoke with the rice mixture.
11. Peel the reserved stalks to expose the lighter colored pith, and cut off the stem end. If very long, cut in two.
12. Remove artichokes from their pot. Layer in the peeled stalks. Place artichokes on top of stalk layer. Pour in remaining lemon juice. Season, including exposed tops of artichokes. Add cold water to ¾ up the artichokes.

> 13. Cook, covered, over medium heat until artichokes are soft and leaves come away easily when pulled (5–10 minutes, depending on earlier cooking time and size of artichokes).
> 14. Remove from fire and allow to cool. Correct seasoning and sourness if necessary.
>
> *Serve cold before a major meal or as a light meal on its own, distributing the stems together with the buds.*

expect a heavier reliance on animal products. Raw vegetables in salads, cooked vegetables in stews, sauces and relishes, legumes in various forms such as hummus, and pickled vegetables are what make up most of the Israeli diet. This means that the switch to vegetarianism and a healthier diet is easy for most people, who may desire meat, but in practice are largely vegetarians even when they act the carnivore. The growing number of Israelis who are becoming conscious vegetarians sometimes try to ape European fashions, forgetting that their own cuisine is largely vegetarian, and that veggie-burgers, meat substitutes, soya meat, nut-burgers, and other innovations of the chattering classes of Europe and America are completely unnecessary in the Israeli diet, or for the average Israeli, who, unknowingly, is a vegetarian *malgré lui*.

Obesity

Israeli food, a variant of what is called the "Mediterranean Diet" has been relatively healthy. In fact, the Israeli diet has been rated the least unhealthy diet (fewer deaths from food-related metabolic diseases than any other) in the world, outbidding Italian, French, and other Mediterranean-diet countries. Plenty of fruit and vegetables, both raw and cooked, are good for the heart and have many longevity benefits.

Growing meat consumption, growing consumption of refined sugars, and the use of prepared foods means that while essentially healthy, Israelis are beginning to become less healthy in their food choices. Notably, this must be counterbalanced by the fact that efficient food distribution systems ensure that, on the whole, everyone has access to the minimum daily intake calories needed, and the structure of the diet more-or-less ensures that malnutrition is rare, and the result of cultural choice.

The problem is partially exacerbated by gender differences. Male dominance means that men are often less concerned about their health (worrying

Roast Mutton and Dried Fruit

Lamb is considered by many to be a tasteless mockery of true mature mutton, but is often substituted for the real deal. The dried fruit cut the fat of the dish to some degree. The dish is for celebrations or can be had at oriental/Moroccan restaurants.

Yield: 4 servings

2 lb leg of mutton, lamb ribs, or other bone-in mutton cut
2 Tbsp olive or argan oil
2 large onions, peeled and sliced
4 bulbs garlic
½ lb dried apricots
½ lb prunes, seeded
½ lb raisins (dried cranberries make a nice, if inauthentic, sour substitute)
1 cup dry red wine
½ tsp cinnamon powder
½ tsp grated nutmeg
2 allspice berries
1 bay leaf
1 red chili hot or very hot, shredded for greater heat
2 cups meat stock
Salt and black pepper to taste

1. Heat a large pan. Add 1 Tbsp oil and brown meat on all sides. Remove and place in baking pan.
2. Add remaining oil to the pan. Add onions and brown thoroughly, stirring all the time. When brown, add to surround meat in baking pan.
3. Cut off the stem end of the garlic bulbs, making sure about ⅛" of the top of each garlic is exposed. Place upright on side of meat.
4. Mix all dried fruit and wine together in a bowl and allow to soak for half an hour.
5. Add spices, bay leaf, and chili to dried fruit.
6. Pour wine and fruit around meat.
7. Season to taste, both meat and fruit.
8. Place in oven preheated to 360°F for half an hour. Open oven and pour 1 cup of stock over fruit.
9. Lower temperature to 310°F for at least 1 hour, then add rest of stock.

> 10. Check doneness. Meat should be cooked throughout and almost falling off the bone. If meat still uncooked, allow another half hour cooking and repeat until done. Adjust seasoning.
> 11. Remove garlic bulbs. Each clove should now be full of a flavorful paste, which can be squeezed out for spreading onto bread or rice.
>
> *Serve with fresh bread, rice of your choice,* chermoulah *(q.v.), pickled peppers (q.v.),* hummusim *in lemon (q.v.), and a fresh salad (q.v.). Place a bowl of* 'arissa *for diners to add heat.*

about one's health is nonmasculine), and less open to dieting. Many lead a sedentary lifestyle, which is barely touched upon by a once weekly basketball game with one's friends.

The Curse of Drink

In the first decades of the State of Israel, and even later, drunkenness, notably public drunkenness, were almost unknown. Populations of hard drinkers—people from India and Russia—who brought with them a culture of drinking to excess, modified their ways or kept them private. Drinking was acceptable as an after-meal pleasure, at important occasions, public and private, and in public on some holidays, such as Purim.

Two phenomena changed that. First, the mass immigration from the Soviet Union in the 1970s, where drinking to excess was an acceptable cultural behavior, brought with it a rise in public drunkenness and acceptability of this behavior. Second, affluence meant that many Israelis traveled and lived overseas in countries in which excessive drinking (by Israeli standards) was a norm, which they brought back with them. From the 1990s onward, Israeli official society recognized alcoholism as a problem, and measures were put in place to combat things such as drunk driving, which rose dramatically (even if not by U.S. or European standards). In the military, where military stores in the 1970s sold beer, brandy, and wine without comment, these were removed from the shelves.

By external standards, Israelis still drink little, on the whole. The problems brought about by alcohol are still under control, and truly unimpressive by the standards of hard-drinking societies in Europe and North America.

Apples Cooked in Wine

Yield: 4 servings

2 cups dry red wine
1 tsp seedless raisins
1 tsp minced dried apricots
1 tsp minced de-seeded dates
1 tsp minced mixed citrus peel
1 tsp lemon zest
1 tsp lemon juice
¼ tsp powdered cinnamon
¼ tsp grated nutmeg
2 Tbsp sugar
4 medium cooking apples, cored from stem side
About 1 cup dry red wine
1 strip of orange zest, about 2" long, peeled from orange just before use
½ tsp cornstarch

1. Soak all dried fruit in wine for 2 hours, then drain, reserving the liquid.
2. Meanwhile, using a corer or small teaspoon, enlarge the core cavity of each apple, being careful not to pierce the skin, leaving a ¼" wall inward of the peel.
3. Mix lemon zest and juice, cinnamon, and nutmeg.
4. Fill cavity of each apple with the fruit mixture.
5. Scatter half the sugar on top.
6. Add 1 cup wine, piece of zest, and the remaining sugar to the reserved wine from the dried fruit.
7. Place filled fruit in an oven-proof dish (or in a *sir peleh* if you have one).
8. Pour wine mixture over fruit, allowing the liquid to drain to bottom of dish.
9. Place in the oven and bring to 300°F (or place *sir peleh* on a medium flame).
10. When apples are soft (about 35 minutes, more if you prefer them softer), remove from dish and reserve. Pour liquid into a pan and keep hot. In the meantime, mix cornstarch with 1 tsp tap water and blend thoroughly to a liquid. Pour into hot wine and stir to mix well. Allow to cook over low heat for 2–3 minutes until liquid coats the back of a spoon.
11. Spoon wine sauce over each apple.

Serve with 1 Tbsp of yogurt or vanilla ice cream, either for dessert or as a snack.

Cultural Appropriation

Israeli food culture is largely derivative. In a bare century, an original cuisine based on nothing but local ecology, without borrowing from other cultures, is an impossibility. Thus, Israelis have happily adopted and adapted cuisines from neighbors, friends, and enemies, near and far, and made those foods and food practices their own. So far, so good. Food practices, by their very nature, are open to both borrowing and lending.

For Israelis, engaged in a century-long struggle with their neighbors in many dimensions, this does have a negative side. Much Israeli food owes its origins to foods that were originally Arab Palestinian. Throughout the *Yishuv* (prestate) period, when food was scarce and European food preferences were adapted to local conditions, many foods—falafel, hummus, and *tahina* are examples—made their way from local Arabs to the incomers. These foods, and many others that are now considered quintessentially Israeli, and still are, were known in the Levant for centuries. Israelis are unfortunately often loathe to admit that their treasured foods originate with a population they are engaged with as opponents and enemies. To a lesser degree, this is true of other Israeli foods as well. Foods soon become Israeli because Israelis consume them, often within the framework of the practices they are familiar with: in salads, with pita, as part of a particular style of eating and dining. The origin of the foods is fast forgotten, or may, at best, be acknowledged by little more than an adjectival, such as "American steak."

Mansaf

Bedouin Israelis—members of nomadic or semi-nomadic tribes, mainly found in the Negev with some in permanent villages in the Galilee—have a long tradition of hospitality going back to the days of Father Abraham. A *mansaf* is a traditional feast dish served to male guests (females, traditionally, may get to enjoy the broken meat remains).

Yield: Serves 4

A large metal or ceramic basin or tray sufficient to contain the *mansaf*
A side of mutton or lamb, about 1 lb per person, including bone. More if the pieces lack fat. Cut or chopped into pieces
Salt and pepper to taste
½ cup uncooked rice per person
1 tsp turmeric powder

½ cup or more, according to taste, *samna* (clarified butter/ghee; available at Middle Eastern and South Asian stores)
½ eggplant per person, cut into 1 cm thick slices
Oil for shallow frying
Freshly baked *lafa*, sufficient to cover the basin or tray with overlap
1 Tbsp purple sumac powder (available in Middle Eastern stores)

1. Arrange the meat in the bottom of a pot. Add cold water to barely cover. Bring to a boil, then simmer covered for half an hour until the meat is soft enough to pull easily from the bone, but not falling off by itself. Season to taste. Remove from heat, drain, reserving the juices/liquid.
    Alternatively, place seasoned meat in a single layer on a baking tray with ½–1 cup water and place, covered, into a 320°F oven for about 1–1.5 hours until the meat is soft enough to pull easily from the bone, but not falling off by itself.
    Correct seasoning. Drain, reserving the juices/liquid, and remove from heat to assemble the dish.
2. While the meat is cooking, cook the rice. Place washed rice in a lidded pot. Cover with cold water until water is the thickness of a finger above the rice level.
3. Add the turmeric and mix well.
4. Bring the rice to a boil, then immediately lower the flame to the lowest possible heat.
5. Close the pot with a well-fitted lid and allow to steam for 10 minutes.
6. Test the rice. If the water has not all been absorbed, allow to steam for another 5 minutes. If all water has evaporated but the rice is not soft and fluffy, add ½ cup or less *boiling* water, and allow to steam for another 5–10 minutes.
7. When rice is ready, stir in the *samna*.
8. While rice is cooking, prepare the eggplant. Salt eggplant slices and lay on an inclined board for 10 minutes or more to allow the bitter juice to extract. (This can be done well before cooking time. New eggplant varieties are less bitter and may not need this step.) Wipe slices well with a paper towel.
9. Heat about ½ cm oil in a pan. When moderately hot, place eggplant slices in the pan and fry, turning until golden brown on both sides. Eggplants absorb a great deal of oil, so you may need to add to the pan. Drain well-cooked eggplants on a paper towel, and season to taste.

Assembly
1. Layer the basin or tray with overlapping *lafa*.
2. Mound the rice on top of the *lafa* and arrange the eggplant slices on the periphery. Pour over additional *samna* if preferred.

> 3. Layer the meat on top of the rice. The liquid from the meat, if any, is served in small glasses as a side.
> 4. Place basin/tray on a floor cloth, with sitting cushions arranged around it, and a glass with the cooking liquid for each person.
>
> *Diners should help themselves from the side of the basin in front of them, using their right hand only (using one's left hand is considered coarse and unhygienic). The proper way is to scoop some rice and meat with the fingertips, squash them together into a small ball, and pop the ball into one's mouth. One can do this with a piece torn from a lafa as well. The host may honor a particular guest by selecting a particularly delectable portion of the meat, making a ball with the meat and some rice, and placing the food in the guest's mouth. Bones, at a Bedouin feast, should not be gnawed upon nor stripped completely: they will be passed on to the women to share in the dish in the women's quarters.*

Conclusion

"What is Israeli food?" Benjamin Bernard-Herman asks (see the Preface). The answer is that it is not only the foods that Israelis eat, but also the ways that they are sourced, prepared, served, and presented. Israelis do have a concept of what image they want to present of themselves through food. However, this is a scattered image, a compound of many quite different facets that not all see in the same way.

Like all food cultures, Israeli food culture is multifaceted. This is inevitable. Socioeconomic differences, differences in orientation and life-experience, differences between generations, all must be accepted as part of the mix. This is as true in the United States as in Israel, or even in an almost-homogenic food culture such as Japan.

Israeli food culture must be seen at two levels. The one level is the material, concrete level. Israelis eat certain foods because they are available, affordable, and have a history of acceptance. Each of these terms has historical, economic, climatic, and other roots. At another level, the ideological and symbolic one, Israeli food is characterized by three factors: one is a religious dimension, that includes differences between religions and within religious belief and practice within the population of the country called Israel. That determines what is eaten or not, served or not. A second dimension is the sheer heterogeneity of the Israeli population of nine million, each atom of that population simultaneously struggling to be part of the whole called Israel, and to defend its own uniqueness and diversity. A third is the influence of the three ecologies: social, natural, and technical. Socially, whether they like it or not, Israelis are physically separated by politics and barriers from the rest of the Levant, of which it is physically a part. Naturally, Israeli food culture needs to address issues of shortages and want of such basics as water and land, uncertain weather, and the intrusion of industry and population pressures. Technically, the environment is highly technological with scientific changes and advances informing and forming much of the food culture, ranging from what foodstuffs are available, to how they are prepared.

Overall, and as can be seen from the growing popularity of Israeli food overseas, Israeli food culture has successfully met its challenges, and been able to flourish despite adversity.

Glossary

'Arak
An anise-flavored alcoholic drink popular throughout the Middle East, including Israel.

'Arissa
A pepper sauce made of red chilies, salt, oil, and spices characteristic of Moroccan cooking and very common in Israel. Not to be confused with *harees*, a meat-and-grain dish common to the Arabian Peninsula and East Africa.

Baklava
A Middle Eastern confection, possibly of Turkish origin, made of layers of puff pastry filled with nuts and sometimes dried fruit, butter, and doused with sugar syrup. It is a common dessert in Israeli Middle Eastern-style restaurants.

Cuisine
A social practice in which food preparation is elaborated upon with the addition of uncommon (often imported) foods and where the presentation of food is complex and highly ritualized. In practice, emerges historically only in those societies that are wealthy and stratified with an elite having surplus resources.

Date honey
See Silan

Falafel
A common Middle Eastern food, now much associated with Israel, consisting of deep-fried balls of mashed chickpeas served in a pita with a choice of salads and condiments.

Gar'inim
Usually refers to sunflower seeds, but can mean watermelon, melon, or pumpkin seeds. One kind of *pitzuchim*.

Hametz
Any food that is even suspect of rising (i.e., fermenting) and is, therefore, forbidden for Passover. This includes all products of the five grains (the wheats and barleys) except those which, under very heavy supervision, are made into unleavened *matza* (flat bread). Ashkenazi ritual adds legumes and rice, and sometimes mustard to the list. Sephardi, Mizrachi, and other do not.

Hamutzim
The range of pickles that normally accompany light meals and particularly *pita* sandwiches. They range from European-style dill cucumbers through *torshi* to *'amba*.

Kashkaval
A firm yellow cheese of Turkish origin popular throughout the Balkans and Israel.

Kibbeh
Ground bulgur wheat mixed with meat. It is served in two forms in Israel. *Kibbeh naye* is of Lebanese and Syrian origin and is made of bulgur, cooked, then mixed with raw finely minced meat and spices. Otherwise, *kibbeh* are small spindle-shaped stuffed balls made of bulgur and stuffed with meat, vegetables, and/or nuts, then fried or cooked in boiling soup. These are considered a speciality in families of Kurdish origin.

Kibbutz(im)
A collective settlement common in Israel, based on the idea that all means of production are owned in common. Food is prepared and served in a common dining room. The kibbutz breakfast has become eponymous as the "Israeli breakfast" for most tourists.

Kugel
A baked noodle dish originating from Eastern Europe. The flavoring can be sweet or savory. Very popular as a filler for a light meal, or as an accompaniment to meat in a main meal.

Lafa
A thin, wide (12″ or more) flatbread popular for wraps.

Lechem achid
"Standard bread." A coarse bread of wheat with rye that was for decades under price control to ensure bread for all.

Moshav(im)
A less extreme form of collective settlement. Land is worked individually, but major items, ranging from tractors to marketing and purchasing, are organized in common.

Moshava(ot)
A noncooperative agricultural village.

Glossary

Parve
A food suitable to be eaten with meat or milk dishes since it contains neither.

Pashtida
A general name for a baked dish generally held together by eggs, somewhat like a heavy quiche. There are numerous vegetable *pashtidot* (plural) for every taste and preference.

Piñones
See Tsnobar

Pitzuchim
Seeds and nuts of various sorts that need to be cracked to nibble on: sunflower, squash, and watermelon seeds in a variety of styles are most common.

Ptilia
Kerosene-fueled vertical cooking burner that was the main cooking element in *tsena* times for many households.

Ptitim
Literally flakes. A commercial dough product of small grain-like pieces that was either crisped as a soup filler, or soft and used as a substitute for rice. Now often known by its marketing name overseas as "Israeli couscous."

Salatim
Literally salads, but specifically means the dishes served with or before a meal in the form of a *mezze*. The Israeli term for *mezze*.

Silan
A syrup processed from dates. Sometimes called "date honey."

Siniya
A popular dish of ground meat baked in *tahina* sauce.

Sir peleh
"Wonder pot." An Israeli invention from the 1930s, still popular today with those having no oven. Consists of a torus-shaped aluminum pot, a cover, and a small funnel-shaped metal base plate. Allows for baking cakes and breads without an oven, during *tsena*, on top of a *ptilia*.

Sumac
A purple grainy powder obtained by drying and grinding sumac berries (*Rhus coriaria*). It has a sour refreshing flavor and may be scattered fresh over grilled meat, fish, or vegetables. It is also a component in spice mixtures. *See also* Za'atar.

Symposion
(Greek. pl. Symposia) A dinner party for sociability and conversation. The Passover Seder is based on the formal structure of a *symposion*.

Ta'amiya

The Egyptian form of falafel made of a mix of *ful* (broad beans) and chickpeas. Popular in Jerusalem instead of falafel.

Tahina

Ground sesame paste. In its natural form, a tan, thick liquid. The oil often separates and lies on top of a thicker base. To make edible, *tahina* paste needs to be blended into a looser emulsion by the addition of water and lemon juice. Once the emulsion is smooth, it can be used as a component of many dishes ranging from *hummus* through *siniya* (q.v.).

Tsena

The period of rationing, roughly 1947–1970. Food such as meat, sugar, and fats were rationed and Israelis learned to make do with vegetable substitutes.

Tsnobar

Stone-pine (*Pinus pinea*) seeds. A hard shell encloses a waxy homogenous core with a delightful scent of fresh pines. Used to decorate a number of different foods. The finest come from the Golan Heights.

Wonder pot

See Sir peleh

Za'atar

A spice mix of hyssop leaves, sesame seeds, sumac powder, and salt for freshening and flavoring bread and other foods.

Selected Bibliography

References Cited

Ashkenazi, Michael, and Alex Weingrod. 1984. *Ethiopian Immigrants in Beersheva: An Anthropological Study of the Absorption Process*. Highland Park, IL: American Association for Ethiopian Jews.

Ashkenazi, Michael, and Jeanne Jacob. 1999. *The Essence of Japanese Cuisine: An Essay on Food and Culture*. London: Curzon Press.

Bernard-Herman, Benjamin. 2014. "'It's Not Israeli But You Eat It in Israel': Power and Difference in the Production of Israeli National Cuisine." Undergraduate thesis, Swarthmore College.

Bottéro, Jean. 1995. *Textes Culinaires Mésopotamiens*. University Park, PA: Eisenbrauns/Penn State University Press.

Khare, R. S. 1980. "Food as Nutrition and Culture: Notes Towards an Anthropological Methodology." *Social Science Information* 19(3): 519–42.

Tuchman, G., and H. Levine. 1993. "New York Jews and Chinese Food: The Social Construction of an Ethnic Pattern." *Journal of Contemporary Ethnography* 22 (3): 382–407.

Yaakobi, Gil. 2006. *Psifas Teamim Bagalil Hamaaravi (Mosaic of Flavors in the Western Galilee)*. Israel: MATI Galil Maaravi.

Other Relevant References

Aldo, Nahoum. 1971. *The Art of Israeli Cooking*. New York: Holt, Rinehart and Winston.

Altmann, Peter. 2011. *Festive Meals in Ancient Israel: Deuteronomy's Identity Politics in Their Ancient Near Eastern Context*. Berlin: Walter de Gruyter.

Ariel, Ari. 2012. "The Hummus Wars." *Gastronomica: The Journal of Food and Culture* 12 (1): 34–42.

Avieli, Nir. 2016. "The Hummus Wars Revisited: Israeli-Arab Food Politics and Gastromediation." *Gastronomica: The Journal of Critical Food Studies* 16 (3): 19–30.

Avieli, Nir, and Rafi Grosglik. 2013. "Food and Power in the Middle East and the Mediterranean: Practical Concerns, Theoretical Considerations." *Food, Culture & Society* 16 (2): 181–95.

Bernstein, Julia. 2012. "Symbolic Meaning of Pork Crossing National Borders in the Migration Process: From a National Collective Anti-Key Symbol to the Manifestation of Russian Jewish Identity in Israel." *HAGAR: Studies in Culture, Polity & Identities* 10 (2): 17–47.

Cohen, Amiram. 2012. "Israel Ranks Third in Consumption of Vegetables, Sweets." *Haaretz,* April 27.

Cooper, John. 1993. *Eat and Be Satisfied: A Social History of Jewish Food.* Northvale, NJ: Jason Aronson.

FAO. 2013. FAOStat Food Balance Sheets. Israel. http://www.fao.org/faostat/en/#data/FBS.

Fernandez-Armesto, Felipe. 2001. *Civilizations: Culture, Ambition, and the Transformation of Nature.* New York: The Free Press.

Fernandez-Armesto, Felipe. 2002. *A History of Food.* New York: The Free Press.

Ganor, Avi, and Ron Maiberg. 1990. *Taste of Israel.* Ontario: McClelland & Stewart.

Garine, Igor de. 2001. "Views About Food Prejudice and Stereotypes." *Social Science Information* 40 (3): 487–507.

Goldman, Rivka. 2006. *Mama Nazima's Jewish-Iraqi Cuisine: Low-Fat, Low-Cholesterol: Cuisine, History, Cultural References, and Survival Stories of the Jewish-Iraqi Diaspora.* New York: Hippocrene Books.

Goodman, Hanna. 2002. *Jewish Cooking Around the World: Gourmet and Holiday Recipes.* Skokie, IL: Varda Books.

Grosglik, Rafi, and Uri Ram. 2013. "Authentic, Speedy and Hybrid: Representations of Chinese Food and Cultural Globalization in Israel." *Food, Culture & Society* 16 (2): 223–43.

Gvion, Liora. 2006. "Cuisines of Poverty as Means of Empowerment: Arab Food in Israel." *Agriculture and Human Values* 23 (3): 299–312.

Gvion, Liora. 2009. "Narrating Modernity and Tradition: The Case of Palestinian Food in Israel." *Identities: Global Studies in Culture and Power* 16 (4): 391–413.

Gvion, Liora. 2011. "Cooking, Food, and Masculinity: Palestinian Men in Israeli Society." *Men and Masculinities* 14 (4): 408–29.

Gvion, Liora, David Wesley, and Elana Wesley. 2012. *Beyond Hummus and Falafel: Social and Political Aspects of Palestinian Food in Israel.* Berkeley and Los Angeles: University of California Press.

Heine, Peter. 2004. *Food Culture in the Near East, Middle East, and North Africa.* Westport, CT: Greenwood Press.

Hillel, David, Yaniv Belhassen, and Amir Shani. 2013. "What Makes a Gastronomic Destination Attractive? Evidence from the Israeli Negev." *Tourism Management* 36: 200–9.

Hinnawi, Miriam. 2008. *Bishul Arvi Glili.* [In Hebrew. Arab Cuisine from the heart of the Galillee]. Ben Shemen, Israel: Modan Publishing House.

Hirsch, Dafna. 2011. "'Hummus is Best When it is Fresh and Made by Arabs': The Gourmetization of Hummus in Israel and the Return of the Repressed Arab." *American Ethnologist* 38 (4): 617–30.

Hirsch, Dafna, and Ofra Tene. 2013. "Hummus: The Making of an Israeli Culinary Cult." *Journal of Consumer Culture* 13 (1): 25–45.

Khuri, Fuad I. 2002. *Being a Druze*. London: Druze Heritage Foundation.

Kirschenblatt-Gimblett, Barbara, and Doreen Fernandez. 2013. "Culture Ingested: On the Indigenization of Philippine Food." *Gastronomica—the Journal of Food and Culture* 3 (1): 58–71.

Klein, Shira. 2008. "An Army of Housewives: Women's Wartime Columns in Two Mainstream Israeli Newspapers." *Nashim: A Journal of Jewish Women's Studies & Gender Issues* 15: 88–107.

Latovitch, Yael. 2005. *A Taste of Teva: The Teva Global Cookbook*. Israel: Teva.

Macdonald, Nathan. 2008. *What Did the Ancient Israelites Eat?* Grand Rapids, MI: William B. Eerdmans Publishing.

Maoz, Darya. 2007. "Backpackers' Motivations the Role of Culture and Nationality." *Annals of Tourism Research* 34 (1): 122–40.

Marks, Gil. 2010. *Encyclopedia of Jewish Food*. Hoboken, NJ: Houghton Mifflin Harcourt.

Mendel, Yonatan, and Ronald Ranta. 2016. *From the Arab Other to the Israeli Self: Palestinian Culture in the Making of Israeli National Identity*. London: Routledge.

Packer, Sarit, and Itamar Srulovich. 2005. *Honey & Co.: Food from the Middle East*. Philadelphia, PA: Salt Yard Books.

Ranta, Ronald. 2015a. "Food and Nationalism: From Foie Gras to Hummus." *World Policy Journal* 32 (3): 33–40.

Ranta, Ronald. 2015b. "Re-Arabizing Israeli Food Culture." *Food, Culture & Society* 18 (4): 611–27.

Ranta, Ronald, and Yonatan Mendel. 2014. "Consuming Palestine: Palestine and Palestinians in Israeli Food Culture." *Ethnicities* 14 (3): 412–35.

Raviv, Yael. 2001. "The Hebrew Banana: Local Food and the Performance of Israeli National Identity." *Journal for the Study of Food and Society* 5 (1): 30–35.

Raviv, Yael. 2002. "National Identity on a Plate." *Palestine-Israel Journal of Politics, Economics, and Culture* 8 (4): 164.

Raviv, Yael. 2015. *Falafel Nation: Cuisine and the Making of National Identity in Israel*. Lincoln: University of Nebraska Press.

Reisinger, Yvette, and Carol Steiner. 2006. "Reconceptualising Interpretation: The Role of Tour Guides in Authentic Tourism." *Current Issues in Tourism* 9 (6): 481–98.

Remennick, Larissa. 2002. "Transnational Community in the Making: Russian-Jewish Immigrants of the 1990s in Israel." *Journal of Ethnic and Migration Studies* 28 (3): 515–30.

Remennick, Larissa. 2004. "Language Acquisition, Ethnicity and Social Integration Among Former Soviet Immigrants of the 1990s in Israel." *Ethnic and Racial Studies* 27 (3): 431–54.

Roden, Claudia. 1996. *The Book of Jewish Food: An Odyssey from Samarkand to New York*. New York: Knopf.
Ron, Amos S, and Dallen J. Timothy. 2013. "The Land of Milk and Honey: Biblical Foods, Heritage and Holy Land Tourism." *Journal of Heritage Tourism* 8 (2–3): 234–47.
Roth, Laurence. 2010. "Toward a Kashrut Nation in American Jewish Cookbooks, 1990–2000." *Shofar: An Interdisciplinary Journal of Jewish Studies* 28 (2): 65–91.
Rozin, Orit. 2006. "Food, Identity, and Nation-Building in Israel's Formative Years." *Israel Studies Review* 21 (1): 52–80.
Sela-Sheffy, Rakefet. 2004. "What Makes One an Israeli? Negotiating Identities in Everyday Representations of 'Israeliness'." *Nations and Nationalism* 10 (4): 479–97.
Sertbulut, Zeynep. 2012. "The Culinary State: On Politics of Representation and Identity in Israel." *HAGAR: Studies in Culture, Polity & Identities* 10 (2): 13–21.
Siporin, Steve. 1994. "From Kashrut to Cucina Ebraica: The Recasting of Italian Jewish Foodways." *Journal of American Folklore* 107: 268–81.
Smith, Anthony D. 1995. "Gastronomy or Geology? The Role of Nationalism in the Reconstruction of Nations." *Nations and Nationalism* 1: 3–23.
Tene, Ofra. 2015. "'The New Immigrant Must Not Only Learn, He Must Also Forget': The Making of Eretz Israeli Ashkenazi Cuisine." *Studies in Contemporary Jewry* 38, 46–64.
Tessler, Mark A. 1978. "The Identity of Religious Minorities in Non-Secular States: Jews in Tunisia and Morocco and Arabs in Israel." *Comparative Studies in Society and History* 20 (3): 359–73.
Timothy, Dallen J, and Amos S. Ron. 2013. "15 Heritage Cuisines, Regional Identity and Sustainable Tourism." In *Sustainable Culinary Systems: Local Foods, Innovation, and Tourism & Hospitality*, edited by Colin Michael Hall and Stefan Gössling, 275–283. London: Routledge.
Ungar, Carol. 2015. *Jewish Soul Food: Traditional Fare and What it Means*. Lebanon, NH: Brandeis University Press.
Zohary, Michael. 1982. *Plants of the Bible*. Cambridge, UK: Cambridge University Press.

In Hebrew

Hinnawi, B'shara. 2011. *Sefer Habishul Shel B'shara [B'shara's Cookbook]*. Israel: Hinnawi.
Kenan, Rachel. 2008. *Habishul Hamarokai Shel Ima [Mom's Moroccan Cooking]*. Kiryat Gat, Israel: Lakorim Publisher Ltd.
Peretz-Rubin, Pascale. 1997. *Mat'amey Iraq [Iraqi Delights]*. Tel Aviv, Israel: Modan Ltd.
Rabin, Elinoar, and Tali Friedmann. *Yerushalayim: Hasipur Hakulinari. [Jerusalem, the Culinary Story]*. Jerusalem: Kor'im/Morotor.
Rousso, Nira. 1995. *Kasher LePesach* [The Passover Gourmet]. Jerusalem: Modan Ltd.

Index

Abraham, 147; and hospitality, 1, 3, 196
Abu Ghosh (village), xviii
Achziv (village), 126
Acre. *See* Akko
Adafina, 130
Additives for plants, 17
Adeloyada, 145
Adulterating foods, 30
Advertising, 61, 170, 189
Adyghe, xxiii–xxiv
Afarsekim. See Peach
Afarsemonim. See Persimmon
Affluence, 12, 14, 112, 117, 160, 171, 175; and Arab-Israelis, 177; and drunkenness, 196; threats to, 188
Afikoman, 4
Agricultural-ritual year, 20
Agriculture, 16–17; diversification, xxviii, 19; and innovation, 2–3, 15, 188
Agroindustrial community, 19
Agronomists, 39
Agvaniya. See Tomato
Ahasuerus, 145–46
Akiva, Rabbi, 138
Akkad, 26, 31
Akko (city), xvii, xix, xxii, xxxiv, 55, 171, 181
Al haesh. See Grilling, over coals

Alcohol, 10, 24, 113, 118, 122–23, 172–73, 196
Alcoholism, 196
Aleppo, 29
Alexander (river), 16
Alexander the Great, 4
Aliya, 6–7, 159
Allspice, 131, 195
Almond, xvii, xviii, 28–29, 45, 106, 107, 110, 111, 146
Almond milk, 107, 140
Almowahids, 137
Amami, 172–74
'Amba, 67, 76, 80–81, 94, 160, 162–63, 164, 204
America, xxxix, 1, 11, 14, 15, 30, 39, 57, 109, 112, 171, 182, 198
Amnun, 59
Amos (prophet), 49
Anise, 123
Anona, 42
Antelope horns (cookies), 139
Anti-glycemic, 66
Anti-Jewish oppression, 6
Apple, xvi, 4, 28, 42, 45, 105, 107, 119, 122, 132, 140, 197
Apricot, 42, 105, 149, 195, 197
Aquifer, 16–17
Arab-Israelis/Israeli-Arabs, xxxix, 2, 63, 86

'*Arak* (liquor), 93, 123, 172
Arava, xvi, xviii, 21, 39, 62
Argaliyot, 109, 170
Argan oil, 136, 195
'*Arissa,* 14, 37, 83–84, 90, 131, 158, 160, 162, 165, 196
Aristocracy, and cuisine creation, 5
Aristocracy, Israeli political, 15
Army, 60, 61, 73, 93, 101, 111; and alcohol, 113; and coffee, 114; messes, xxxvi, 13, 14, 36, 38; and Seder, 134; stores/Shekem, 12, 113; and sweets, 111, 170
Artaxerxes/Ahasuerus, 145–46
Artichoke, 34, 193
Artik (ice cream stick), 112
Artisans/artisanal goods: bakeries, 50, 52, 109; breweries, 118; cheesemakers, xvi, 18, 62, 63; *gazoz,* 121; olive oil, 23; *tahina,* 79
Atayef, 148, 151, 154
Aubergine. *See* Eggplant
Authenticity, 179, 181
Automatization, 18
Automobiles, 125
Avatiach. See Watermelon
Avicenna, 67
Avocado, xvi, xvii, 42, 73, 184, 188
Avoidance, of particular foods, 134
Awasi, 18, 54

Baba ghanouj, 72
Bacalau, 57
Backgammon, 171, 173
Backpackers, 15, 179
Bacon, 55
Bafla, 169–70
Bagel, 70, 87, 167
Baguette, 50, 165
Baha'i, xix
Baharat, 65–66, 68, 79, 96, 98
Bakalah, 57

Baked goods, xxxi, 1, 21, 41, 48, 50, 68, 93, 96, 97, 100, 103, 108–10, 142, 153, 189
Bakeries, xxxiv, xxxviii, 42, 43, 50, 51, 52, 92, 103, 144, 146, 157, 167
Baklava, 29, 68, 176
Bamardan, 149, 151
Bamba, 169
Bamiah, 34–35, 38, 95
Banana, 42, 104, 107, 112
Bar (candy), 15, 30, 69, 110–11, 169–70
Bar Kochva, Shimon, 39, 138–39
Bar Yochai, Shimon, 138
Barbecue, xxxviii, 125–27, 192
Barley, xxx, 1, 2, 18, 20, 21, 32, 118, 132, 140, 148
Bar-mitzvah, 52, 154
Barrow (street vendor), 111, 159, 169
Bars (drinking location), xxxix
Batata. See Sweet potato
Bean, xxii, 18, 30, 31, 33, 35, 91, 130–32, 158, 160
Bedouin, xvii, xxii, xxxi, 1, 6, 18, 28, 54, 86, 104, 114, 198–200
Beef, xviii, xxx, 53; and *kashrut,* 54; and spices, 65, 79, 95, 101, 126–27, 130, 132, 134, 150, 187
Beekeepers, 28
Beer, 74, 93, 113, 117–18, 172, 196; making, 118
Beersheva (city), xvii, xviii, 69, 112, 160
Beetroot, 40, 72, 75, 80, 160
Beit Shean (city), xvi, 24, 35
Bene Israel, 105, 143
Bene Menashe, 105
Berliners, 167
Bet Alpha (kibbutz), 35
Bible, xix, xxvi, 1, 3, 20, 21, 24, 26, 31, 70, 145, 147, 158
Bira schora, 117–18
Birthday, 169, 185

Index

Biscuit, 170
Bisli, 169
Black/malt beer, 117–18
Blessing, xxxviii, 51, 111, 117, 140, 145, 154
Blood (religious prohibition against), xxvi, xxix
Bokhara, xx, 6, 130, 132
Bolognese sauce, 53
Bonfire, 39, 138–39
Bonito, 58
Borscht, 35
Boten. See Peanut; Pistachio
Bourekas, 52, 63
Boycott, 118
Boyos, 92
Brandy, 74, 93, 110, 122–23, 172, 196
Bread, xxvi, xxvii, xxxvi, 1, 3, 9, 13, 16, 20, 21, 24, 30, 38, 41, 50–52, 63, 68, 69, 71, 87, 93, 95, 101, 129, 142, 191
Breakfast, xxxiii, 13, 24, 28, 36, 38, 43, 62, 63, 64, 67, 71, 87–92, 119, 121, 162–63
Bream, 58
Brinza, 62, 136
Brit milah, 123, 154
British Mandate, 6–7, 8
Broadbeans. *See* Ful
Bronze Age, 32
Buckwheat, 11, 28
Buffet, 13, 72
Bukra ful mishmish, 42
Bulemas, 92
Bulgarian-style cheese, 87
Bulgur/burgul, 33–34, 35, 72, 93, 96, 98, 99–100
Buna coffee service, 114
Bundt pan, 189
Buri, 57–58
Burmese Jews, 9
Butter, 54, 65, 87, 88, 90, 91, 104, 109, 135, 137–38, 146, 175, 178, 199; peanut butter, 30

Buttermilk, 65, 122
Byzantine Empire, 4

Cabbage, 35, 72, 77, 89, 96, 133, 159, 160
Café, xxxvi, xxxviii, xxxix, 88, 89, 92, 109, 112, 116, 165, 184
Café culture, xxxvi, 109, 114, 123, 171, 172–75, 185
Cake, xxxi, 1, 11, 28, 29, 42, 48, 62, 65, 108, 109–10, 140, 146, 154, 157, 173, 189
Calamari, 55
Calendar, xxxiv, 125, 141, 145, 147
Camel, xvii, xxvi, xxviii, 18, 54; milk, 61
Camembert, 62
Canaan, 3, 28, 31, 32
Candied fruit, 44, 47, 112
Candies, 104, 110–11
Candy bars, 30, 69
Capers, 69
Caraway, 50
Carcioffia. See Artichoke
Cardamom, 28, 76, 106, 114, 115, 158, 163–64
Cardoon, 34
Care packages, 14, 15
Carmel (mountain), 63, 117, 143
Carnival, 69, 117, 145
Carob, 25, 168
Carp, xxx, 59
Carrot, 4, 32, 72, 75–76, 95, 99, 130–33, 178, 191
Casserole, 93, 100–101, 130–33, 154
Cassia, 66
Catalan, xx
Caterer, 154
Catfish (non-kosher fish), xxvi
Catholics, xix
Caucasus mountains, xix, xxiii, xxiv, 9, 11
Cauliflower, 35, 72, 80, 177
Caviar (from Kibbutz Dan), 59

Celebration, 141
Celeriac, 32, 35
Celery, 32, 59
Cereal (breakfast), 93
Cereals, 21
Chalcolithic (New Stone Age), xvii, xxx
Challah, xxxvi, 30, 50–51, 69, 129, 142
Charity (in Muslim feasts), xxix, 148
Charoset, 134
Cheese, xxiv–xxv, xxx, 13, 16, 18, 31, 41, 52, 61–64, 72, 87, 92, 100, 109, 135, 136, 140, 148, 152–53, 167, 172, 179; in Bible, 1, 3; spread, 9, 10
Cherkess/Adyghe, xxiii–xxiv
Chermoulah, 90, 196
Cherries, 43, 105
Chevremaniyut, 172
Chicken, xviii, xxx, 53, 55–56, 67, 95, 97–98, 101, 126–28, 130–32, 134, 148–49, 179
Chicken giblets, 56, 93, 98, 163–64, 176; *kishke*, 182
Chickpea. *See* Hummus
Children's fruit, 47, 49, 157, 168
Chilies, 11, 25, 36, 37–38, 40, 63, 77–78, 80–84, 89–90, 99, 122, 127, 130, 159–60, 169, 178, 180, 191, 195
Chinese food, xxvii, 15, 86, 171, 175, 179–80, 181
Chips, 38–39, 102, 176
Chives, 193
Chocolate, 110, 112, 116
Cholent, 130, 131–32. *See also* *Adafina*; *Hamin*
Chopped liver, 93
Christians, xvii, xviii, xix, xxii, xxiii, xxxiv, xxxvii, 5, 13, 18, 24, 24, 55, 93, 117, 154, 177
Christmas, xxxiii, xxxiv, 143, 145
Ciabatta, 50

Cilantro, 66, 130, 160, 161. *See also* Coriander
Cinnamon, xxiv, xxx, 33–34, 52, 66, 96, 105, 106, 109, 110, 131, 136, 142, 152, 195, 197
Circassian. *See* Adyghe
Circumcision, xxxv, 154
Citron, 44
Clarified butter (ghee), 54, 199
Clementine, 43, 45
Cloven hoof sign of kosher animal, xxvi
Cloves (spice), 142
Coca Cola, 113, 119, 121
Cochinese (Indian Jewish community), 105
Cocoa, 87, 91, 116
Coconut, 106, 107, 174
Cod, 57
Coffee, xxxi, xxxiii, xxxvii, 13, 15, 52, 68, 87, 93, 103, 109, 111, 113–15, 140, 142–43, 155, 163, 164, 171, 172–74, 176, 181; iced, 112
Coffeehouse. *See* Café
Collard greens, 35
Commensality, xxxv
Communal agriculture forms, 7, 19, 56
Communal meals, xxxvi, 28
Connoisseurs, 162
Conscription/conscripts, 13–14
Cookies, 67, 109, 115–16, 139, 151, 154, 170
Cooperative farming, 17, 18, 19
Cooperatives (commercial and social), 23, 170
Coptics, xxxiv
Cordon Bleu, 175
Coriander, 11, 33–34, 66, 77–78, 79, 80–81, 82, 83, 90, 96, 126–28, 131–33, 136, 142, 150, 160–61, 164, 166, 184; cilantro, 66, 130, 160, 161

Index

Corn (maize), 27
Cornstarch (corn flour), 102, 106, 107–8, 197
Corruption (venal), xxvii–xxviii
Cottage cheese, 87
Couscous, 20, 95
Cracker, 9, 10, 60, 68
Cranberries, 168, 195
Cream, xxxi, 61, 110, 111, 112, 170, 175. *See also* Ice cream; Sour cream
Cream cheese, 10, 31, 87
Croissant, 109
Croquettes, 72
Crusaders/Crusades, 5, 6, 38
Crustaceans, 181
Cucumber, xvii, xviii, 26, 34, 35–36, 38, 63, 64, 71, 75, 76, 77, 87, 89, 180; pickled, 69, 75–77, 191
Cumin, 4, 11, 32, 66, 67, 68, 71, 74, 79, 81, 82, 83, 90, 126–27, 130–33, 136, 149, 150, 158, 159, 160, 161, 164
Cupcakes, 1, 11, 109
Currants, 105
Cutlery, xxxvi

Dabo, 142
Dan (river), 59
Date, xvi, xxx, 1, 24–25, 28, 104, 109, 146–47, 151, 188, 197
Day of Atonement. *See* Yom Kippur
Daysat solet, 91
Dead Sea, xvi, xviii, 4, 16
Decorum, 172
Degania (kibbutz), 7, 24
Denis (fish), 58
Desalination, 16
Desayuno, 92
Desert truffle, xviii, 41
Deuteronomy (book of Bible), xix
Diabetes, 66, 119, 122, 157
Dibs. *See* Silan
Dill, 69, 75, 76–77, 133, 191, 193
Dim sum, 181

Dimlama sabzavod, 130–33
Dimona (town), 11, 66
Distilled alcoholic drinks, 67–68, 122–23
Dla'at, 39
Dobosh (cake), 109
Doctor Leck, 112
Dolmades, 96
Domim (jujube tree), 168
Dorade, 58
Doughnuts, 92, 109, 144–45, 167, 172
Dried fruit, 104–6, 145–47, 148, 168, 169, 195, 197
Drought, xvi; tolerant plants, 17
Drunkenness, 113, 118, 196; religious injunction to indulge in, 117
Druze, xvii, xix, xxiii, xxv, 1, 2, 13, 33–34, 63, 154; and *labaneh*, 62
Dugri, xxxi
Dumba, 132
Duvdevan. *See* Cherries
Dvash. *See* Honey

Eau-de-vie, 93
Eggplant, xxx, 9, 10, 13, 36–37, 51, 72, 92, 96, 126, 128, 132–33, 160, 162–63, 167, 190
Egozey melekh. *See* Walnut
Elections (and role in imposing *kashrut*), xxvii
Elijah, 143
Elite (chocolate company and road junction), 111
Esau, 31
Esther, 145–46
Ethiopia, 35, 37, 51, 141–43; coffee ritual, 114
Etrog, 44
Ewe (sheep) cheese, 62, 63, 87
Exodus, 25, 26, 129
Exogamous, 78
Ezov, 69

Fads in food preference, 172–73
Falafel, xv, xxxvi, xxxviii, 2, 12, 30, 31, 38, 40, 58, 72, 76, 77, 78, 81, 82, 102, 141, 158–60, 162, 198
Famine, 4, 25, 187; and locusts, xxvi
Farida, 58, 176
Fast-food, 15, 38, 51, 73, 157
Fasting, xx, xxi, xxxiv, xxxvii, 62, 79, 128, 140, 141, 147–48; Ramadan, 148–51
Fava beans, 31. *See also Ful*
Feasts and feasting, xxiv, xxix, 3, 4, 11, 28, 29, 54, 141, 147–48, 198–200
Feijoa, 45
Fennel, 36, 95, 99
Fenugreek, 32, 52, 66–67, 81–83, 142
Ferdinand and Isabella, 6
Fermented dates, 25
Fermented milk, 62, 64, 65, 121–22
Fermented pancakes, 28
Feta cheese, xxiv
Fideus (noodles), 32
Fig, 1, 21, 105, 112, 141, 169
Finoccio, 36, 99
Fish roe, 57, 58, 59
Fishing, 59–60; fish ponds, 59; overfishing, 182
Fistuk halabi. See Pistachio
Fistuk sha'ami. See Pistachio
Fizzy lemonade, 170. *See also Gazoz*
Flatbread, xxxii, 11, 20, 31, 50–52, 72. *See also Lafa;* Pita
Flax, 38
Foie gras, 57
Food preparation, 30
Foodies, xvii
Foodscape, 181
Franchise, 11, 15, 173
French fries, 38, 58, 102
French haute cuisine, xxxix, 182
French-style dining, 171, 180

Friday (Jewish observances), xxiii, 50–51, 92, 96, 97, 117, 129–30
Friday (Muslim observances), xxiv
Friday night, xxxii, xxiv, xxxv–xxxvi, 30, 59, 85, 95, 97, 100
Frikkeh, 20
Fruit salad, xvii, 43, 44, 45, 46, 47, 103, 104, 179
Fruit soup, 45, 49, 103, 105
Ful, 31, 91, 159–60, 161–62
Ful medames, 91, 160–62
Funeral: Jewish, 154; Muslim, 155

Garlic (in Jewish cooking), 26, 36
Gaza, xvii
Gazoz, 49, 118, 121, 122
Gefilte fish, 59, 60, 80, 134
Gelatin, 100
Gelatinous vegetables, 35, 38
Gemara, xix
Generosity (displays of in Israeli culture), xxvi
Genesis (book of Bible), xix, 1, 3, 20, 31, 54
Georgia (Caucasus), 11
Georgian-Israelis, 9, 11, 48
German-style coffeehouse, 109
German-style sauerkraut, 35, 159
Gezer. See Carrot
Ghee, 199
Giblets, 98
Gid hanasheh, 54
Gilt-head bream, 58
Ginger, 81, 122
Giudea (beans), 30
Glatt kosher, 176, 182
Glidah. See Ice cream
Glitterati, 109, 116
Globalization, 26, 55, 173, 181, 191–92
Goat, xvi, xvii, xxviii, 18, 54, 147, 148; hair tents, xx; milk, 61; milk cheese, 62, 63, 72
Gogoim, 42

Golan Heights, 6, 206
Government agencies: and Ethiopian Jews, 141; and recipes, 9
Grape, xvi, 1, 21, 46, 107, 122, 123
Grape leaves, 72, 92
Grapefruit, 43–44
Greek salad, 36, 72
Greek yogurt, 123
Greeks, 4, 39, 111, 143, 174
Green beans, 31, 35, 99
Gregorian calendar, 147
Grey mullet, 57, 58
Grill flavor, 169
Grilling, xxviii, xxxix, 10, 11–12, 14, 36, 38, 54, 66, 67, 72, 83, 97, 101, 159, 163–64, 166, 176, 177–78, 179–80; desert truffle, 41; fish, 57–58, 59, 182; over coals, xxxiv, 125–28
Groats, 28
Guava, 45
Guvetch, 36
Gvina levanah, 63

Hadith, 147
Haggadah, 4, 133–34
Hajj, 147
Halal, xxv, xxviii
Halamit, 41
Halva, 30
Ham, 55
Ham (mock), 57, 190–91
Hamburger, 11, 157, 176
Hametz, xxvi, xxxiv, xxxvii, 29, 133–35
Hamin, xxxiv, 30, 97, 129–33
Haminados, 92, 97–98, 161–62, 162–63
Hamutzim, 76–78, 180
Hanukkah, 39, 143–45, 167
Harees, 83
Harem, 145
Haroset, 4, 29, 42, 134

Harshaf. See Artichoke
Hashemite Kingdom, 6
Hasmonean kingdom, 4
Hassidic, 86
Hatzil. See Eggplant
Hazelnut, 29
Hebraicized words, xxxiii, 101
Hel. See Cardamom
Hellenistic kingdoms/culture influence on Seder, 4
Herring, 87
Hibiscus tea, 151
Hilbeh. See Fenugreek
Histadrut trade union, 179
Holocaust, 7, 182
Holon (city), xxv
Honey, xxiv, 2, 25, 28, 42, 52, 69, 91, 104, 105, 110, 122, 134, 135, 137–38, 140, 142–43, 147, 154
Horseradish, 80, 82
Hospitality, xxiv, 114, 115, 155, 198
Hummus, xxxvi, 1–2, 13, 14, 24, 30, 31, 33, 71, 72, 76, 87, 91, 92, 128, 158, 162–63, 179, 194; ethnic dimension, 176, 198; spicing, 66, 68, 69
Hummusim, 74, 196
Hummusiyah/hummusiyot, 31, 178–79
Hungary, xvii, 68, 168
Hybridizing, 43
Hydrolyzing, 190
Hyssop, 69

Iberian Peninsula, 6, 111
Ice cream, xxxiii, 15, 46, 62, 103, 104, 111–12, 113, 197; sundaes, 15
Iceboxes, 126
'Id al 'Adha, xxxiv, 147, 148, 149
'Id al Fitr, xxxiv, 148, 151–52
Immigrants, xv, 1, 12, 14, 35; adapting to new foods, 65; Arab and Jewish, 7–9, 10, 11, 14; from USSR, 9–11; and hot chillies, 37;

Immigrants (*cont.*)
  Middle Eastern, 11; and pork, 55; postwar refugees, 9; providing major culinary influences, 10–11; religious and secular, 6; Yemenite and German, 77
Imports, 4, 5, 8, 18, 20, 28, 29, 30, 42, 44, 53, 55, 57, 58, 110, 111, 113, 118, 122, 123, 169, 181
Independence Day (*Yom Ha'atzmaut*), xxxiv, 125–28
India, xx, 3, 9, 15, 61, 66, 80, 105, 122, 143
Indian food, xxxix, 11, 14, 36, 37, 66, 67, 80, 83, 106, 109, 167, 176, 180, 196
Industrialization, 172
Injirah, 28, 35, 51
Inquisition, 26, 36
Intermarriage between Jewish communities, 77–78, 86
Intestines (chicken), 182
Iran, 29, 47
Iraq, 7–8, 24, 92, 105, 143
Iraqi food, 1, 2, 5, 20–21, 38, 51, 76, 80, 92, 97, 99, 143, 160, 162; breads, 20, 51
Iron Age, 21–22, 118
Irrigation, xvii, 17, 19, 188
Isaac (son of Abraham), 137
Ishmael (son of Abraham), 147
Islam, xix, xxiii, xxviii, 5, 117, 155
Israeli-Arabs/Arab-Israelis, xxxix, 2, 63, 86
Italians, xx, 11, 15, 34, 36, 44
Itriya. See Noodle

Jacob (son of Isaac), 3, 31–32
Jacob's sheep, 54
Jaffa (city), 6, 7, 43, 55, 112, 171
Jaffa Sweetie, 43, 44
Jahnoon, 88
Jain, xix
Jalabi, 67, 109, 167

Jam, xxiv, 48, 87, 116, 135
Jambo, 57, 191
Jamon, 192
Jerusalem, xvi, xviii, 2, 5, 6, 18, 21, 24, 29, 38, 41, 67, 69, 70, 100, 119–20, 126, 134, 137, 159, 160, 163–64, 167, 171, 173, 180
Jerusalem mixed grill (*meorav yerushalmi*), 81, 163–64
Jesus, 24
Jezreel valley, xvi, 19
Jibneh, 63
Jordan (river and valley), xvi, 16, 24, 28, 42, 59
Jubilee, xxvi
Judea, xvii, 3, 25, 39, 69, 138
Jujube, 45

Ka'ak, 30, 69, 70, 167
Kabab, 57, 126–28, 176
Kabbalah, 139
Kadayef, 152
Kafé hafuch, 114
Kamun. See Cumin
Karkade, 151
Karpas, 69
Kartiv, 112
Kartofelim. See Potato
Kasha, 11, 28
Kasher. See Kosher
Kashkaval, 87
Kaved katzuz, 93
Kerosene burner, 114, 159, 189
Ketchup, 10, 40, 127
Kfar Kama, xxiii–xxiv
Khaluzh, xxiv
Khardal. See Mustard
Kharshaf. See Artichoke
Khauran, 6
Khavushim. See Quince
Khimtza, 30
Khreime, 59, 134
Khren. See Horseradish
Khubeza, 41

Index

Kibbeh, 72, 99
Kibbeh nayeh, 99
Kibbutz, xvi, xvii, xviii, xxxv, xxxvi, xxxix, 7, 12, 13, 19, 24, 35, 46, 47, 56, 59; breakfast, 87; and fish farming, 62, 66, 93, 128, 134, 192; and pork, 55
Kinneret, Lake (Sea of Galilee), 59
Kinras. See Artichoke
Kiosk, 11, 80, 82, 114, 119, 121, 157, 159, 160, 165, 167, 170
Kippa (skullcap), xxi
Kishke, 182
Kishon River, 16
Kishuim. See Zucchini
Kiwi fruit, 46
Kmehin, xviii, 41
Knesset, xxvii, xxviii, 190
Kohlrabi, 76, 87
Koran, 147–48
Kosher, xx, xxi, xxv, xxvii, xxx, 11, 15, 28, 54, 56, 94, 117, 134, 175, 176, 180, 182, 190, 192
Kosher certificate, 55
Krembo, 169–70
Kreplach, 181
Krisha, 38
Kruv. See Cabbage
Kruvit. See Cauliflower
Kshatriyah, 105
Kugel, 52, 53, 93, 100–101
Kumquat, 43, 44
Kurdish Jews, 99, 143
Kurkum. See Turmeric
Kusbara. See Coriander
Kvaker, 91
Kvass, 118

Labaneh, 1, 62, 63, 64, 72, 152
Ladino, 100
Lafa, 20, 51, 54, 64, 162, 199–200
Lag Ba'omer, 39, 138–39
Lager, 118
Lahouh, 51–52

Lake Huleh, 28
Lakerda, 58
Lakhsha, 52
Lakhshman soup, 53
Lamb, 65, 69, 79, 97, 130–31, 150, 160, 195, 198–99
Lambic beer, 118
Latin, 52
Latin America, 73
Latke, 39, 65, 144
Latvia, 80
Lavash, 51
League of Nations, 6, 7
Leavening, xxvi–xxvii, xxxiv–vii, 20, 29, 134
Lebanese food, xv, 1, 2, 80, 99, 117, 123
Lebanon, xxiii, 1, 6, 7, 8, 99, 123
Leben, 64–65, 71, 179
Lebeniyah, 64, 121–23
Lechem achid, 50, 191
Leek, 38
Lefet. See Turnip
Legume, 26, 30–34, 194
Lekach honey cake, 28, 110
Lemon, 25, 37, 43, 44, 48, 58, 67, 69, 72, 73, 74, 76, 78, 79, 83, 99, 102, 104, 107, 113, 115, 121–22, 126–28, 149, 150–51, 152–53, 158, 172, 174, 177, 180, 184, 191, 193, 196, 197
Lemon flavor, 112, 169, 170
Lemon, pickled, 77–78, 164, 165
Lemonade, 43, 44, 118, 119, 121–22, 170
Lent, 145
Lentil, 3, 31–34
Lettuce, 76
Leviticus (book of Bible), xxvi
Levivot. See Latke
Libya, 5, 6, 8, 9, 86
Licorice, 69, 119–20
Licorice-flavored drink, 119
Liquor, 113, 122–23

Litchi. *See* Lychee
Liturgical communities, xx, xxii, xxxiii, 134
Liturgy, 134
Liver, 10, 36, 54, 56, 93–94, 163–64, 176, 182, 190
Locust (insect), xxvi
Locust tree. *See* Carob
Lokshen, 53–54, 100
Lokshim (salary slip), 53
Lollies (ice cream sticks), 112
Longevity, 67, 194
Loof (leek), 38
Loof (military meatloaf), 14, 101
Loquat, 49
Lunar-based calendar, 125, 148
Lungs, 54
Luxe, 112
Lychee, xvi, xvii, 46

Ma'agan Michael (kibbutz), 59
Ma'amoul, 109, 115, 116, 151, 154
Macaroni, 53
Mackerel, 58
Maftir, 140
Maghreb, 54
Mahane Yehuda (market), 163
Mahleb, 68
Maimonides, 137
Maize, 27, 36, 169
Majadarah, 33–34, 93
Makluba, xxv
Malabi, 106–8
Malawach, 1, 82, 88–89
Male-dominated society, 185
Maleeda, 106, 143
Maleness, 38, 47
Mallow, 41
Malnutrition, 187, 194
Malt beer, 117–18
Mamaliga, 27
Mandarin orange, 43, 44, 45
Mangal, xxxiv, 126–28
Mango, 46, 47, 67, 76, 80, 81, 160

Manliness, 38, 47
Manners, 63
Mansaf, 28, 54, 198–200
Marak adom (red lentil soup) and Jacob and Esau, 32
Marak perot, 45, 49, 103, 105
Margarine, 87
Markets (traditional), xviii, xxii, xxiii, xxviii, 17, 18, 19, 24, 29, 35, 41, 42, 55, 56, 63, 109, 116, 120, 121, 151, 163, 167
Maror, 134. *See also* Horseradish
Marrow, 130
Marshmallows, 146
Marzipan, 29
Masada, 24
Mastic, 49, 111, 112
Matboucha, 72–74
Matza, xxvii, 10, 65, 102, 134, 135
Matzabrei/matziya, 65, 135–36
Maultasche, 146
Mayonnaise, 36, 38, 59, 72, 191
Mecca, xviii, xxix
Melafefonim. See Cucumber
Melkite Catholics, xix
Melon, xvii, 26, 46, 47; seeds, 166
Membrillo, 174
Memulaim, 72, 95–97, 193
Menarche, 154
Mentha (sp.), 68
Meorav yerushalmi, 81, 163–64
Merguez, 90, 131
Mesopotamia, 3, 31
Mess-hall (Army), 12, 36, 38, 73, 101, 111
Messiah, 6
Messianic, 6, 159
Mexican restaurants, 180
Mexico, 48, 56
Mezzalune, 94
Mezze, xxxvi, xxxix, 24, 40, 63, 72–74, 76, 81, 93, 99, 158, 162, 177. *See also* Salads
Michelin-starred restaurants, 171, 183

Index

Military, xxvii, 12, 13–14, 36, 60; Arab, 7; and avocados, 73; stores, 116, 141, 196
Millet, 28
Mimouna, xxxviii, 15, 136–37, 141, 143
Mimrach tzimkhi, 190
Mint, 46, 68, 72, 89, 116, 122, 123, 149–50, 172
Mis'adot poalim, 179, 190
Mishloakh manot, 146
Mishmish. See Apricot
Mishnah, xix
Misoshiru, 175
Mitzpeh Ramon (city), 47
Mitzvot, xxi
Mixed grill, 163–64
Modernization, 192
Mohel, 154
Mohn, 146
Molokhiya, xxv, 38
Moorish, 130
Mordechai, 117, 145
Moroccans, 9, 14, 15, 39, 44, 54, 59, 66, 68, 72–73, 83–84, 89–90, 116, 117, 136–38, 139, 143, 160, 195–96; pepper sauce, 37
Mortadel, 72
Moshav, xvi, xvii, xxviii, xxxix, 7, 12, 19, 56, 77
Moshava, 18
Moufleta, 137–38
Mourning, 155
Mt. Grizim, xxv
Mt. Hermon range, 59
Mt. Meiron, 138
Muhammad, xxxvii, 147, 148
Muhammara, 72
Mulberry, 47, 122
Mulberry fig. *See* Sycamore fig
Mumbai, 80, 105
Mushroom, 41, 167
Musht. See St. Peter's fish

Muslims, xvii, xviii, xix, xxii–xxiii, xxv, xxviii–xxix, xxx, xxxv, xxxvii, 5, 54, 55, 93, 117, 118, 137, 147–51, 154, 155, 173, 177, 185, 191; holidays, xxxiv; and Jewish holidays, xxxiv; military service, 13
Mustard, 25, 37, 66, 75, 81, 102, 191
Mutton, xviii, xxx, 12, 28, 48, 53, 56, 126, 127, 134, 151, 160, 195–96; desirable meat, 54; fat, 132; turkey substitute for, 56, 160
Mystical, 139

Na'ana. See Mint
Nabatean, 21
Nablus (city), xxv, 78, 151
Nahalal (moshav), 7, 19
Nahariya (city), xvii, xix, 114, 181
Nazareth (city), xvii, xxxiv
Nazis, 7, 8, 63
Neanderthals, 2
Negev, xvii–xviii, xxii, 16, 17, 18, 20, 21, 41, 47, 48, 62, 65, 68, 86, 198
Neolithic period, 3, 22
Nepal, 105
Nepotism, 27
Nesher beer, 118
Nesichat hanilus, 59
Netanya (city), 114
Nigella, 4, 51, 68, 72, 88; *tahina,* 78
Nile perch, 59
Nishnushim, xxxiii, 169
Nistader, 189
Noah, xx
Nomads, xxii, xxiii, 1, 18, 86, 104, 115, 198–200
Non-kosher, xxviii, 11, 15, 56, 57, 60, 61, 175, 180, 181, 183, 189
Noodle, 20, 52–53, 100–101, 148
Norwegian sheep, xxviii
Nosh, xxxiii
Nut, xxxvi, 25, 28–30, 42, 107, 108, 111, 146, 147, 152, 157, 167

Nut-burgers, 194
Nutmeg, 110, 195, 197

Oats, 91
Obesity, 122, 157, 194, 196
Ogen melon, 47
Okra, 34, 38
Oleuropein, 25
Olive, xvi, xvii, xxx, 1, 18, 22, 23, 24, 25, 31, 38, 71, 72, 75, 87, 162, 163, 165, 173, 191
Olive oil, xxiv, 3, 22, 23–24, 32, 33, 58, 63, 64, 71–74, 76, 79, 82–83, 88–89, 99, 126, 128, 130, 135, 136, 149, 158, 160, 161, 163, 166, 177, 178, 179, 180, 193, 195
Omer. See Lag Ba'omer
Onion, 10, 26, 28, 32, 33–34, 36, 38, 52, 58, 71, 72, 76, 87, 88, 90, 94, 96, 98, 99, 126, 127, 130–33, 136, 144, 150, 160, 161, 166, 167, 178, 190, 193, 195; husks, 92; sweet, 75
Orange, 43, 45, 73, 104, 197
Orange blossom water, 68, 108, 152–53
Orange juice, 87, 104, 107, 119, 164
Orchid, 106
Oregano, xxx
Orthodox Christians, xix, xxxiv, 117
Orthodox Jews, xx, xxi, xxii, xxv, xxvi, xxvii, xxviii, xxxii, xxxiii, xxxviii, xxxix, 6, 53, 59, 86, 100, 115, 117, 125, 128, 130, 134, 138, 145, 182–83, 184, 185, 190; and official rabbinate, 56
Orthodox Muslims, 155
Ostrich, xxvi, 56, 65
Ottoman, xxiii, 5–6, 22, 56, 88, 119, 120
Oznei haman, 69, 146–47

Palaestina, 4, 138
Palamida, 58

Palestine, xxv, 6–8, 63, 78, 138, 151, 189
Palestine, British Mandate of, 6–7, 189
Pancake, 28, 35, 39; *atayef,* 148, 152; *lahouh,* 51–52
Paprika, xvii, xxx, 32, 63, 68, 71, 73–74, 90, 127, 158
Parade, 145, 154
Parag. See Poppy seeds
Parfaits (ice cream), 112
Paris, 186
Park, xxxviii, 24, 124, 126, 137
Parliament. *See* Knesset
"Parliament" (discussion), 173, 175
Parsley, xxx, 32, 33, 34, 35, 36, 38, 68, 71, 72, 79–80, 82, 96, 127, 130, 150–51, 158, 163, 178, 193
Parve, 65, 90, 100, 190
Pashtida, 41, 93, 100–101
Passover, xxii, xxvi, xxvii, xxxii, xxxiv, xxxvii, 4, 28, 29, 30, 34, 41, 42, 54, 59, 65, 80, 82, 102, 117, 133–36
Pasta, 53, 95
Pastide, 100
Pastries, xxxvii, 13, 30, 47, 69, 92, 109–10, 146–47, 157, 167
Peach, 46, 47, 107, 122, 123
Peanut, 29, 30, 169
Peanut butter, 30
Pear, 48, 105
Peas, 95
Peasants, 7, 17–18, 160
Pecan, xvii, 28, 29, 111, 147
Penguin, xxviii
Pentateuch, 3
Pepper (black, peppercorns), 16, 32, 36, 68, 74, 93, 100–101
Pepper (chilies), xxx, 11, 35, 36, 40, 68, 82, 83, 99, 122, 180, 184, 191; sauces, 37–38, 66
Pepper (sweet, bell), 34, 39, 59, 72, 73–74, 76, 83, 87, 90, 126, 127–28, 132, 160, 166, 180, 196

Pepsico, 119, 121
Perch, Nile, 59
Persecution, 8, 159
Persia, xxxix, 5, 14, 22, 27, 29, 42, 52, 53, 68, 105, 145
Persimmon, xvii, 45, 47–48
Pesach. See Passover
Pesek zman, 170
Petel. See Raspberry
Petrol stations, 178
Petrozilia. See Parsley
Philadelphia pretzels, 167
Philistines, 138
Phyllo dough, 52
Pickle, xxxvi, 12, 24, 25, 31, 35, 38, 39, 40, 44, 69, 72, 75, 76–78, 87, 89, 90, 102, 128, 158, 159, 160, 162–64, 165, 176, 179, 180, 194, 196
Picnic, xxxii, xxxviii, 12, 62, 126
Pig, xxiii, xxvi, xxviii, xxix, 18
Pigeon, 148
Pilgrimage, xxv, 21, 59, 140, 141, 143, 148
Pilgrims, 24
Pilpel. See Pepper
Pilpelim. See Pepper (sweet, bell)
Pine nut, 52, 158
Pineapple, 45, 168
Pistachio, 29, 30, 106, 107, 152, 153
Pita, 12, 20, 31, 39, 40, 51, 64, 72, 77, 81, 87, 89, 102, 157–64, 179, 198
Pitanga/pintango, 48
Pitzuchim, xxxvi, xxxvii, 27, 28, 29, 30, 74, 105, 111, 157, 166–67, 168
Pizza, 11, 15–16
Pizzerias, xxxix
Platat Shabbat, 130
Plum, 46, 48, 73, 107
Pogrom, 8, 145
Poland, 52, 80
Polenta, 27

Pollock, 60
Polluted temple, 143
Polluting flesh, xxix
Polyethylene milk bags, 61
Pomegranate, xvii, xxx, 1, 22, 23, 46, 119, 122, 141, 168; molasses, 22
Pomelo, 43, 44
Poppy seeds, 30, 50, 69, 146–47
Pork, xxi, xxii, xxiii, xxvii, xxviii, xxx, 10, 11, 55, 126, 177; substitutes, 190, 192
Porridge, 28, 91, 93
Portuguese, xx, 43
Post-army youth, 15, 179
Post-fast dinner, 62
Post-*tsena* immigrants, 9
Post-Yom Kippur War, 171
Potato, xxx, 35, 36, 37, 38–39, 52, 69, 72, 75, 95, 130–33, 136, 139, 144, 167, 179
Poultry, xviii, 53. *See also* Chicken; Turkey (bird)
Poverty, 6, 8, 159, 187
Povidl, 48
Prawn-shaped *surimi,* 192
Prawns, 55, 182
Prayer, xxv, xxvi, xxxiii, xxxiv, 4, 92, 129, 140
Prejudice, 142
Premodern times, 20, 26, 49
Preserves, 40, 44, 58, 62, 63, 101, 103, 105, 147
Pre-State period, 14, 42, 64, 111
Pre-Talmudic observances, 141
Pretzels, 167
Priests, 129, 141
Proletariat, 19
Prosperity, 7, 11, 41, 49, 62, 113, 159
Prunes, 48, 105, 146–47, 195–96
Ptiliya, 189
Ptolemaic Egypt, 4
Pudding, 28, 40, 41, 100–101, 103, 106–8

Pumpkin, 39, 50, 132, 166
Purim, 69, 117, 145–46, 196

Quaker oats, 91
Quark, 63
Quince, 48, 132, 174

Rabbinate, xxvii, 53, 54, 55, 56, 118, 175, 176, 183
Rabbit, xxvi
Radish, 39, 40, 76, 87, 160, 191
Ragout, 53
Rahat lokum, 68, 111, 154
Raisins, 28, 91, 106, 107, 110, 146, 147, 152, 195, 197
Ramadan, xxxiv, 79, 148–51, 152
Ramat Gan (city), 111, 162
Ramle (city), 11, 66
Ras al hanut, 66, 68
Raspberry, 112, 121–22, 169
Rationing, 9–10, 13, 187, 190; water, 19
Rations, Army field, 14, 60, 101, 134
Refrigeration technology, 56
Rehaniya (Adyghe village), xxiii
Rehovot (city), 77
Reibkuchen. See Latke
Relish, xxxiii, 37, 38, 52, 67, 72, 73–74, 78–84, 88, 163, 180, 194
Resin. *See* Mastic
Ribs, mutton or lamb, 195
Rice, xxii, xxxii, xxxvii, 1, 9, 27–28, 33–34, 35, 36, 54, 67, 80, 93, 95, 96, 98–99, 102, 105, 106, 107–08, 111, 149, 151, 193, 196, 198–200
Ricotta, 152
Rishon Letzion (city), 117
Rivyon. See Buttermilk
Romans, 4, 6, 24, 25, 39, 138
Rose water, 67, 68, 106, 107–08, 109, 148
Rosh Hanikra (beach), xvii
Rosh Hashana, xxxvii, 22, 28, 42, 59, 104, 140

Rothschild Foundation, 117
Roulade, 88–89
Russia, 35, 196
Ruth (book of Bible), 158
Rye, 9, 21, 50, 87, 191

Saag, 83
Sabbath. *See* Shabbat
Sabich, 51, 81, 92, 162–63
Sabra (cactus fruit), 49, 112
Sabras (native-born Israelis), 1, 49
Sabzavot dimlama, 132–33
Sacher Park (Jerusalem site), 126, 137
Sacrifice, xxiv, 50, 134, 147, 148
Sahlab (orchid and sweet), 106
Sahrana, 143
Salad ingredients, xxv, 12, 24, 31, 34, 35, 36, 38, 39, 42, 43, 65, 68, 69, 71–73, 80
Salads, xvii, xxx, xxxvi, 52, 58, 59, 64, 75–76, 87, 89, 92, 93, 95, 98, 102, 126, 128, 135, 149, 158, 159–64, 165, 166, 176, 179, 180, 194, 196, 198
Salat. See Salads
Salat perot. See Fruit salad
Salat russi, 75
Salat yevani, 36, 72
Salata mechoui, 64, 165, 166
Salatim. See Salads
Salmon, 11
Salt, 4, 10, 31, 47, 51, 69, 70, 73, 91, 139, 167, 169
Salt water, 64, 134
Salted foods, 24, 25, 28, 29, 30, 36, 44, 58, 77–78, 87, 166, 169
Salting for *kashrut,* xxvi
Salt-tolerant crops, 17, 39
Samaritans, xix, xxiv–xxv, xxix, 16, 54
Samna, 54, 199
Sandwich, 20, 31, 39, 40, 59, 60, 67, 76, 77, 80, 92, 102, 158, 159, 162–66, 172, 190–91

Sandwich tunisai, 165
Sardines, 60
Sashimi, 182
Sauerkraut, 35, 77–78, 159, 160
Sausage, 55, 66, 90, 93, 131, 182
Schmalz, 93
Schnitzel, 57, 101–02, 157, 179; eggplant, 36–37
Sde Boker (kibbutz), 47
Sea bass, 58
Seafood, xxi, xxxix, 55, 57, 171, 181–82, 192
Secularization, 85
Seder, xxxii, xxxvii, 4, 29, 42, 69, 97, 117, 133, 134, 136
Selek. See Beetroot
Seleucids, 4, 39, 143
Seltzer, 121, 123, 149, 172
Semolina, 91
Sesame, 30, 50, 52, 69, 70, 78, 160, 167
Shabbat, xx, xxv, 128, 129–33
Shahada, xxix
Shakshouka, 87, 88, 89–90
Shallots, 38
Shamenet hamutza. See Sour cream
Shamir. See Dill
Sharab, 22
Shark, xxvi, 60
Sharon fruit. *See* Persimmon
Sharon plain, xvi, 43, 44, 46, 79, 150
Shashlik, 126–27, 176
Shavuot, xxv, xxxiv, 21, 28, 43, 62, 104, 140
Shawarma, 12, 40, 54, 56, 160, 162, 190
Sheep, xvi, xxviii, xxxiv, 1, 18, 54, 148, 151; milk, 61
Shellfish, xxi, 57, 181, 192
Shesek, 49
Shesh-besh. See Backgammon
Shi'a, xix, xxiii
Shikma. See Sycamore fig

Shiva, 154–155
Shivat haminim, 20–25
Shkedim. See Almond
Shochet, xxvi
Shomrei Mitzvot, xxi
Shomronim. See Samaritans
Shoresh. See Celeriac
Shrimp, xxvii, 55, 57, 182, 192
Shum. See Garlic
Shumar. See Fennel
Sicily, 44
Siesta, 93
Sigd, 141–42
Silan, 25, 28, 149
Simchat Torah, 62, 141
Simple cooking methods, 30
Sinai desert, xviii
Sinew, 54
Siniya, xxv, 79–80
Sir peleh, 189–90, 197
Slaughter, 1; Jewish practice, xxvi, 54, 56; Muslim practice, xxviii–xxix, 148
Slivovitz, 123
Slow-cooker, 130
Small-beer (malt/black beer), 117–18
Smetana. See Sour cream
Smoothies, 46
Snapper, 58
Soda. *See* Seltzer
Sodastream, 121
Solet, 91
Sophistication in food choices, 53, 178, 182
Sour cream, 61, 62, 65, 105, 144
Sourdough, 51
Spinach, 52, 136, 167
Spleen, 54, 163–64
St. Peter's Fish, 4, 59
Starch, 27, 95, 106, 144, 192
Steak, 11, 54, 58, 66, 126, 176, 177
Steakhouse, 177, 178, 179

Steaming, 75, 142
Stekiyot. See Steakhouse
Stew, xxvi, xxxiv, 1, 3, 21, 27, 30, 31, 33–34, 35, 36, 38, 39, 40, 54, 66, 68, 97, 129, 130–33, 157, 194. *See also* Hamin
Stone Age, xvii
Strawberry, xvii, 49, 105, 123, 167, 168
Strawberry flavor, 112, 170
Strudel, 42
Stuffed foods, 25, 34, 35, 39, 40, 56, 57, 59, 72, 88, 92, 95–97, 97–98, 99, 146–47, 151, 150–51, 152–53, 176, 181, 193–94
Sturgeon, 59
Stylistas, 116
Subsistence farming, 17
Succah, 22, 141
Succoth, 22, 141
Sudan, 38, 86
Suet, xxvi
Sufganiyot. See Doughnuts
Sultana, 105, 106
Sumac, xxx, 69, 70, 79–80, 127, 149, 199
Sumerians, 118
Sumsum. See Sesame
Sunflower, xxxiii, 50, 111, 166, 169, 173
Sunni, xix, xxii
Surimi, 192
Suriname cherry, 48
Surplus, agricultural, 21
Sushi, 73, 86, 171, 182
Suss, 119–20
Sweet potato, xxxiii, 36, 39, 130
Sycamore fig, 49, 168
Symposium, 4

Ta'amiya, 159
Tabbouleh, 72
Tabi, 109
Tabla. See Backgammon

Tahina, 30, 31, 35, 36, 44, 69, 71, 78–80, 92, 102, 148, 158, 159, 160, 161–64, 176, 177, 189, 198
Tahini. *See Tahina*
Talmud, xix, xx, xxvi, 20, 28, 30, 34, 35, 40, 48, 130, 141
Tamarhindi. See Tamarind
Tamarind, 69, 120
Taninim (river), 16
Tank (engine as food heater), 114
Tanur oven, 51
Tapuach. See Apple
Tapuach adama. See Potato
Tapuz. See Orange
Tea, xxiv, 13, 43, 44, 68, 87, 89, 93, 103, 110, 113, 115–16, 140, 142–43, 163, 167, 172–73, 174; hibiscus, 151
Tears of Chios. *See* Mastic
Tebit, 97–98
Technology: agricultural, xviii, 9, 16, 17, 19, 34, 168; Israeli innovation, 183; refrigeration of foods, 56, 112
Tef, 11, 28
Tel Aviv, xvii, xxii, 7, 15, 36, 55, 111, 114, 157, 162, 168, 171, 173, 180, 181, 182, 184
Tel Aviv-Yaffo, 171
Tempo Drinks Co., 118, 121
Thai restaurants, xxvii, xxxix, 180
Tiberias (city), 6
Tilapia, 59
Timer-controlled Sabbath cooking, 130
Tisch, rabbi's dinner, xxxvi, xxxviii
Tkemeli, 48
Tnuva, 56
Tomato, xvii, xviii, 16, 28, 34, 35, 36, 38, 39–40, 53, 57, 58, 64, 67, 71, 72–74, 76, 87, 88–90, 96–97, 98, 99, 101, 126, 132–33, 149, 160, 161–62, 166, 178, 188; ketchup, 10, 127

Index

Torah, xix, xx, 22, 141
Torshi, 40, 72
Tree-gum. *See* Mastic
Trends, xxiii, xxv, 109, 157, 173, 175, 181, 183, 185
Tsena. See Rationing
Tsfat (city), 6, 62, 138
Tsnobar. See Pine nut
Tsnon. See Radish
Tu Bishvat, 104, 145
Tuna, xxvi, 58, 60, 165
Turkey (bird), xviii, xxx, 12, 42, 53, 54, 55, 56–57, 101–2, 126, 134, 160, 179
Turkey (country), 12, 52, 65, 92, 111, 162, 169, 190
Turmeric, 28, 38, 54, 67, 98, 126, 159, 163–64, 167, 198–99
Turnip, 40, 77, 89, 132–33
Turnovers, xxiv
Tut etz. See Mulberry
Tut sade. See Strawberry
Tzalaf. See Capers
Tzatziki, 69

United Nations, 7
Urbanization, 6

Vegan lifestyle, 98, 128, 171, 183
Vegetarian, 33, 34, 80, 86, 92, 96, 98, 99, 100, 125, 130, 132–33, 154, 183, 191, 192–93
Vinegar, 24, 25, 39, 40, 69, 72, 75, 76, 81, 180
Virility, 66
Vodka, 77, 123

Wafer, 169–70
Waffle, 169–70
Walnut, 29, 111, 147, 152
Wastewater, 16
Watermelon, 47, 123, 168; seeds, 166
Weaning, 91

Wedding, xxxv, 102, 111, 123, 154
Wheat, xvii, xxx, 1, 2, 18, 20–21, 28, 36, 118, 140, 191
Whiskey, 123
Wine, xvi, xxxiii, xxxvi, 3, 4, 9, 11, 21, 29, 42, 45, 93, 113, 117, 123, 128–29, 134, 145, 154, 172, 195, 196, 197; pomegranate, 22; vinegar, 75
Wot, 1, 35
WWII (World War II), 7, 8–9

Yaffo. *See* Jaffa
Yavne'el (moshava), 18
Yeast, 50–51, 52, 137–38, 142, 152–53
Yekke, 77, 114
Yemen, xx, 1, 66
Yemenites, 6, 8, 37, 51, 66, 88–89, 159; *challah*, 50; and falafel, 82; and German (Yekke) immigrants, 77–78
Yeruham (town), 175
Yiddish words, xxxiii, 52
Yiddishkeit restaurants, 182–83
Yishuv period, 14, 198
Yogurt, xxiii, xxx, 3, 34, 43, 45, 61–65, 69, 87, 103, 121–22, 123, 167, 179, 197
Yom Ha'atzmaut (Independence Day), xxxiv, 125–28
Yom Kippur, xx, xxi, xxxiv, xxxvii, 62, 140, 141
Yom Kippur War, 171
Yotveta (kibbutz), 62

Za'atar, xxx, 16, 63, 64, 69, 70, 167
Zakat, 148
Zakushki, 10
Zchug, 37, 52, 66, 67, 82–83, 89, 158, 160, 162, 164
Zichron Ya'akov (city), 117
Zionist, 6, 14, 19
Zucchini, 40, 95, 100, 126

ABOUT THE AUTHOR

Michael Ashkenazi, PhD, is an anthropologist who has conducted fieldwork and research on four continents. He has taught at universities in Israel, Canada, Japan, and the United Kingdom, and has worked as a senior researcher at a German academic research institute. He has studied Ethiopian immigrants in Israel, small arms issues throughout Latin America, Africa and Asia, Japanese religion and ritual, martial arts, and business organization. His major love, however, remains the study of food culture, and throughout his travels, he has kept a weather eye on interesting foods and food customs. He has published two books on Japanese food culture, numerous articles on topics related to food, and coauthored *The World Cookbook*. He cooks a mix of Israeli, Japanese, and other cuisines, and currently helps raise exotic fruit in his wife's garden and serves as chief tester of its products.

www.ingramcontent.com/pod-product-compliance
Lightning Source LLC
Chambersburg PA
CBHW060947230426
43665CB00015B/2092